BALLET

A Guide

The authors

PETER BRINSON

is founder/director of the Royal Ballet's Ballet for All Company at the Royal Opera House, Covent Garden; author of many books and television scripts on ballet, including Thames Television's *Ballet for All* series; and has recently been awarded a Winston Churchill Travelling Fellowship for his work in this field.

CLEMENT CRISP

writes ballet criticism for *The Financial Times*, *The Spectator* and *Les Saisons de la Danse* of Paris; and is librarian/archivist of the Royal Academy of Dancing.

with contributions by

DON McDONAGH

dance reviewer for the *New York Times*, associate editor of *Ballet Review* and one of the contributing editors (USA) for *Dance and Dancers*. He writes articles on ballet and modern dance for a number of periodicals and recently prepared the Martha Graham entry for *Collier's Encyclopaedia*.

JOHN PERCIVAL

ballet critic for *The Times*, associate editor of *Dance and Dancers*, and London correspondent of *Dance Magazine* (New York), besides writing regularly on ballet for the *New York Times* and other publications.

The cover photograph by Andrzej Sleżak shows Margaret Barbieri rehearsing Giselle

CONDITIONS OF SALE

PETER BRINSON and CLEMENT CRISP

BALLET FOR ALL
A Guide to One Hundred Ballets

With contributions by
Don McDonagh and John Percival

A PAN ORIGINAL

PAN BOOKS LTD : LONDON

First published 1970 by Pan Books Ltd,
33 Tothill Street, London, S.W.1

330   02430   2

Printed in Great Britain by
Hazell Watson & Viney Ltd, Aylesbury, Bucks

Contents

Chapter Four

Chapter Five

Chapter Six

Chapter Seven

Chapter Eight

List of Illustrations

1

Dancers of the Royal Ballet in the Prologue of
Petipa's *The Sleeping Beauty*, St Petersburg, 1890,
as staged for the Royal Opera House,
Covent Garden, 1946
(*Photograph: Houston Rogers*)

2

Dancers of the Royal Ballet in George Balanchine's
Serenade, Hartford, USA, 1934, as performed at the Royal
Opera House, Covent Garden, 1964
(*Photograph: Michael Richardson*)

3

Dancers of Ballet Rambert in Glen Tetley's
Embrace Tiger and Return to Mountain, London, 1968
(*Photograph: Alan Cunliffe*)

4

Louis XIV as Apollo in *Les Noces de Pelée et de Thétis*, Paris,
1654, with costumes and settings by Giacomo Torelli

5

John Weaver's *The Loves of Mars and Venus*,
London, 1717, recreated by Mary Skeaping for the Royal
Ballet's *Ballet for All*, London, 1969, with costumes
by David Walker.
Alison Howard as an Hour, Oliver Symons as Vulcan,
Jacqueline Lansley as Venus
(*Photograph: P. Alexander Lloyd*)

6

Noverre's *Medée et Jason*, Stuttgart, 1763,
with costumes by Boquet. This print by John Boydell
from a drawing by Nathaniel Dance, RA, shows a
version produced by Gaetano Vestris at the King's Theatre,
London, in 1781, designed by Novosielski, with
Vestris himself as Jason

7

Filippo Taglioni's *The Return of Springtime*,
Stockholm, 1818, recreated by Mary Skeaping for the
Royal Ballet's *Ballet for All*, London, 1965,
with costumes by David Walker. Shown here, Ann Dennis
as Flora, Gail Thomas as Cupid,
Oliver Symons as Zephyr

(Photograph: Anthony Crickmay)

8

Filippo Taglioni's *La Sylphide*, Paris, 1832, in Chalon's
engraving showing Ciceri's decor for Act I with
Marie Taglioni as the Sylphide and Joseph Mazilier as James

9

Giselle, by Jean Coralli and Jules Perrot,
Paris, 1841. Giselle is crowned Queen of the Wine Harvest,
from the wood-engraving in Gautier's
Les Beautés de L'Opéra, 1845

10

Dancers of the Royal Danish Ballet in August
Bournonville's *Napoli*, Copenhagen, 1842. Still in the repertory
of the Royal Theatre, this scene from Act III
shows a production of the ballet, about 1942, with
Kirsten Ralov, Knud Henriksen, Inga Gotha,
Margot Lander, Leif Ørnberg and Mona Vangsaa

11
Giuseppina Bozzacchi, the first Swanilda, in
Arthur St Léon's *Coppélia*, Paris, 1870: Act I,
scene I; Act I, scene 2;
Act II
(*By courtesy of Ivor Guest*)

12
Lev Ivanov's Act II of *Swan Lake*, St Petersburg,
1894, as performed by the Royal Ballet at the
Royal Opera House, Covent Garden, in a reproduction
by Nicholas Sergueyev
(*Photograph: Anthony Crickmay*)

13
Michel Fokine's *Petrushka*, Paris, 1911, Scene 2, showing
Alexander Benois' decor for Petrushka's cell with Tamara
Karsavina as the Ballerina and Vaslav Nijinski as Petrushka
(*Photograph: Bert*)

14
Vaslav Nijinski's *L'Après-midi d'un Faune*,
Paris, 1912, with Nijinski as the faun in the costume
designed by Léon Bakst
(*Photograph: Bert*)

15
Leonide Massine's *La Boutique Fantasque*, London, 1919.
Shown here, Massine in a costume designed by Derain
(*Photograph: Foalsham and Banfield*)

21

Dancers of the Royal Ballet in Antony Tudor's *Shadowplay*,
London, 1967, designed by Michael Annals with
Anthony Dowell as Boy with Matted Hair and
Frank Freeman as an Arboreal
(*Photograph: Anthony Crickmay*)

22

Dancers of the Wurtemberg State Ballet in John Cranko's
The Taming of the Shrew, Stuttgart, 1969, designed
by Elisabeth Dalton with Richard Cragun as Petrucchio
and Marcia Haydée (in white) as Kate
(*Photograph: Anthony Crickmay*)

23

Kenneth MacMillan's *Romeo and Juliet*, London, 1965,
designed by Nicholas Georgiadis with Lynn Seymour as Juliet
(*Photograph: Reg Wilson*)

24

Jerome Robbins' *Afternoon of a Faun*, New York, 1953,
with decor and lighting by Jean Rosenthal and costumes by
Irene Sharaff. In the repertory of Robbins'
Ballets: USA, it is danced here by Wilma Curley and
John Jones
(*Photograph: Roy Round*)

25

Yuri Grigorovich's *Spartacus*, Moscow, 1968,
designed by Suliko Virsaladze, with Maris Liepa
as Crassus and Mikhail Lavrovsky as Spartacus
(*Photograph: Edward Griffiths*)

Introduction and Acknowledgements

This is a guide to what can be seen on the ballet stage today. By providing background information to over a hundred ballets we hope to increase the enjoyment of ballet-going as well as introduce a complex, fascinating art which has become one of Britain's chief cultural achievements in our time. Nowadays ballet attracts hundreds of thousands of people every year in theatres throughout Britain, and many more in cinemas and on television; its history and practice have become subjects of school study in the General Certificate of Education. It is a form of theatre which combines music, literature, painting and dancing to create visual dramas which are the result of centuries of endeavour – as well as of public taste at this moment.

The perfect ballet requires a perfect balance between each of its elements, and therefore a perfect collaboration between composer, designer, librettist and choreographer. Most often the choreographer is in control. Not only does he organize the performers on stage through his dances, but he usually supervises the production. He has been the central figure around which ballet has developed ever since it became able to tell stories in movement without the aid of words two hundred and fifty years ago. This book is about his work shown through the ballets of thirty-eight choreographers, living and dead, who represent together what is called the international repertory. In other words, we have been guided in what to include largely by whether or not the work of a choreographer can actually be seen on stage now.

The title of this book comes from a ballet company which is a section of the Royal Ballet and whose repertory has become a television series, called *Ballet for All*. This company, founded in September, 1964, presents special programmes, called ballet-plays, which combine words with ballets, actors with dancers and musicians, to inform as well as entertain. The success of these programmes showed the interest there is in ballet appreciation, thus providing this book's starting point as well as many of its illustrations.

Our synopses cover in detail just over one hundred ballets by choreographers from Clément in the seventeenth century to Frederick Ashton and Kenneth MacMillan today. Many other ballets and choreographers are mentioned in passing. Of the ballets treated in detail, the early historical ones are selected according to what the *Ballet for All* company has re-created in the theatre and so made available to audiences. All others are in the repertory of some ballet company somewhere in the world, selected according to our own prejudice and enthusiasm, though space problems have meant that some favourites have had to be omitted. Each is discussed in three parts: production credits – synopsis – commentary. They are grouped under their choreographers arranged in roughly chronological order. A narrative links each period with the one preceding, thus providing a compressed history of ballet itself; at the end is a short reading list to guide further study.

Our thanks are due to the Editors of *The Financial Times* and *The Spectator*, the General Administrator, Royal Opera House, Covent Garden and The Friends of Covent for permission to reproduce material originally published by them. Although we have seen for ourselves every ballet we discuss (and therefore the opinions expressed are solely our own) we have checked our research of detail against recognized sources and must particularly record our indebtedness to Mr Cyril Beaumont's monumental *Complete Book of Ballets* and its Supplements (Putnam); *A Dictionary of Modern Ballet* edited by Francis Gadan and Robert Maillard (Methuen); Mr G. B. L. Wilson's *A Dictionary of Ballet* (Cassell); and *The Choreographic Art* by van Praagh and Brinson (A. and C. Black).

Our thanks are due also to Mr Don McDonagh and Mr John Percival for undertaking at short notice the sections on

America and the ballets of John Cranko respectively; to Miss
Mary Skeaping for historical information in Chapter II; to Mr
Alan Fridericia for additional information on *Konservatoriet*; to
Mr Ivor Guest for the photographs on Plate 11; to Miss Mary
Clarke of *The Dancing Times* for the loan of photographs from
her collection; to Mr Werdon Anglin for much help; and to
Mrs Margaret Moores, Mrs Jennifer Bungey, Miss Bibby
Whittam, Mrs Joan Maxwell-Hudson and Miss Elizabeth
Scammell, our team of secretaries, without whom the work
would never have reached the publishers.

PETER BRINSON
CLEMENT CRISP
London, 1970

Chapter One

The Background

Ballet's image today is *The Sleeping Beauty*, opulent, spectacular, a fairy-tale told in dance, known to most people through the version presented by The Royal Ballet at Covent Garden (Plate 1). Or it is the clean lines of Balanchine's *Serenade* from America, no story, just dancing to music (Plate 2). It might also be something which uses bodies rather differently, combining the clean lines of Balanchine with other modern influences to produce a contemporary work like *Embrace Tiger and Return to Mountain* (Plate 3).

Whatever it is, the dancers' movements, their training and the ballets in which they appear on stage are the product of two things, like any other art: first, the past; second, the ideas and pressures of people today.

If you study the pictures of *The Sleeping Beauty* and Balanchine's *Serenade* you will notice a similarity in the way the dancers move and hold themselves. This is because the dancers are classical dancers in ballets which are expressions of *classical* style – classical because the body is held as a central upright while arms and legs move always in balance and harmony around it. In architecture, painting, music, every art in fact, classicism implies these same qualities of balance and harmony. So in ballet.

The foundation of classical ballet and classical dancing is the academic vocabulary of what dance teachers call the *danse d'école*. This vocabulary of steps, always developing and changing, is what dancers learn in the classroom. It is their language, as words are the language of an actor. For historical reasons its terminology is French, and the steps, too, are the product of history. So to enjoy ballet in the fullest possible way one needs to know something of how it began.

The *danse d'école* is the product of five hundred years of study and creative work by dancers, teachers and choreographers. It is also a part of social history because, throughout this long period dancing, like other arts, has always been an expression of the ideas of the time. Any movement we make as individuals reflects some idea or intention in our minds; in the same way dancing is human movement organized to music reflecting the ideas of a group or class of people.

Five hundred years ago such 'organization' produced the first ballets. These were nothing like ballets today, but elaborate combinations of music, singing, poetry, 'machines' (i.e. stage effects), costumes and dancing to praise in allegory the qualities of some prince or important guest. They were a product of court life with all the performers drawn from the same circle – kings, princes and courtiers – often very good at dancing or singing, but essentially amateurs. Professionals were used only as dancing masters, to arrange and produce the whole show, or as dancers in burlesque interludes which it might be undignified for a nobleman to perform. Men were the founders of these grand court ballets, dancing also the feminine roles, much as boys performed female roles in Shakespeare's plays. Women might dance privately at court, but never in the more public performances which were given to impress the king's subjects and the world at large with his wealth and importance.

Such ballets arose five hundred years ago as a result of the Renaissance, the great social and intellectual movement which freed European thought from the restraints of medieval Christian philosophy. Parallel with this intellectual liberation went a political liberation. Individual kings and princes allied themselves with the lesser nobility and merchant class in order to end the power of the great nobles, concentrate state power in the King's hands and so enable him to organize the social peace necessary for the expansion of trade and social wealth. It was important, therefore, to establish the King publicly as the centre of the life of the state in every sense, not just politically and economically, but artistically and intellectually. The princes realized this too, gathering around their persons as many artists as they could afford, to embellish their homes and their reputations. Court ballet assisted this political use of the arts in two ways. First and most obviously it combined many arts for a single purpose, the impact of such a combination being more powerful and immediate than the impact of a single art alone. From the combination arose almost incidentally a new art, greater than its individual parts, Court Ballet. Second, the new art was flexible enough to be adapted easily to particular themes, important at the time. Hence court ballet, new in form and flexible in content, became a leader of the arts and to some extent their principal influence in the service of the monarch.

The idea began in Italy because the Renaissance began there, and it was there that the concept of the absolute prince first established itself. In very early days – the late 1400s – the entertainments were combined with meals, as dinner ballets, each course being accompanied by an entry, or new scene, to carry forward the story. A reminder of this beginning still appears in the term 'entrée' on menus today.

When Charles VIII of France invaded Italy in 1494 to claim the throne of Naples, he and his nobility were astonished at the size and quality of the 'balli' they saw there, and the fact that so many leading artists contributed to them. Back in France the French copied the Italians and developed their own court ballets, often assisted by Italian dancing masters and by the taste of Italian princesses marrying into the royal house. A hundred years after the French invasion of Italy Catherine de Medici, Queen Mother of France, inspired the *Ballet Comique de la Reine*, largely created by her Italian dancing master, Belgiojosa. Accounts of its splendour were distributed around Europe so that this spectacular event ushered in the greatest period of court ballet when every European monarch of any standing included ballet among his entertainments. In England ballet took the form of the Masque, popular under Henry VIII, and rising under James I, through Ben Jonson and Inigo Jones, to become briefly the envy of Europe.

Court ballet, however, belonged absolutely to the monarch and existed solely for him. Restrain the monarch, or curb his absolutism, and the reason for Court ballet would disappear.

This happened in England under Charles I. Conversely, if the monarch grew in glory and power so did Court ballet. Thus it was Louis XIV of France, most absolute monarch of his time, who raised *ballet de cour* to the heights and gave it thenceforth a French image.

Because of this the French have tended to overshadow the Italians in their contribution. Yet the Italians invented the idea of ballet as a combination of all the arts; have been largely responsible for its spectacular tradition; and inspired since very early days the virtuoso element in its dancing with ingenious rhythms and originality of steps. For two centuries before Louis XIV's time Italian dancing masters played the leading part in most European court entertainments, and it was an Italian, Lulli (or Lully) who translated Louis XIV's love of dancing into the court ballet's most splendid form.

France contributed to the new art the prestige and wealth of the most influential court of Europe, plus French qualities of grace and charm in executing steps and in the performance as a whole. Since the French court was the European centre of manners and polite society it was here, rather than Italy, that the *danse d'école* grew up. Until Louis XIV's time there did not exist any formal vocabulary of steps such as professional dancers learn today in the classroom. Dancing masters had always used the steps of ballroom dances fashionable at court – which every courtier knew – and arranged them to make groups and patterns across the floor much as formation dancers do now. Pattern, in fact, was more important than step, because court ballet was often performed in a large hall, the audience looking down upon the performers from tiers of seats round three sides of the room.

In time, as the new art developed under Louis XIV, and heavier demands were made upon the performers by Lully and others, it became impossible for the noble amateurs to achieve the necessary standard. Louis XIV, moreover, 'growing portly', danced less often so that his courtiers, sycophantically, took less interest in ballet. Hence, in 1661, the King established an *Académie Royale de Danse* 'to increase the said art as much as possible', followed in 1669 by an *Académie Royale de*

Musique, now the Paris Opéra. It was this latter academy, to which a dancing school was added in 1672, which produced the professional dancers Lully needed. Their studies embraced manners as well as dance steps, because ballroom dancing has always involved the niceties of social behaviour. In the 17th century these niceties required knowledge of social ceremonial to the smallest detail: how to walk elegantly with feet and legs turned out (though not as fully turned out as a dancer's today); how to raise the hat; and how to bow. Behind all this lay the mastery of posture, dignity in the carriage of the body, and grace in the deportment of the arms. When the steps of dancing began to be codified around the 1660s by Pierre Beauchamps, the King's dancing master, and his colleagues, the rules and style of aristocratic bearing were naturally included. Thus today's classical ballet steps are descended largely from ballroom dance steps fashionable at the courts of Renaissance monarchs, while their style is developed from the manners of polite society in Louis XIV's time. Together, steps and style make up the vocabulary of the *danse d'école* whose growth can be traced through the ballets of three hundred years.

Chapter Two

Pre-Romantic Ballet

Le Ballet Royal de la Nuit

Ballet de Cour in four parts and forty-three entrées. Music: Camberfort, Boesset, Lambert and others; designs and machines possibly by Torelli. First performed Palais du Petit Bourbon, Paris, February 23rd, 1653. Danced by Louis XIV with the principal personages of his court. A short extract from the fourth part of this ballet has been re-created in the style of the period by the Royal Ballet's 'Ballet for All' company with choreography by Mary Skeaping and costumes by David Walker, using the original words and music.

Apart from the text and music of the original production, from which the *Ballet for All* extract is taken, further details are presented in Per Bjurström's *Giacomo Torelli and Baroque Stage Design* (Stockholm 1961).

The four parts of the ballet each span three hours of the night, preceded by an Overture in which Night appears accompanied by the twelve hours.

Part I

From six in the evening until nine, 'showing the ordinary events of country and town'.

In a succession of scenes, hunters, bandits, shepherds and shepherdesses are seen followed by gentlemen buying ribbons for their ladies, gipsies who tell fortunes, knife-grinders, pedlars, lamp-lighters (with dancers dressed as lamps) and young ladies who are accosted. This part ends in a *Cour des miracles* where vagabonds, beggars and cripples throw away their crutches and dance a comic serenade.

PART II

From nine in the evening until midnight, 'representing the diversions of these hours such as Balls, Ballets and Comedies'. Venus floats down from the skies accompanied by Games, Laughter, Hymen and the god Comus. A ball follows, followed in turn by 'a ballet in the ballet' and finally a four act comedy.

PART III

From midnight until three in the morning; introduced by a recitative from the Moon in her chariot, while two astrologers follow the stars in their course. The moon is in love with Endymion and disappears, much to the astonishment of the astrologers. In the ensuing darkness corybants, demons and magicians appear, the noise recalling the Moon to her duties. A burning house is seen with people running from it. Thieves try to steal something and are caught.

PART IV

From three in the morning until six; introduced by a recitative from Sleep and Silence. Demons representing the four elements and the four temperaments perform one by one. Counterfeiters finish work and leave their den, and blacksmiths start up their forge, representing the first workers before dawn. Dawn appears leading the twelve hours of day accompanied by the Morning Star carrying an urn representing the dew. The whole builds to a climax with the arrival of the Sun, danced by Louis XIV accompanied by Genii of the Noble Virtues, all of whom take part in the concluding grand ballet.

Few court ballets show the political purpose of this early form more clearly than *Le Ballet Royal de la Nuit*, nor at the same time the high artistic quality of what was then a major influence upon the arts. The years 1648–1653 were marked by civil wars of the Fronde, in which first the Parliament of Paris, then the nobility, challenged the power of the Crown and of Mazarin, its chief minister. In 1652, led by Condé and supported by Spain, the rebel nobles had even occupied Paris, although the King returned to his capital by the end of the year. Early in 1653 it was clear the rebellion was failing and the last strongholds of the Fronde were being crushed.

With victory in sight the Court resumed its normal life and lavish arrangements went forward for the *Ballet de la Nuit*. Mazarin's political purpose in presenting the young King, aged 15, in such a role and such a ballet at this point becomes clear in the extracts re-created by the Royal Ballet's *Ballet for All* company – the first time, so far as we can discover, that any part of this important production has been seen or heard since 1653. A long recitative between Sleep and Silence at the opening of the fourth part begins the build-up to the arrival of the Sun.

Musically, this recitative is very interesting as well as being very beautiful. It is one of the first examples of its kind and reflects the influence of Italian opera vigorously championed by Mazarin. As a result of this influence ballet began to be performed publicly in France by professional dancers and courtiers towards the end of the 1640s (the first public opera house had been opened in Venice in 1637), but Italian opera never achieved the same popularity.

Except in such recitatives, the texts of *ballets de cour* were usually not delivered from the stage area at this period; the ballets were intensely visual with magnificent costumes and effects, and many changes of scene. To follow the events depicted, the audience were given printed booklets from which have been drawn the words which introduce the Sun in the *Ballet for All* production, and which still express Mazarin's political purpose.

On Mountain Tops glowing with my first fire
Already I shine for the world to admire.
On my vast course have I far to run
But already to all things I have begun
To give form and colour. And who does not meet
My light with homage, shall feel its heat.

Louis XIV had danced in his first ballet two years earlier, but this is probably the first time he danced the role of the Sun from which he acquired his famous title *Le Roi Soleil*. Already, at 15, an excellent dancer in the noble style, his skill and interest gave to dancing the decisive influence which insured its triumph over Mazarin's interest in opera. Louis was aware of the political value of his allegorical roles and continued, like Mazarin, to use his writers to convey the propaganda message of the Crown against any rival. Hence many ballets ended with an apotheosis of the King which had the useful effect of renewing the homage of the nobility who took part.

The Loves of Mars and Venus

'Ballet d'action' in six scenes. Libretto and choreography: John Weaver. Music: Symonds and Firbank. First performed Drury Lane Theatre, London, 2nd March, 1717. Short extracts from this ballet have been re-created in the style of the period by the Royal Ballet's 'Ballet for All' company with choreography by Mary Skeaping and costumes by David Walker, using Symonds' music.

The full libretto can be summarized, as follows:

Scene I: A Camp
Entry and dance of Mars and his followers.

Scene II: Venus in her Dressing Room
Venus is visited by Vulcan who declares his love, but is rejected by Venus.

Scene III: Vulcan's Shop
Vulcan plans revenge. He and his Cyclops work at the forge to prepare a giant net.

Scene IV: A Garden
Mars and Venus meet, declare their love and sit together on a couch where they sleep.

Scene V: Vulcan's Shop
The net is ready. The Cyclops carry it off.

Scene VI: A Garden
Mars and Venus express again their love. Vulcan and the

Cyclops enter and catch the lovers in their net, after which enter all the other gods and goddesses to see their shame. Neptune intercedes on their behalf. Vulcan forgives them, they are released and all take part in a grand dance.

Since *The Loves of Mars and Venus* is the first recorded *ballet d'action* (i.e. ballet without words) it might be thought to occupy a dominant place in ballet history and in the history of the English theatre. Important and memorable, perhaps; but dominant, no. At this time it was a freak growth, premature, standing almost on its own. To understand its significance one must recall the essential characteristic of *ballet de cour*, a combination of all the arts in which words were essential to convey the meaning. In France, once the monarchy had become firmly established, and a number of Royal Academies had been founded for different arts to guide them in their service to the King, court ballet largely lost its political function. Its aesthetic value as an art form, however, was unquestioned, encouraging development into opera-ballet under Lully's guidance, and its transfer from palace hall to public stage performance by professional artists. The title 'Opera-ballet' arose because it was a combination of Italian opera and French ballet in which words remained essential to explain the story and the feelings of the characters. Dance steps were still those fashionable in the ballroom. Modern formation dancing shows how adequately such steps can create pattern and spectacle but how lacking they are when it comes to portraying finer emotions. Hence dancing masters early began to tackle the problem of making dance steps expressive enough to tell a story without the aid of words.

Although a mimed representation of an episode in Corneille's *Horace* had been given at Sceaux in France in 1708, the credit for the first major attempt to solve the problem belongs to John Weaver, one of the leaders of a brilliant group of dancing masters in London during the reigns of Queen Anne and George I. Weaver argued that words could be replaced by gestures. He demonstrated his idea in *The Loves of Mars and Venus* by giving to each feeling expressed by his characters – Neglect; Coquetry; Contempt, etc. – an appropriate gesture.

From his own description, this first *ballet d'action* 'which drew the whole town after it', seems to have had mimed passages of 'conversation' alternating with danced passages which still used the ballroom steps of the period. The result must have been a production of great novelty, although it failed to catch on because experimental theatre always needs a patron. The England of George I was not interested in theatre which could not pay its way. Nevertheless, this addition of gestures to ordinary dance steps marks the beginning of ballet as we now know it.

The event also emphasized that the traditions of 'the dancing English', for which Elizabethans were noted, were not yet lost in early eighteenth-century London. Weaver himself danced Vulcan, and all the named cast but one were English, including Venus, 'danced by Mrs Santlow'. The exception was Mars, danced by M. Dupré, most famous French dancer of his day, and subsequently a teacher of Noverre, founder of the *ballet d'action* in France. Through Dupré, Weaver's ideas may have influenced Noverre.

The extracts from this ballet, re-created by the *Ballet for All* company show the entry of Mars from Scene I; the quarrel between Venus and Vulcan in Scene II with its 'conversation of gestures' and Venus attended by one of the Hours; the meeting of Mars and Venus from Scene IV; their capture by Vulcan in Scene VI and eventual reconciliation in a final dance. Using ballroom steps of the period the choreography thus also provides a review of the dance technique used in ballet in early years of the eighteenth century.

Les Petits Riens

Ballet in three scenes. Libretto and choreography: Jean Georges Noverre. Music: Mozart (12 pieces) and others (6 pieces). First performed 11th June, 1778, Paris Opéra. Performed by some of the most distinguished dancers of the Opéra at that time, including Marie Allard, Madeleine Guimard, Mlle Asselin, Jean Dauberval and Auguste Vestris. There have been several versions by later choreographers including de Valois and Ashton, both in 1928. The only piece now to be seen on stage is a solo for

*one of the two shepherdesses, re-created in the style of Noverre's
period for the 'Ballet for All' company with choreography by
Mary Skeaping and costume by John Phillips.*

The ballet comprised a series of tableaux, forming three
disconnected scenes in the style of Watteau and Lancret. (1)
Cupid caught in a net and put in a cage; (2) A game of blind
man's buff; (3) Cupid causing two shepherdesses (Allard and
Guimard) to become jealous of a third (Asselin) disguised as a
man. The dénouement, in which Mlle Asselin, the shepherdess
in male garb, enlightened the two jealous women by uncover-
ing her breast, was greeted with mingled protests and applause.

As its title implies, the ballet was light-hearted, its three
scenes being linked only by the slenderest theme. It is chiefly
notable for its music, illustrating in Noverre's choice of Mozart
his maxim that music for ballet should be specially composed
by the best composers. In fact Mozart composed exactly two-
thirds of the music, the other six pieces he said, consisting of
'trumpery old French airs'. The solo in the repertory of *Ballet
for All* uses one of Mozart's pieces to illustrate the development
of choreography and dance technique by 1778. Women at this
time were still hampered by long skirts, wigs, and heeled
slippers but whereas Weaver had separated mime and dance
passages, Noverre and choreographers like Angiolini were now
combining these two elements into expressive choreography.
And dance steps were no longer just ballroom steps but the
beginnings of classical technique capable of expressing simple
feelings with a skill beyond anything the most gifted amateur
could achieve. In the interval since Weaver, the singing and
dancing of Louis XIV's opera-ballets have begun to form
separate arts. Singing becomes opera; dancing becomes
ballet, because dancing at last was learning to speak without
the aid of words. Rather unfairly, Noverre has been given most
of the credit for this important advance because his *Letters on
Dancing and Ballets*, published in Stuttgart in 1760, became the
first really widely read book on the theory and practice of
ballet d'action. But many other ballet masters had dreamed and

worked to the same end since Weaver's day. Among them the Austrian Hilferding van Wewen, and the Italian, Gasparo Angiolini, deserve at least as much honour. The first worked mainly in St Petersburg; the second collaborated with Gluck in Vienna.

Les Caprices du Cupidon et du Maître de Ballet

Ballet Comique. Libretto and choreography: Vincenzo Galeotti. Music: Jens Lolle. First performed Royal Danish Opera, 31st October, 1786. Still performed by the Royal Danish Ballet.

The scene is the Temple of Cupid in an eighteenth-century formal garden. Cupid armed with bow and arrow holds court, attended by his priests. Couples from all over the world come to his temple to ask his blessing. He gives an audience to each couple resulting in a wide range of *divertissements* in *pas de deux*. The audiences over, Cupid commands the priests to blindfold everyone for the marriage ceremony. Then, at a whim, he changes all the couples round, pronounces them wed and orders the bandages removed. The finale is a lively comic ensemble in which one half of the dancers tries frantically to escape the arms of the other.

The Whims of Cupid and the Ballet Master in the repertory of the Royal Danish Ballet is the oldest ballet still danced in its original choreography. Never long out of the repertory since 1786, it is safe to say the choreography has been preserved largely as Galeotti created it. Thus the work is an important indication of the technical level of one *genre* of ballet just before the French Revolution, and also of Galeotti's quality as a choreographer, although he never regarded it as anything more than a trifle. It is indeed a trifle, albeit a charming one, intelligently conceived, with well-observed comments on a succession of married states easily recognizable today, and with an inventive use of dance material carefully contrasted to obtain maximum effect. Styrian, Norwegian and Amager couples appear in adaptations of folk dances. An old-people's dance burlesques eighteenth-century court dance. A French Dance is created in terms of academic ballet of the period while a Greek Dance is presented as an academic *pas de deux* in a version of ancient Greek costume. Best is the American Dance of the Quaker Couple, a witty joke at the expense of starchy respectability.

Equally important is the reminder, through Galeotti, of Italy's profound contribution to the development of *ballet d'action*. Galeotti was born in Florence in 1733 and studied principally under Angiolini, absorbing the principles of *ballet d'action* mostly from that master, although he worked later with Noverre and saw the results of the work of both choreographers during wide travels throughout Europe. By the time he was appointed ballet master to Copenhagen in 1775, at the age of 42, he was established as a dancer and choreographer with a reputation among the highest in his profession. He found in Denmark a well-established theatre and company, trained in the French style and deriving some tradition from the court ballet of the Danish Kings in the previous century. There were many such ballet companies in Europe at that time, all operating under some form of royal patronage and tracing their existence from the days when Renaissance princes had felt it necessary to demonstrate their importance through suitable court ballets. Although he continued as a dancer, Galeotti's principal contribution in Copenhagen was as teacher and choreographer. He created a wide range of ballets, using Danish composers like Jens Lolle to write his music, and in his own style developed the *ballet d'action* much as others were doing elsewhere. More important still, the regular classes he conducted for his dancers established the school which became the foundation of Bournonville's company during the nineteenth century.

The Return of Springtime

Anacreontic Ballet in one act. Libretto: Filippo Taglioni. Choreography in the period style of 1818: Mary Skeaping. Music: Cesare Bossi. Scenery and costumes: David Walker. First pro-

duced by the Royal Ballet's 'Ballet for All' company at the
Abbeydore Festival, Hereford, 10th September, 1965. Sub-
sequently reproduced by the Royal Swedish Ballet at the
Drottningholm Court Theatre, Sweden, 31st August, 1966, as
part of the theatre's bicentenary celebrations.

The scene is a garden in springtime; on one side a tall urn of
flowers, on the other a statue of Cupid. Zephyr, god of the
gentle winds, causes the flowers to open. One flower, the rose,
especially pleases him, so he gives it human form, as Flora a
nymph. Falling in love with Flora, Zephyr begs her attention,
but she spurns him. In desperation Zephyr appeals to Cupid.
The little god appears complete with bow, arrow and carrying
a heart. He agrees to help if Zephyr will teach him a gracious
dance. Zephyr is reluctant to give away his secrets by teaching
such a dance but relents when Cupid threatens not to help. The
lesson over they search for Flora and see her, cold and chaste as
ever, dancing by herself. Cupid tells Zephyr to hide and
conceals himself behind his own statue appearing only when
Flora stops dancing. At first Flora is very much startled to find
she is not alone. Then she is intrigued by this extraordinarily
attractive little fellow whose charm warms her heart. Without
thinking, she kisses him but at once becomes shy. To put her at
ease and win her confidence, Cupid invites her to join in the
gracious dance he has learned from Zephyr. When this is done
he pretends to pick a rose from the tall urn, but cannot reach
the flower. Flora offers to pick it for him. As she turns her back
to do so, Cupid raises his bow and pierces her heart with an
arrow. She flings the rose from her, thinking a thorn has hurt
her. At that moment Zephyr appears summoned by Cupid.
Seeing him, Flora instantly falls in love. The little god joins
their hands for a dance of celebration, re-appearing at the end
to contemplate the success of his work.

In Stockholm in 1818, the 30-year-old Italian dancer Filippo
Taglioni, then in his first year as ballet master, was invited by
the Spanish Ambassador to compose a short ballet to be given
in the Embassy at a party attended by the Crown Prince of

Sweden. The occasion represented a considerable compliment to Taglioni.

His libretto is based on a classical myth popular for many years among ballet masters. The most famous *Flore et Zephyr* was created at the King's Theatre, London, in 1796 by Charles Didelot, the great French ballet master and pupil of Noverre, who had been born in Stockholm and went on to become a founder of ballet in Russia. Into it Didelot introduced dancers made to fly with the aid of wires. Taglioni omitted from his libretto all such provision for a *corps de ballet* and concentrated only on the three principal characters. The result was a distillation of eighteenth-century anacreontic ballet, that is a ballet which was required to show 'free, joyous, and erotic' qualities – personified as Zephyr, Flora and Cupid respectively.

This was a period of intense change, a preparation for the triumphs of Romantic Ballet launched fourteen years later in Paris by Filippo Taglioni's *La Sylphide*, with his daughter Marie in the leading role. Themes like *The Return of Springtime* were still variations of eighteenth-century mythological formulae, as were music, stage lighting and production techniques. But costumes, especially for women, had abandoned eighteenth-century restrictions and now allowed a much wider range of movement, to the feet in soft heel-less slippers, and to the body in flowing Empire-line draperies. Dance technique followed suit. Men still dominated the ballet stage, as they had done since ballet began, but the dancing of men and women now commanded resources of technical display and expression which were the fruit of new exercises in the classroom and new, more advanced methods of teaching.

The choreography of *The Return of Springtime* draws on these period resources. Since Taglioni was Italian-trained – although, like all other leading professional dancers of the day, he studied in Paris and made his debut at the Opéra – Mary Skeaping based her work entirely on Italian technical dance manuals of the late eighteenth and early nineteenth centuries, up to and including Carlo Blasis' *Treatise on the Dance*.

Published in 1820, this early manual, by a man who became the greatest teacher of the nineteenth century, can safely be assumed to summarize technique and training methods at that time, and therefore present the knowledge upon which the Italian-trained Taglioni would draw.

Chapter Three

Romantic Ballet

AUGUST BOURNONVILLE (1805–1879)

Of the two great choreographers of Romantic Ballet, August Bournonville and Jules Perrot, Bournonville's work has been preserved more completely and becomes the best guide today to the style and quality of a movement which revolutionized choreography in the mid-nineteenth century. Born in Copenhagen, trained there first by his father, Antoine, and by Galeotti, both pupils of Noverre, he became a student of Auguste Vestris in Paris in 1820. Thus he inherited the best classic traditions of the eighteenth-century French and Italian schools. The French tradition was one of grace and style, epitomized in the teaching and ballets of Pierre Gardel, chief ballet master at the Paris Opéra from 1787 to 1827. The Italians contributed virtuosity in performance, invention of steps, and a more thorough academic approach. It is notable that all the technical manuals which have descended to us from the late eighteenth and early nineteenth centuries are Italian, so that we have no very clear idea of Gardel's teaching methods. We can be more certain of Vestris', partly because he inherited Italian traditions from his father and because Carlo Blasis' *Treatise on the Dance* of 1820 sums up the best of these traditions; partly because August Bournonville has left a choreographic portrait of a Vestris class in his ballet, *Konservatoriet* (q.v.).

Vestris, born in Paris in 1760, *premier danseur* at the Paris Opéra for thirty-six years – and even, for one performance at the age of 75, the partner of Marie Taglioni, then aged 31 – thus became the undisputed master and guardian of the best traditions of both schools. On the basis of his teaching, further explored by younger masters like Filippo Taglioni and Carlo

Blasis, was created the whole technical edifice of Romantic Ballet. Here began its exploration of the air through all kinds of jumps, the unprecedented lightness its female dancers achieved through the new skill of dancing on *pointe*, the qualities of its *port de bras*, and the grace of its movement.

In 1820, of course, much of this was still to come, although the exercises and training methods were there already and feminine fashion, in the flowing Empire line and new kinds of shoe, had begun to free body and feet for a much wider range of dance movement than was possible before. Filippo Taglioni, too, was busy on the harsh régime of training – six hours a day – which by 1832 produced in his daughter, Marie, the new image of ballet which has lasted to our own day.

As always, the technical discoveries of teaching in the classroom could not be considered complete until adapted and developed by choreographers on stage. It was the choreographers of Romantic Ballet – Taglioni, Bournonville and Perrot – who gave the movement the directions which have passed into history. Bournonville in Copenhagen is unique for the balance he maintained between the male and female dancer, where all other choreographers of Romantic Ballet emphasized the woman at the expense of the man. Such an emphasis proved fatal in the end, almost destroying ballet as an art because it destroyed the balance between the sexes on which dancing depends. By contrast, Bournonville's work has survived not only because of the particular isolation of ballet in Denmark but because all his ballets challenge male dancers as strongly as they challenge the female. To this day his choreography remains the basis of the style and school of Danish dancers.

After becoming soloist at the Paris Opéra in 1826 and dancing a season in London, Bournonville returned to Copenhagen in 1829. Here he created his first ballet and was appointed ballet master soon after. Except for short interludes of absence, due to disagreements or quarrels, he retained this position until his retirement in 1877. In his half century of life-work was created the Bournonville style, based on the style of Vestris. It was evolved through methods of teaching whose principles are described in his technical notes, *Etudes Chorégraphiques* published in 1861, and through the creation of thirty-six ballets and *divertissements*, many of which remain in the Danish repertory.

La Sylphide

Ballet in two acts. Libretto: Adolphe Nourrit. Choreography: August Bournonville after Filippo Taglioni. Music: Løvenskjold. First performed Royal Theatre, Copenhagen, 28th November, 1836, with Lucille Grahn as the Sylphide and Bournonville as James. Taglioni's version – music: Schneitzhöffer; décor: Ciceri; costumes: Lami. First performed Paris Opéra, 12th March, 1832, with Marie Taglioni in the name role and Joseph Mazilier as James.

ACT I: The interior of a farmhouse in Scotland.

At dawn on his wedding day, James sits asleep in a chair in front of the fire with Gurn, a friend, also asleep in a corner. Around him are the things he loves: the panelled walls of his Scottish home, warmed and lit from the great fireplace; in an upper room his mother and fiancée, Effie, also asleep. Beyond the farmhouse door lies the forest, 'green, mysterious, silent'. He ought to be happy, yet he is troubled. In his dreams, a white figure has appeared between him and his betrothed, a Sylphide, an ideal of love and beauty out of the forest and the Scottish mist. She is beside him as the curtain rises, kisses him lightly and disappears through the chimney as he wakes. He rouses Gurn, but at that moment Effie and his mother enter. Gurn protests his love for Effie, but she declares for James and kneels with him to receive his mother's blessing.

Effie's friends bring her presents while James, still looking for the Sylphide, suddenly finds old Madge, a witch, beside the chimney. The girls beg him to let Madge tell their fortunes, but Madge reads in Effie's hand that it is Gurn, not James, she will marry and James orders Madge away. Effie retires to prepare for the wedding and the Sylphide appears to James a second time, confessing her love for him. At the wedding celebrations the Sylphide flits in and out among the guests, seizes James's wedding ring and finally induces him to follow her into the forest. Effie, in despair, hears Gurn again protest his love.

ACT II: In the forest at night.

Old Madge and her attendant witches cast a spell upon a scarf. At dawn they vanish. James enters, searching for the Sylphide who appears beside him. She brings him water from a stream, fruit from the forest. James wants her to remain always with him instead of disappearing among the other Sylphides. Seeing Madge cross his path, he begs her forgiveness and she offers him help by means of a magic scarf which, she says, will make the Sylphide his forever. When the Sylphide returns, James puts the scarf about her. Instantly her wings fall off and she dies while Madge gloats over the results of her work. The Sylphides carry their sister into the tree tops while below them James sees in the distance the bridal procession of Gurn leading Effie to the altar.

In Filippo Taglioni's original version, at the Paris Opéra in 1832, *La Sylphide* became one of those unique ballets which change choreographic history and introduce a new era. Its significance lies in the influence and philosophy of the Romantic Movement which altered the arts of Europe as decisively as the Renaissance had done three centuries before.

The social upheavals manifest in the French Revolution and the Napoleonic régime gave a new perspective to man's thought. He moved beyond eighteenth-century rationalism to look deeper into the emotions. Foreshadowed in the writings of Rousseau and Madame de Staël, this romanticism found expression in France in a passionate interest in the writings of Walter Scott and Goethe, in the early poems of Lamartine, the paintings of Delacroix, Hugo's *Hernani*, and the music of Berlioz. So profound a change in the arts of Europe reflected in turn the change in social relations caused by the industrial revolution, including the relationship of artist and patron. A new bourgeois audience, which knew nothing about the theatrical conventions of the past, came into the theatre. Outside the theatre, a world of dirt, smoke, and industrial squalor had arisen in which the artist found himself equated with the worker. No longer able to expect the patronage of the rich, the artist must sell the fruits of his labour or starve.

To help forget the harshness of this new world and as a manifestation of the new romantic ethos, public and artist alike sought colour, fantasy and delight. They tried to evoke in art the creatures they would like to be, or to dream about – faraway exotic peoples with strange customs; spiritual beings from the occult and the supernatural; history become romance. People asked to see, in fact, a different, idealized world. This was the impulse behind the Romantic Movement, new, rebellious, led by young people who resembled, in outward forms at least, young critics of society and the arts today. They wore their hair long, upset their elders with strange ideas of behaviour and dress, experimented with drugs. 'Our cry' declared Théophile Gautier, the poet and one of their leaders, 'was liberation from the past, the bonds of classical restraint and all restriction!'

In ballet the new themes demanded by the new audiences gave inspiration and direction to the work of teachers, dancers and writers of ballet libretti. In 1831, Meyerbeer's *Robert le Diable* owed much of its success to a Ballet of Nuns who were summoned from the grave by the opera's hero. Their ghostly shapes on stage inspired the tenor in the opera, Nourrit, to propose the following year a libretto for a ballet which became *La Sylphide*. This responded so perfectly to the feeling of the time that it established a formula for all romantic ballet during the next forty years. Its story mirrored the tragic conflict between ideals and reality, which runs through all romantic art. The ending of this story, like the end of most romantic ballets after it, was unhappy because romantic art carried within itself its own fatal end. Dealing only in dreams and fantasies, its ideals could never be realized; there had to be the moment of awakening and return to reality.

Marie Taglioni was schooled exactly to create the image of the Sylphide. Her father's choreography of the ballet exploited the gifts she had developed in the classroom, and those gifts established her in the hearts of her audience as the image of the new style. The great and essential feature of this style was the exploration of the air through all kinds of steps of elevation. In other words, the lightness and grace on which Vestris had insisted as attributes of female dancing were developed to exploit the special qualities which women could bring to ballet. These qualities were emphasized further by new gas lighting and the simplicity of the Sylphide's costume, which began the gradual introduction of a silhouette quite different from the high-waisted Empire line of the preceding period. Of white muslin, leaving neck and shoulders bare, the skirt reaching midway between knee and ankle, it became the prototype of Romantic Ballet costume, providing in its later bell-shaped form an image retained until today. Similarly with Taglioni's utterly simple hair style, parted down the centre and gathered tight around the head to be tied at the back; and with Ciceri's farmhouse and forest bringing reality onto the ballet stage.

All this was continued and preserved in Bournonville's *La Sylphide*. The two versions cannot be compared since no choreographic record remains of Taglioni's staging, but Bournonville rejected Taglioni's mime-and-partnering conception of James ('In addition,' remarked Gautier of Taglioni's *Sylphide*, 'there are hardly any dances for men, which is a great comfort') in favour of the more lively conception which has descended to us, including a great deal of dancing in the first act and excellent male solos in the second. Very probably, Bournonville's whole treatment of Nourrit's libretto was fresher and less sophisticated than the original treatment. His was a younger approach, with a 17-year-old Sylphide in Lucille Grahn, compared with Marie Taglioni who was 28; a 21-year-old composer in Løvenskjold compared with the older Schneitzhöffer; and Bournonville himself, aged 31, at the height of his dancing career, 27 years younger than Filippo Taglioni. Nevertheless, the style of choreography, costume, scenery and, of course, libretto closely follow Taglioni's original. Thanks to Bournonville and the Danes, we have a simile of one of the most influential ballets ever created.

Napoli, or The Fisherman and his Bride

Romantic Ballet in three acts. Libretto and choreography: August Bournonville. Music: Paulli, Helsted, Gade and Lu nbye.

Scenery: Christersen. First performed Royal Theatre, Copen-hagen. 29th March, 1842.

ACT I: The square and beach of Santa Lucia, Naples.

To the left, the house of Veronica, a widow. To the right, a palace. In the square, people, children, macaroni and lemonade stalls, and so on. Enter Teresina with her mother, Veronica. It is clear that Giacomo and Peppo, the macaroni and lemonade sellers, are in love with Teresina, but she waits only for the return of the fisherman, Gennaro. The fishermen return. After some quarrelling over division of the catch, which Gennaro solves by giving a major portion to the Madonna, he offers Teresina an engagement ring. She accepts, Veronica giving them her blessing. To be alone, the young couple decide to go out in Gennaro's boat but a storm arises, Teresina is lost over-board and Gennaro, rescued by his friends, is blamed for her death. He appeals to the Madonna, and Fra Ambrosio, a monk, advises him to search the sea for his beloved, giving him an amulet of the Madonna for protection.

ACT II: The blue grotto on the Island of Capri.

Golfo, a sea-sprite, appears and Tritons attend to receive his commands. Naiads bring in the lifeless form of Teresina. Captivated by her beauty, Golfo restores her to life, but when she begs to return to her betrothed he turns her into a Naiad so that she loses all memory of human existence. Even so, she cannot reciprocate Golfo's affection. Gennaro enters the grotto searching for Teresina and finds the guitar she had carried with her, but when Teresina herself appears she fails to recognize him. He remembers the amulet and prays that Teresina be re-stored to him. Gradually her memory returns. Golfo, enraged, orders the Naiads to seize Teresina and the Tritons to crush Gennaro, who again raises the amulet. Golfo submits to its superior power and Teresina and Gennaro depart, their boat loaded with riches.

ACT III: Noon. An open space below a bridge connecting two hills outside Naples.

The bridge's centre pillar displays a picture of the Madonna, before which pilgrims come to kneel. Teresina arrives with her mother and Gennaro, but the people, encouraged by Peppo and Giacomo, think Teresina has been rescued by witchcraft and separate the couple. Fra Ambrosio, sent for to cast out the evil spirit, tells the crowd that Teresina was rescued by the divine power of the Madonna. Fear changes to joy and the return of the couple is celebrated with dances.

This, the most popular of Danish ballets, illustrates particularly well the direction which Bournonville's own talents and interest gave to romantic ballet. A distinguished male dancer – he was the first Gennaro in *Napoli*, the first James in his own *Sylphide* – he never accepted the secondary role ascribed to men by French romantic ballet, a fashion copied almost everywhere else. All his ballets include challenging dances for men but nowhere more than in the brilliant Tarantella which is the principal item in the celebrations at the end of *Napoli*. Dances of this kind sustained public interest in male dancing and provided essential proof – at a time when such proof was lacking everywhere else – of the male dancer's importance.

Napoli's theme stresses Bournonville's abiding interest in the folk *genre*. It shows how he added the gaiety of folk characters to the mystery and melancholy of Paris romanticism, building a Danish form of *ballet d'action*, the romantic folk-life ballet. The Bournonville repertory is filled with fisherfolk from Italy, townsfolk from Flanders, Spaniards, Norwegians, Czechs and Russians, besides a collection of Scandinavian elves and trolls. His work favoured the real-life element of romantic ballet rather than the supernatural element fashionable in Paris; and Bournonville reaches the summit of his art as the scenic narrator of genius who gives dance form to the romantic-bourgeois outlook of his time. Each ballet reflects the inspiration of travels abroad, but never exploits technique as an end in itself.

Konservatoriet eller et avisfrieri (*The Dancing School, or A Proposal by Advertising*).
Ballet in two acts. Libretto and choreography: Bournonville.

Music: Paulli. First performed Royal Theatre, Copenhagen, 6th May, 1849. Revised and revived as 'Konservatoriet' (The Dancing School) by Harold Lander and Valborg Borchsenius, using extracts from the original music. First performed Royal Theatre, Copenhagen, 24th October, 1941.

Only the Lander-Borchsenius one-act version of Bournonville's original two-act work now survives. Set in a classroom of the 1820s, it recalls and re-creates Bournonville's classroom experiences under Vestris in the Paris of that time. Its principal character is the ballet-master, violin in hand, who sets the exercises, demonstrates and controls everything. The *corps de ballet* and principal dancers comprise his pupils – from the youngest to the oldest. The result is an elaborate and charming *divertissement* linked by the exercises and rivalries of dancers in class.

Konservatoriet is one of the few – and perhaps the first – choreographic memoirs. Slonimsky, the Russian critic, recalls how in 1900 *Les Millions d'Arlequin*, also known as *Harlequinade*, came to enshrine the octogenarian Petipa's memories of his young days in Paris. So *Konservatoriet* recalls the 43-year-old Bournonville's memories of Paris; first when he was taken by his father to study under Vestris at the age of 14, then four years later when he settled there with the help of a royal subsidy from Copenhagen. Subsequently, he visited Vestris' classes every time he returned to Paris for as long as the old man was teaching.

Nor is this 'choreographic memoir' based only on a memory dimmed after 20 years. At the age of 18 Bournonville made a complete scheme of the Vestris *enchaînements*, many of which he used in his daily lessons, and so preserved them. Besides this, and his booklet *Etudes Chorégraphiques*, there remain two further manuscripts, unprinted and unfinished, dealing mainly with notation problems and the classification of dances and steps. Some of these latter were innovations by Bournonville, others were named as being particularly characteristic of leading contemporary dancers or ballets, such as Taglioni, Elssler, *La Sylphide*.

All this material indicates how aware was Bournonville of the

value of what he learned in Paris and the care he took to preserve
his knowledge in easy reference form. *Konservatoriet* remains
the purest choreographic expression of the School of Vestris
so that its historical importance is enormous. It illustrated the
French-Italian style which evolved over the hundred and fifty
years since Louis XIV formed his Royal Academies: lightness,
grace and charm from the women; elegance, strength and
a virile nobility from the men; from both, a considerable technical virtuosity.

JEAN CORALLI (1779–1854)
JULES PERROT (1810–1892)

These joint creators of *Giselle* span in their careers the
ambitions and weaknesses of Romantic Ballet. Coralli, born in
the early years of Louis XVI, Italian of Bolognese extraction
but trained at the Opéra in what was then the best school in
Europe, never acquired distinction as a dancer. He aimed
always at choreography. In this he displayed competence with
occasional distinction as in *Giselle,* but never that creative
originality which distinguishes the important artist. His
strength lay in the arrangement of *corps* dances, a certain gift
for spectacle and a grasp of what was appropriate to public taste
at a particular moment.

Perrot, son of a carpenter who became chief machinist at the
Grand-Théatre, Lyons, began to study dancing there, then
worked in the boulevard theatres and the Porte-Saint-Martin of
Paris. Later, through his own ambition, he became a pupil of
Auguste Vestris who instantly recognized his talent. Thus
Giselle joined two opposite talents: Coralli, by that time *maître
de ballet en chef* at the Opéra, achieving through *Giselle* his
small place in history; and Perrot, self-made, a natural theatre
man of enormous talent. Already established as a distinguished
dancer, he was the lover of Carlotta Grisi, the first Giselle, and
collaborated in the production entirely on her account, having
left the service of the Opéra in 1835 after disagreement with
Véron, the Director. How great a loss to the Opéra this was
became clear only after 1841 when Perrot was ballet master at

Her Majesty's Theatre, London, where he created most of his greatest works.

Giselle, ou Les Wilis

Fantastic ballet in two acts. Libretto: Théopile Gautier, Vernoy de St Georges and Jean Coralli. Choreography: Coralli and Perrot. Music: Adam, and some numbers by Burgmüller. Décor: Ciceri. First performed Paris Opéra, 28th June, 1841, with Carlotta Grisi as Giselle, Lucien Petipa as Albrecht and Adèle Dumilâtre as Myrtha.

ACT I: Outside Giselle's cottage.

'We set the action,' said Gautier, 'in some mysterious corner of Germany, among hillocks weighed down with russet vines: those beautiful vines from which hang the amber-coloured grapes which produce Rhine wine, these form the background.' In the distance, 'at the summit of a grey and bare rock stands like an eagle's nest one of those castles so common in Germany, with its battlemented walls, its pepperbox turrets, and its feudal weathercocks. It is the abode of Albrecht, young Duke of Silesia.' Here, on the edge of the forest, 'half buried among the leaves, cool and clean, is Giselle's cottage. The hut facing is occupied by Loys; Loys whom Giselle loves as much as she loves dancing; Loys whom she believes to be a village boy of her own kind; Loys who is, in fact, Duke Albrecht in disguise.' Betrothed already to someone else, he is not free to marry the peasant girl Giselle, however much he loves her. But as yet Giselle knows nothing of this. She loves Loys and she loves dancing, until one morning Hilarion, a gamekeeper, discovers Loys' secret.

Hilarion, who is deeply in love with Giselle, comes to lay flowers at her door and sees 'Loys' hiding a cloak and sword in his cottage. His suspicions aroused, Hilarion warns Giselle against Loys, but Giselle is sure of Loys' devotion. She disregards Hilarion's suspicions and the worries of Berthe, her mother, and joins happily with 'Loys' in the celebrations which mark the end of the grape harvest.

Horns sound faintly in the distance, and Albrecht's squire,

Wilfrid, comes to warn his master that a hunting party is approaching. Albrecht retreats into the forest, but Hilarion observes this encounter and breaks into Loys' cottage to try to uncover the mystery of the cloak and sword.

The hunting party arrives led by the Prince of Courland and his daughter, Bathilde, betrothed to Albrecht and staying at his castle. They ask for rest and refreshment at Berthe's cottage; Bathilde is charmed by Giselle and gives her a necklace on discovering that she, too, is betrothed. The Prince and Bathilde retire to rest in the cottage leaving orders that a hunting horn be hung outside so that they may be summoned in case of emergency. At this moment Hilarion appears from Loys' cottage with Albrecht's sword. Its crest tells him what he suspected – Loys is only trifling with Giselle's love. Choosing the moment when Giselle has been crowned Queen of the Vintage he unmasks Loys, but Giselle refuses to believe him, until he blows the horn. Bathilde appears with the Prince and claims Albrecht as her fiancé. The shock of such duplicity, unsuspected even by Hilarion, unhinges Giselle's reason. In her madness she enters another world between reality and unreality. She recognizes no one, but relives for herself the happiness she knew with Albrecht, the way they danced, until, heartbroken, she dies.

ACT II: Beside Giselle's tomb in the forest.

'The heart of our ballet,' said Gautier, 'lay in its second act. There is the poetry. It is where I began . . . A world of which the German poet speaks, where maidens who have died before their wedding day, because of faithless lovers, return as Wilis to dance by night.'

First Hilarion, then Albrecht, come to keep a night-time vigil of penitence beside Giselle's grave. Meanwhile the Wilis appear, led by Myrtha, their Queen, and summon Giselle to join their band. Giselle must obey the Queen, but when she sees Albrecht she is moved because he is so sad. The Wilis return, pursuing Hilarion, who is driven to death in the lake. Next they capture Albrecht and the Queen commands him to dance to his death. Giselle urges him to the protection of the cross on her grave. He is safe from Myrtha's power until the Queen compels Giselle to dance and thus entice Albrecht from the cross. But Giselle dances with him and for him until dawn breaks, the power of the Queen of the Wilis over Albrecht evaporates with the sun, and Albrecht is saved.

Coming nine years after *La Sylphide*, *Giselle* perfected the romantic formula. As Gautier said, each collaborator – composer, designer, and choreographer – raised to a higher sphere what had been achieved before. Especially was this true of Jules Perrot, 'the greatest male dancer and choreographer of his day', who devised most of the dances for Giselle herself. In these dances he combined acting with dancing so closely as to create danced action which was a more expressive kind of ballet, and 'a new development in the art of choreography'.

In fact, the role of Giselle represented not only a great advance in choreography when Perrot created it, but a great advance in the demands it made upon the dancer. It is one of the most emotionally exhausting roles in classical ballet today because of the contrast it requires between realism in Act I and fantasy in Act II and because the dancer must be able to mime joy and sorrow while dancing. 'Perrot', said Gautier, 'had dreamed of combining the two sides of Romantic Ballet – the real and the supernatural – in one person. And he did. In Carlotta Grisi, the first Giselle.'

Never before had character been explored so deeply in dance form. Perrot achieved this through the combination of dance steps with acting; through a contrast of choreography between the two acts – bright, quick, folk-inspired steps for the peasant Giselle in the first act compared with a larger, more remote and joyless style requiring exceptional elevation in the second act; also through the use of elementary motifs in movement similar to Adam's elementary motifs in the score. These motifs were phrases of dancing given to the leading characters and repeated with variations to show their dramatic development. Because Albrecht remains the same living, human person throughout the ballet, his motif remains the same in both acts.

Hilarion, a mime role, receives only a motif in the music. But for Giselle it is different. As a ghost in Act II, her dancing moves into a different key, while in Act I, she has two motifs, sometimes danced alone sometimes with Albrecht, to show her happiness and love of dancing. Both these return in distorted form to reflect her pain and madness when Albrecht's duplicity is revealed.

Choreographically and in every other way, as Gautier pointed out, *Giselle*'s greatness lies in its second act. The conception was Gautier's, whereas St Georges was responsible for the skilled carpentry of Act I. In Act II, all the innovations of music, costume and lighting, style and theme, all the technical developments introduced through *La Sylphide*, were perfected and used at their highest level to evoke a world of spirits. Perrot's choreography, in particular, reveals the purest romantic feeling through movements in a different key, with the music taken more slowly.

In this act Coralli had been responsible for the organization of the *corps de ballet* and its dances – as he had been in Act I, enjoying particular success with an interpolated peasant dance for two principals and *corps de ballet* to music by Burgmüller – but *Giselle* owes its excellence to Perrot's genius reflected especially in the choreography for the title role in Act II.

For so significant a ballet it was created in record time. Adam composed the score in just a week, producing music which was a considerable advance on previous ballet music. At the same time Ciceri set to work to build the scenery and the whole was completed in little more than two months. Its triumph was absolute, 'the greatest success of a ballet at the Opéra since *La Sylphide*,' said Gautier. 'After it even *La Sylphide* seemed but a beginning.'

Versions were staged throughout Europe. Perrot produced it for London on 12th March, 1842, again with Carlotta Grisi as Giselle but with himself instead of Lucien Petipa as Albrecht. In 1848 he produced it in St Petersburg (which had already seen a garbled version by the old ballet-master Titus) with Elssler as Giselle and Marius Petipa, Lucien's brother, as Albrecht. Two years later he produced it again in St Petersburg, this time for Grisi.

Appointed as a ballet master to the Imperial Theatre in 1862, Petipa maintained *Giselle* in the repertory during the remaining 40 years of his career as master of the Russian ballet, making a series of alterations and emendations to the text, notably in 1884. He retained, for example, Elssler's acted version of the mad scene at the end of Act I in preference to Grisi's original danced version because Elssler was the more popular of the two ballerinas in Russia. He also blended, naturally and rightly, the simple, charming French style of Perrot's *Giselle* with new dance developments of the period, particularly the more brilliant technique and greater virtuosity acquired by the Russians from Italy. That is why the Queen of the Wilis moves now with greater jumps than Perrot ever knew, sharper and quicker turns, a longer line of the leg in arabesque, stronger use of the pointes, and shoes with blocked toes to make such things possible. In this way the Russians preserved *Giselle* while retaining the essential qualities of Perrot's choreography. It is the same with Gautier's theme. The story remains but the Russians have added a deeper dramatic truth, emphasizing Giselle's pathetic dilemma, that Myrtha can force her to destroy the man she loves; and, especially, the triumph of Giselle's love over the vengeance demanded by the Queen of the Wilis.

Elsewhere in Europe, *Giselle* slipped into oblivion. It was not until 1910, when Diaghilev presented it in his second Paris season, with Karsavina and Nijinski, that this romantic masterpiece was rediscovered by audiences in its original home. Subsequent stagings of the ballet have all stemmed from the St Petersburg version descended to us in a direct link from Perrot through Petipa and Nicholas Sergueyev's productions based on his Stepanov notation of the Maryinski repertory.

The first modern British production was staged by Sergueyev for Olga Spessivtseva during the Camargo Society's season at the Savoy Theatre, London, in June, 1932. It was revived two years later for the Vic-Wells Ballet at Sadler's Wells and has remained in repertory regularly since then.

ARTHUR ST LEON (c. 1815–1870)

Coppélia, or La Fille aux Yeux d'Email
Ballet in two acts and three scenes. Libretto: Charles Nuitter and Arthur St Léon. Choreography: St Léon. Music: Delibes. Scenery: Cambon, Despléchin and Lavastre. Costumes: Paul Lormier. First performed Paris Opéra, 25th May, 1870.

ACT I: A square in a little town on the border of Galicia.

To the left, an inn with Swanilda's house upstage in the background. To the right, opposite, Coppélius' house with a large dormer window.

As the curtain rises Coppélius pushes into the dormer window his newest and best creation – Coppélia, a mechanical doll so lifelike that he wants to see who will believe she is real. The first person to fall for the trick is Swanilda who comes into the square and is very annoyed when the beautiful girl in Coppélius' window seems to ignore her. The second person to be taken in is Franz, Swanilda's fiancé, who tries to flirt with Coppélia and is caught doing so by Swanilda. During a general dance the burgomaster announces a fête to celebrate the presentation of a new bell to the town. All who are betrothed at that time will receive dowries from the Lord of the Manor. He asks Swanilda if she is to be among them. To test Franz's faithfulness Swanilda takes an ear of corn. If it rustles, then Franz *does* love her. But however much she listens, and her friends listen, the ear of corn is silent. She is comforted when Franz assures her all is well. Everyone dances for the burgomaster, then leaves as evening falls. Coppélius, pleased at the success of his trick, comes out of his house for an evening stroll. Teased by a crowd of youths, he is rescued by the innkeeper but drops the key of his house in the scuffle. Swanilda and her friends find the key and use it to enter the house to discover more about Coppélia. Coppélius returns to look for the key, finds the door of his house open and steals in to surprise the intruders. Franz also determines to meet Coppélia. He brings a ladder and is climbing to her window as the curtain falls.

Act II: Dr Coppélius' workshop.

Inside the workshop Swanilda is urged by her companions to approach the alcove where they think Coppélia must be. They are astonished to discover she is only a doll. The other mechanical dolls are set in motion and the girls dance round them. Coppélius bursts in and drives them all out except Swanilda, who hides in the alcove and disguises herself by dressing in Coppélia's clothes. Franz appears at the window and Coppélius, pretending to be one of his own dolls, allows him to enter before seizing him by the ear and threatening punishment. Then Coppélius has an idea. Inviting Franz to share a bottle of wine, he drugs the wine and, using a book of magic, tries to bring Coppélia to life by transferring Franz's spirit to the doll. Swanilda, disguised as the doll, pretends to come to life. The old man is delighted, but the doll becomes more and more difficult and demanding. To keep her occupied Coppélius teaches her a Spanish dance and a Scottish dance, but, finally, Swanilda's friends return, Franz regains his senses and the old man realizes he has been tricked.

Act III: The Square of the Town.

Next evening, at the presentation of the bell, the Lord of the Manor bestows purses of gold on all the betrothed couples. Coppélius arrives and complains that his dolls have been ruined. Swanilda offers her dowry as compensation, but the Lord of the Manor gives one of his own purses to Coppélius and so placates him. As part of the celebrations the young people of the town dance 'A Masque of the Hours'. Franz and Swanilda are forgiven and their marriage is made the crowning event of the occasion.

Just as romantic ballet required a sad or fatal ending to most of its stories, so romantic ballet itself suffered from a fatal weakness. It relegated male dancers, first to become partners, foils and *porteurs* for the all-important ballerina, then mimes and dancers in speciality spots. By the time of *Coppélia*, in 1870, leading male roles were often danced by women *en travestie* and regiments of women could be seen on London and Parisian

stages at the turn of the century impersonating soldiers and
sailors. Thus the romantic movement nearly destroyed the art
of ballet by destroying the balance between the sexes upon
which all dancing depends.

In its historical development *Coppélia*'s significance is two-
fold: with Franz danced by a woman and the production itself
being the last new ballet before the closure of the Opéra in the
siege of Paris in 1870, it marks the end of Romantic Ballet; at
the same time the positive elements of the production,
especially Delibes' score, serve as a link between romantic
ballet and the new classical style arising under Petipa in Russia.

The ballet was the work of three people in collaboration –
Arthur St Léon as choreographer, Léo Delibes as composer
and Charles Nuitter, librarian of the Opéra, as the librettist. Of
these, St Léon and Nuitter were close friends, well established
in their professions; Delibes, then aged 34, was still building
his reputation. Each of them, through *Coppélia*, enhanced the
separate arts of their contribution to create a work which
remains a model of ballet construction. The basis of *Coppélia*'s
success – and the reason it has survived – is the music of
Delibes. Delibes was a dancer's composer with the gift of
illustrating action, creating atmosphere and inspiring movement. He attempted in the music of *Coppélia* what the impres-
sionists had achieved already in painting – to make colour the
thing that mattered most. The result was the first symphonic
ballet score, developing many of the devices which composers
like Adam in *Giselle* had tried tentatively already. The colour
in the music is a development of the descriptive passages introduced in most romantic scores. The rudimentary use of *leit-
motif*, initiated in *Giselle*, is developed here and woven into the
score to describe the principal characters – old Coppélius,
Swanilda and, of course, Franz, who has two themes, both very
suitable for a woman playing a man's role.

St Léon, the choreographer, had been born in Paris and
studied under his father while he was ballet master at Stuttgart.
Becoming an excellent dancer, actor and choreographer, he
appeared subsequently all over Europe dancing and mounting
his ballets. His taste was somewhat erratic and inclined to be

commercial, reflecting also the wide interests of the man as teacher, historian, author, violinist – and one of the best choreographers of his time. In 1870, he was *maître de ballet* at the Opéra as well as having fulfilled much the same function in St Petersburg for the previous ten years, commuting between the two capitals. His health now was failing, and for these reasons the creation of the new ballet was spread over three years.

Nuitter's contribution was a libretto which helped to restore the fading reputation of the *ballet d'action* as well as being almost unique in its time. No supernatural beings nor ethereal heroines like Giselle. Instead, real people, both nice and nasty. But it was St Léon's professional expertise which drew everything together. At his suggestion, Delibes included a Hungarian Czardas for the first time in any theatre score. And he made certain the libretto had all the elements which would allow him to hold the interest of audiences, especially through national dances with plenty of spectacular effects. In this way choreography reflected the rising nationalism of the time and gained an extra variety of steps.

None of St Léon's dances for the ballet remain today but sections of the traditional Opéra version, with Franz *en travestie*, are included in the repertory of the Royal Ballet's *Ballet for All* company. This allows comparison with the version created in Russia, in the early years of the present century, with choreography by Ivanov and Cecchetti. Ivanov's version is based on that produced by Petipa earlier at the Maryinski Theatre, St Petersburg, in 1884, keeping St Léon's ideas and story but presenting them through dances of his own. In these, Franz became a role for a man. The music remains as Delibes created it, linking two great historical periods of ballet, the French Romantic style of the first *Coppélia* and the Russian classical style of *Coppélia* today.

Chapter Four

The Imperial Russian Ballet

MARIUS PETIPA (1819–1910)

Marius Petipa is the colossus of nineteenth-century ballet; other choreographers may well have rivalled him for genius, or have had as great – or greater – influence on the art of ballet – but none can rival him for productivity; none achieved the creation of a monument so grand or influential as the Imperial Russian Ballet, of which he was master, in effect, for more than forty years. This ballet was created out of the combination of French style, traditional in Russia, with newly imported Italian technique expressed through Russian bodies and Russian temperament. The result was a new national school of ballet which remains a yardstick for dancers today. Over the birth of this school Petipa presided; it is his principal legacy.

Marius Petipa was born into a family of itinerant dancers in 1819 in Marseille, where his father was at that time ballet master. Like many of the dance families of that day, the Petipas were ever on the move. By the time Alphonse Victor Marius was three years old, his father was in Brussels with his wife, elder son Lucien, and elder daughter Victoria. They stayed there until 1831 – Marius starting dancing lessons from his father at the age of seven, and first appearing on stage at the age of nine. Revolutionary activity in 1830–31 drove them to Antwerp, then back to Brussels. They next went to Bordeaux for four years, and at the age of 16 Marius launched out on his own, obtaining work in Nantes where he was called upon to compose a few short ballets. While there, he broke his leg and was obliged to return to his family who, in 1839, set out for New York. Their stay was brief. Jean Petipa staged some ballets (including Taglioni's *Jocko, the Brazilian Ape*), but a manager absconded with their funds and the Petipas hastened back to Europe.

Lucien was already *premier danseur* at the Paris Opéra, and Marius joined the classes given by the 80-year-old Auguste Vestris. He also partnered Carlotta Grisi at a benefit gala, and then was offered a post as *premier danseur* at Bordeaux where he danced in *Giselle*, *La Péri* and *La Fille Mal Gardée*, as well as staging four ballets of his own. After a year he was engaged to go to the Royal Theatre, Madrid, creating four more ballets and dancing leading roles during the next four years. A duel with an aristocrat over an affair of the heart necessitated his fleeing Spain, and in 1846 he was back in Paris, out of work. He was saved, so to speak, in 1847 by an invitation from the veteran ballet master Titus (*maître de ballet* in St Petersburg) to go to that city as *premier danseur*, arriving there in May. Since his father, Jean, was a professor at the Imperial School, one may well assume a certain parental influence in the offer of the post.

His experience as dancer and choreographer stood him in good stead. In his first season he staged three ballets: *Paquita*, *Satanella* and *La Péri*, for himself and the principal ballerina, Andreyanova, as well as dancing Albrecht in *Giselle*. (Marius, incidentally, was very much under the shadow of his more famous brother Lucien, who was one of the great dancers of the Romantic age and the first Albrecht.)

Any hope of his further developing as a choreographer was killed by the arrival in St Petersburg of Jules Perrot, who remained as ballet master until 1859. During this time Petipa danced leading roles, but his choreographic output amounted to a few brief works, staged principally for his first wife, Marie Surovschikova, whom he married in 1854. Even with Perrot's departure Petipa was not to be given a real chance to stage ballets. Arthur Saint-Léon was appointed, an accomplished and prolific choreographer, whose ballets were often described as protracted *divertissements*. He could invent charming solos and duets, but he was less accomplished at the dramatic ensembles which so distinguished the work of Perrot. Despite St Léon's attempts to prevent Petipa being entrusted with any creative work, the Director of the Imperial Theatres offered him a ballet in 1861. The fact that the work was to star the fading technical abilities of the Italian guest ballerina, Carolina Rosati, who was well past her prime, may have accounted for Petipa's being given what was, in effect, a very difficult task. But he realized that an important chance was being offered him. With a clear sense of occasion – which never deserted him throughout his creative life – he realized too, that, things Egyptian were the current fashion (Russia was at that time fascinated with the news of archaeological excavations in Egypt). Accordingly he went to Paris to consult Vernoy de St Georges, the most accomplished ballet librettist of the time, and together they concocted an intrigue of massive complication, based upon Gautier's *Le Roman de la Momie*. On his return to Petersburg, Petipa was told that the ballet had to be completed within six weeks, in time for Rosati's benefit performance. He agreed, and while Pugni ran up the score, Petipa laboured and completed five acts with prologue in an unprecedentedly short time. *La Fille du Pharaon* was a huge success, and Petipa's reputation was made. The work was a grand spectacular – indeed it is the first of the ballets *à grand spectacle* that were to delight audiences for the next 40 years. Petipa was a genius, of that there can be no doubt, and his genius lay not only in his sheer ability to make dances, but in his powers to absorb ideas, to accept influences from other choreographers. In *La Fille du Pharaon*, he was making use of everything he had learned while working with Perrot and St Léon, and he shaped these elements into the massive work that won him acclaim.

Six weeks was, in fact, the period in which the piece was staged; it had been gestating for much longer. The skill with which Petipa built each act, balancing solos with ensembles, processions with set pieces, was the result of a profound and lengthy consideration.

The next 40 years present the picture of a career that was filled with disappointments as well as triumphs; from 1862 until 1869 when St Léon left, Petipa laboured as second ballet master, producing (almost alternately it now seems) flops and successes. With St Léon's departure he was named chief ballet master, responsible for the Imperial Theatres in St Petersburg and Moscow and the Imperial Schools. His duty was 'to produce a new ballet at the beginning of every season'. This Petipa did, offering his audiences the sort of grand and complicated productions which had first won him fame. Alas, his audiences became bored, attendances fell off at the ballet performances, but Petipa had to go on producing spectacle after spectacle: *Don Quixote* (1869), *Trilby* (1871), *Camargo* (1872), *The Butterfly* (1874), *The Bandits* (1875), and many more.

That he was not happy with the need to turn out spectacle after brilliant spectacle we know from the testimony of August Bournonville, who visited St Petersburg in 1874 and commented on the hollow magnificence of these dance extravaganzas. Petipa agreed but pointed out that the public expected them and were not to be weaned from them. In 1881, however, the Imperial Theatres were placed under the direction of Ivan Vsevolozhsky (for further details about this admirable man see *The Sleeping Beauty* note), and it is to his guidance that Petipa's later career owes its greatness. He supported and advised the choreographer, gave him a new long contract as ballet master-in-chief and helped in the re-organization of the Imperial Theatres. With the arrival of a troupe of visiting Italian dancers in a summer theatre in St Petersburg in 1885, a new interest in ballet arose. The Italians were led by Virginia Zucchi, and danced in a farrago called *A Flight to the Moon*. What gripped the Russian audiences was their technical brilliance and Zucchi's dramatic power. She was promptly invited to appear at the Maryinski, and during the next two years her great gifts lured back an audience to the theatre. She was followed by a whole series of Italian virtuosi: Pierina Legnani, Antonietta dell'Era, Carlotta Brianza, Enrico Cecchetti. They offered the most stimulating example to the Russian dancers, who sought to emulate and rival their prodigious brilliance. (Cecchetti stayed on in Russia to teach for some years and created both the first Bluebird and Carabosse).

In the late golden years of the century when the Imperial Ballet knew its apogee, Petipa continued producing ballets –

notably the last two great works of his career, *The Sleeping Beauty* and *Raymonda*. In 1899 Vsevolozhsky resigned, to be succeeded by an equally amiable and charming aristocrat, Prince Volkonsky. But his tenure of office was short, and following a disagreement with the ballerina, Kschessinskaya, he was forced to resign. His successor, Colonel Telyakovsky, was inimical to everything Petipa stood for. The old ballet master's memoirs recount insults and reproaches, and his final ballet, *The Magic Mirror* in 1903, was a tragic and terrible débâcle. Petipa had outlived his own career; Telyakovsky was intent upon change – much influenced by the new artistic world of Moscow – and Petipa represented the old establishment. The première of *The Magic Mirror*, with the Imperial Family present, was to be Petipa's benefit; it turned into a mad house of hooting and cat-calls. Soon after, Petipa retired, and the Imperial Ballet (though not the Imperial Schools), left without a major choreographer, went into a decline from which it was only to be saved by the Revolution.

Petipa made the Imperial Ballet. With an audience bent on spectacle and splendour, he provided all the requisite magnificence and technical dazzle. He had at times to sacrifice his own tastes to those of his audience; he was a purveyor of pleasures, and fortunately his genius was such that he could produce magnificent ballets to order. He insisted, above all, on the supremacy of dancing, and under his rule the Imperial Schools produced and went on producing many of the finest artists of their time, whom the new Russian School made supreme. He constantly sought to extend the range of his dancers – and at the same time was extending his own powers. In sum, he made the Imperial Ballet great at a time when ballet in the rest of the world was sunk into depths from which it was soon to be rescued by the next generation led by Diaghilev and Fokine.

La Bayadère

A ballet in five acts and seven scenes. Libretto: Khoudekov. Choreography: Petipa. Music: Minkus. First performed Maryinski Theatre, St Petersburg, 4th February, 1877.

The libretto of this Indian extravaganza in romantic style tells of Solor, a warrior, who falls in love with a temple dancer (a Bayadère), Nikiya. A Brahmin priest loves her too, but she rejects his attentions. Solor is offered the hand of Gamsatti, daughter of a Rajah, and he is unable to refuse. Gamsatti learns of his love for Nikiya, and quarrels with her. Eventually Nikiya is given a basket containing a poisonous snake which bites her, and she dies. Solor dreams that he has followed her to the Kingdom of Shades and there dances with her and begs her forgiveness. (In the now suppressed fifth act Solor marries Gamsatti; their palace is struck by lightning and crashes to the ground in ruins, killing everyone beneath it, including Solor and Gamsatti).

When the Kirov Ballet made their first London appearance in July, 1961, they brought nothing more beautiful or exciting than the Kingdom of Shades scene from *La Bayadère*. As the first of the thirty-two Bayadères appeared on the ramp and began that slow unfolding of arabesque penché after arabesque penché, we became aware of something novel and beautiful. To realize that this choreography was nearly a hundred years old was to be reminded once again of Petipa's genius. As given subsequently by the Royal Ballet (27th November, 1963) – staged by Nureyev and decorated by Philip Prowse – the sequence of dances is as follows: Entry of the *corps de ballet*; *pas de trois* for three soloists; entry of Solor and appearance of Nikiya; *pas de deux*; entry of *corps de ballet* and solos for Nikiya; solo for Solor; variations by three soloists; duet for Solor and Nikiya; solo for Nikiya; *pas de trois* with *corps de ballet*; *pas de deux* for Solor and Nikiya; solo for Nikiya; solo for Solor; finale.

The Kingdom of Shades is a masterpiece of choreography; it relies entirely upon its dancing – drama is minimally present – but what delights is the superb fashion in which Petipa has manipulated his forces. One Soviet critic has called it 'symphonic' in structure, and this is certainly true in the way the *corps de ballet* echoes or enhances the work of the principals. It recalls, too, the second act of *Giselle*, but the profusion of dances are here far superior to the choreography of *Giselle*. Each of the variations for the three soloists is a gem and the work for Nikiya (particularly) and Solor is by turns dazzling and moving – because Petipa was writing Nikiya for his favourite ballerina, Vazem. Perhaps the most extraordinary thing about the ballet is its modernity; it looks far less dated and old-fashioned than many another piece half its age: a witness, were witness needed, to the enduring freshness of the classic dance, of which *La Bayadère* is a glorious example.

The Sleeping Beauty

A ballet in prologue and three acts. Choreography: Marius Petipa. Libretto: I. A. Vsevolozhsky after Perrault. Music: Tchaikovsky. Scenery: Levogt, Botcharov, Shishkov, Ivanov. Costumes: I. A. Vsevolozhsky. First performed 15th January, 1890, Maryinski Theatre, St Petersburg.

Carlotta Brianza as Aurora, Paul Gerdt as the Prince, Cecchetti as Carabosse, Cecchetti and Varvara Nikitina as Bluebirds, Marie M. Petipa as Lilac Fairy.

PROLOGUE: The Christening.

In a hall of King Florestan XXIV's palace the courtiers are assembling for the celebration of the christening of the King's infant daughter, Aurora. Catalabutte, the Master of Ceremonies, marshals the guests; the King and Queen arrive to receive the greetings of their court, and soon a group of five fairies arrive with their cavaliers, to be followed by the Lilac Fairy. Each fairy dances a variation but just as they have presented their gifts to the infant princess, a roll of thunder announces the appearance of another fairy. It is Carabosse, who comes in with attendant creatures; she is furious at having been forgotten when the invitations to the christening were sent out. She mocks the other fairies and announces that her gift to Aurora is death: when the Princess grows up she will prick her finger on a spindle and die. As she bursts into peals of evil laughter, the Lilac Fairy steps forward; she has yet to make her present to Aurora and she says that, though she cannot remove all of Carabosse's curse, she can save Aurora's life.

Instead of dying, Aurora will sink into a hundred years sleep, from which she shall be awakened by a Prince's kiss. Carabosse exits in a furious temper, and the relieved court turn and pay their respects to the infant princess.

Act I: The Spell.

It is Aurora's twentieth birthday and, in a garden of the palace, peasants and courtiers are assembled to celebrate the happy day. Although anything sharp-pointed has been banned from the kingdom, three knitting women are discovered by Catalabutte, who seizes their needles and threatens them with punishment. When the King and Queen enter, with four Princes who are suitors for Aurora's hand, they are furious at the sight of the needles, and the King condemns the three old women to death; the Queen intercedes for them and, because it is Aurora's birthday, the King forgives them. The peasants dance a joyous waltz, after which, heralded by a group of her friends, Aurora appears. She greets her parents, who present the four princely suitors to her; Aurora dances for them, accepting the roses that they offer. As she dances, an old woman mysteriously comes forward, offering her a curious gift the like of which Aurora has never seen before. It is a spindle. Her parents are horrified, but Aurora has already pricked her finger with it. She sinks to the ground in a faint, then revives and seems fully recovered; but as she starts to dance again her head swims, she circles round in a series of dizzying turns and collapses. At once the old woman throws off her cloak and reveals herself as Carabosse. The courtiers try to seize her, but she vanishes in a cloud of smoke, leaving the distraught assembly contemplating the body of Aurora which lies on the ground at the Queen's feet. Now the Lilac Fairy arrives to fulfil her promise; Aurora is carried away, and the Lilac Fairy casts a spell of sleep over the scene, causing a forest of trees and twining brambles to rise up and hide the entire palace and gardens.

Act II, *Scene I.* The Vision.

A hundred years later Prince Florimund is out hunting with

his court in this same forest. His companions dance and sport, but when beaters enter announcing that a wild boar has been sighted, Florimund stays behind, urging his whole retinue to go after the animal, while he remains alone. The Lilac Fairy now appears to him, telling him of the enchanted forest and the sleeping Aurora. She shows him a vision of Aurora and the Prince is immediately struck by her beauty. The vision appears surrounded by a group of nymphs, and dances with the Prince before melting away into the night. Florimund, by now in love with Aurora, begs the Lilac Fairy to take him to the spot where she sleeps, and they move off in the Lilac Fairy's boat to the palace of the Sleeping Beauty.

ACT II, *Scene II*. The Awakening.

The Lilac Fairy guides Florimund through the forest and the cobwebby palace to the room where Aurora sleeps. The Prince awakens her with a kiss.

ACT III: The Wedding.

Characters from all the fairy tales come to the wedding of Aurora and Florimund and pay their homage to the newly-wed pair: a quartet of fairies; a Bluebird and the enchanted Princess Florisse; Puss in Boots and the White Cat; Red Riding Hood and the Wolf; Cinderella and Prince Fortuné; these and many more, with the Lilac Fairy and her attendants, dance in celebration. Aurora and Florimund dance, too, and the whole court joins in a general mazurka which leads into an apotheosis of happiness as the curtain falls.

There is a name missing from the credits for *The Sleeping Beauty* on our ballet programmes, and ironically it is that of the man who planned, guided and inspired its creation, and in no small measure made possible the very existence of this masterpiece.

Ivan Alexandrovich Vsevolozhsky (1835–1909) was Director of the Imperial Theatres from 1881–99, and during his eighteen years of service, ballet in Russia flourished as never before – just how much we may judge from the crowning achievement of his régime, *The Sleeping Beauty*. The Maryin-ski Theatre was a direct adjunct of the Imperial Court and it reflected, probably better than anything else, the taste of that closed, aristocratic world; appropriately enough its Director was appointed either from the higher ranks of the army or from the diplomatic corps. Vsevolozhsky, who succeeded the penny-pinching Baron Kister (Petipa records that his insistence on re-using rickety old scenery occasioned an incident when a set collapsed in pieces during a performance, and the stage manager 'lost his reason right there on stage') was a diplomatist who had been *en poste* in Paris and was considered very fran-cophile by his contemporaries. A man of wide culture, a play-wright and essayist, he was also a talented amateur artist, sufficiently gifted to design costumes for the theatre. But his claim to fame and to our gratitude rests on the very consider-able impact he had on the Imperial ballet.

Natalia Roslavleva's valuable *Era of the Russian Ballet* records that within a year of his appointment his salary had been doubled 'for excellent management'; that he instituted the rehearsal hall in Theatre Street that is still in use today; that at his instance the first syllabus of the ballet school was drawn up, and that he created a system of advisory panels – comprising composer, librettist, choreographer, designer and stage manager – to ensure the highest standards of collaboration in the creation of ballets, in which he seems a notable forerunner of Diaghilev.

In 1886, in an act which we can still applaud even at this distance in time, he abolished the post of official ballet composer – alas, poor Minkus – as part of his scheme to encourage better music in the theatre; and it is significant that as early in his official career as 1883 he had championed Tchaikovsky. In that year the composer had written in amazement to Mme von Meck: '*Without any advances on my part, Petersburg and Mos-cow contend for my work* [*the opera* Mazeppa] . . . *I cannot understand the reason for such attentions on the part of the theatrical world – there must be some secret cause for it, and I can only surmise that the Emperor himself must have expressed a wish that my opera should be given as well as possible in both capitals.*'

The 'secret cause' was Vsevolozhsky, whose admiration for Tchaikovsky was to manifest itself in even more practical form five years later when he obtained an annual pension of 3,000 roubles for the composer from the Emperor. In 1886 he had already made his first attempt to get a ballet score from Tchaikovsky, whose diary for the October of that year records a couple of visits to Vsevolozhsky's home and then on November 8th '*At home, where everything was packed [for his return home to Maidanovo] found a letter from Vsevolozhsky with an invitation for Sunday to talk over ballet. Fell into despair but decided to stay and made arrangements accordingly. Ran to Vsevolozhsky's where both Petipa and Frolov [a critic] turned up. Immediately started discussions. My rejection of Salammbô. Undine.*'

Nothing came of the projected ballet, in part because, reportedly, Modeste Tchaikovsky's libretto was found unsuitable, but two years later Vsevolozhsky tried again. In May 1888 he wrote to Tchaikovsky: '*It wouldn't be a bad idea, by the way, for you to write a ballet. I have been thinking of writing a libretto on Perrault's La Belle au Bois Dormant. I should like the scenery to be in the style of Louis XIV, and in this setting one could stage a magical fantasy and compose melodies in the style of Lully, Bach and Rameau, etc. . . . In the last act we must have a quadrille of all the Perrault fairy tales: Puss in Boots, Tom Thumb, Cinderella, Bluebeard and so on.*'

The style of this proposed ballet was clearly inspired by the theatrical fashion of the time for extravagant, complicated *féeries*, whose chief attribute was a profusion of *divertissements*. The inspiration for this type of gorgeously undemanding entertainment may well have been the success of Manzotti's *Excelsior* (Milan 1881), which sparked off many imitations, and which itself was seen in St Petersburg in 1887 in two separate but simultaneous stagings in one of which Cecchetti appeared. The *ballet féerie* had become de rigueur at the Maryinski – it was both Petipa's strength and his weakness that he could so successfully turn out ballets to suit the vagaries of public taste, and ignore his personal feelings as to what his ballets might be – and in *The Sleeping Beauty* its limitations are

more than transcended by Petipa and Tchaikovsky, who transformed it into a great work of art.

On receipt of Vsevolozhsky's scenario, Tchaikovsky replied:
'*I have just seen the scenario of* The Sleeping Beauty . . . *and I
should like to tell you straight away how charmed and enthusiastic
I am. The idea appeals to me and I wish nothing better than to
write the music for it.*'

This last remark is revealing, since he had earlier in the
same year completed his fifth symphony, and after its first two
performances had written to Mme von Meck: '*I have come to
the conclusion that it is a failure. There is something repellent,
something superfluous, patchy and insincere which the public
instantly recognizes. . . . Am I really played out as they say?*'

But Tchaikovsky's enthusiasm for his new project may well
have been somewhat dampened in the late autumn when he
received Petipa's immensely detailed working draft of the action. This fascinating document is preserved in the Bakhrushin
Museum, Moscow, and we are indebted to Joan Lawson's
important translation (published in *The Dancing Times* between
December 1942 and March 1943) for quotations from it. It was
Petipa's habit to draw up a complete plan of a ballet before
appearing in the rehearsal room, thus furnishing his composer
with fullest details of his musical requirements. (He also on
occasion provided notes for the designer and costumier.) His
notes for *Beauty* indicate just how precise were his preliminary
ideas. The draft sent to Tchaikovsky comprises duplicate notes
for each section: the first contains the plans for the dance/mime
action, the second (bracketed with it) gives minute indications
of the type of music, its duration in bars, tempo, rhythm, even
in certain instances, orchestration. We can assume from this
that Petipa went into rehearsal with certain of the dances
already partially composed in his head – as evidenced by the
Fairy Variations in the Prologue.

'*The Fairies descend from the platform. Each in turn, they
go to bless the child.*

'(*A little introduction for a pas de six.*) *Pas de six. A sweet
adagio. A little allegro. Variations: Candide. Fleur de Farine
(flowing). Kroshka (Breadcrumbs) (Which interweaves and*

twines?). *Canary (who sings). Violante (2/4 animated) (Plucked strings). The Lilac Fairy (A sweetly happy variation). Coda (3/4, fast and stirring).'*

In his *The Story of the Russian School* Nicolai Legat gives a fascinating description of Petipa at work. *'Whenever Petipa set about producing a ballet he waited till absolute silence reigned in the hall. Then, consulting the notes he had composed at home, he would methodically begin work. He worked out many of his groupings at home, where he used little figures like chess pawns to represent dancers, arranging them all over the table. He would spend long hours studying these groupings and write down the successful ones in his note book. Separate numbers, solos and pas de deux he composed at rehearsals.*

'First he had the music played through. Then he would sit for a time in deep thought. Then he would usually ask for the music to be played through again, imagining the dance, making little gestures, and moving his eyebrows. In the middle he would jump up and cry: "Enough". He would then compose the dance in eight bars at a time, call the dancer to him, and explain the movements at first in words rather than gestures. The whole dance having been explained, the dancer began again from the beginning, while Petipa frequently stopped, corrected or modified the movements. In the end he would cry: "Now try nice," which meant that the artist might try to execute the finished dance.

'. . . The most fascinating moments of all were those when Petipa composed his mimic scenes. Showing each participant in turn he would get quite carried away by the parts, and the whole hall would sit with bated breath, following the extraordinary expressive mimicry of this artistic giant. When the scene was set there would be a terrific outburst of applause, but Petipa paid little attention. He would return quietly to his seat, smiling and licking his lips in a characteristic gesture, lighting a cigarette, and sitting silent for a time. Then the whole scene would be repeated while Petipa put finishing touches to the actions of the individual artists.'

A study of Petipa's notes reveals just how thrilling these 'mimic scenes' must have been – and how much of the dramatic detail, dramatic logic even, we no longer see properly. The celebrated note to Tchaikovsky concerning the knitting women gives some idea of the minutiae of the mime between the King and Catalabutte: '*Four beats for the questions and four for the answers; this to be pronounced four times. A broad 2/4, i.e. Question: "Where are you taking the women?" four beats. Answer: "To prison" four beats. Question: "What have these peasant women done?" four beats. Catalabutte shows the evidence (from 32–48 all together). The King's anger is now aroused. "Let them be punished for their offence." Energetic music. But the princes plead for clemency since no tears must be shed on Aurora's birthday.*'

With all this Tchaikovsky proved he could cope, even with the constricting requirements for the most dramatic moment in the ballet, when one might expect genius to need a somewhat freer rein. Listening to the vivid writing of the end of Act I, so effortlessly brilliant in its theatrical effects, it is hard to believe that Tchaikovsky was working to the following notes: '*Suddenly Aurora notices the old woman who beats the time of her dance with her spindle – 2/4 which develops. It is beaten out all the time, into a 3/4 tempo, gay and very flowing. When the 3/4 begins, Aurora seizes the spindle, which she waves like a sceptre. She expresses her delight to everyone – 24 bars valse. But suddenly (pause – the pain – blood flows!) Eight bars, tempo 4/4 – broadly. Full of terror, now it is not a dance, it is a frenzy, as if she had been bitten by a tarantula. She turns and falls senseless. This will require from 24/32 bars. A few bars tremolo, with sobbing and cries of pain. "Father! Mother!" Then the old woman with the spindle throws off her disguise. At this moment the entire orchestra must play a chromatic scale. Everyone recognizes the Fairy Carabosse, who laughs at the sorrow of King Florestan and the Queen. Short masculine-like music, culminating in a diabolical laugh tempo, when Carabosse disappears in a flurry of flame and smoke. The four princes run away in terror. At this moment the fountain in the centre stage is illuminated: here, tender, fantastic, and magical music. This passage must be long, as it has to last until the end of the act.*'

Tchaikovsky settled down to his extraordinary task in December, 1888 and by great good fortune his diary for the next six months has been preserved (we quote from Vladimir

Lakond's translation), and through it one can chart the composer's progress. He was at this time living at Frolovskoye, some distance from Moscow, but during the time he was writing *Beauty* Tchaikovsky also undertook his second lengthy European concert tour as a conductor, appearing in Germany, Switzerland, Paris, London and proceeding thence, via the Mediterranean, to Tiflis and St Petersburg.

Some of the relevant entries read as follows:

'*Jan 1. Celebrated so much that, in due time, I did not even remember. Worked all morning* (*Entrance of Aurora*) [Petipa's note asked for from 16–24 bars which develops into another tempo. For Aurora's entrance – abruptly coquettish 3/4. 32 bars. Finish with 16 bars, 6/8, forte].

Jan 2. The day went by, as always, when I am absorbed in work. Was writing the grand adage in the second scene, and it came hard.

Jan 3. The work went so-so. But I did not strain myself too much and for that reason my head did not hurt.

Jan 4. How beautiful the days continue! Not very frosty, bright, and, starting at about 3 or 4 o'clock, the moon! . . . worked, as always now, beyond my strength. It seems to me I am played out!! . . . after dinner, walked long and was down by the river. Wonderful! Worked after tea, but very differently. It's not the same!

Jan 5. Still the same amazing, beautiful, bright weather. Worked well today on the whole. Finished the second scene. Played it through (*lasts half an hour*).

Jan 10. The work went well: wrote the entire entr'acte to the Sleep scene, and I think it's all right. . . . In the evening played the overture to The Voyevode *and examined the orchestra score of the ballets given me once upon a time by Gerber.* [Music supervisor at the Bolshoi Theatre].

Jan 11. The work went especially well today, as of old. Did many things. Finished the second scene of the second act.

Jan 14. Worked still as painstakingly. Hope arises of finishing the first four scenes before my departure.

Jan 16. . . . worked till I was tired out. A passion for chocolate.

Jan 17. Worked beyond my strength. How very tired I am.

Jan 18. It seems to me that never has there been such a divine,

beautiful winter day. The beauty was truly stunning. Finished the
work: i.e. the first four scenes.'

On January 19th Tchaikovsky went to Petersburg for consultations with Petipa and Vsevolozhsky, and within a week had
set out on his concert tour. During his travels he completed
part of the fifth scene (Act III of the ballet) and by the time he
had reached Tiflis on April 26th he wrote to Petipa (a letter
which is to be found in Lilian Moore's edition of Petipa's
Memoirs) announcing that the sketches for the ballet were
complete, and hoping that a newspaper report which suggested
that *Beauty* was to be postponed for a year was true, so that he
might have more time to undertake the orchestration of the
work. The rumour was not true; on his arrival in St Petersburg
in May he found Vsevolozhsky engaged on designing the
costumes for the ballet and had further consultations with
Petipa, before returning to Frolovskoye to complete the actual
composition and start on the task of orchestration. By May
26th he had finished the writing, after working *'strenuously and
successfully'* and reading the orchestral score of *Giselle*, and
from May 30th until the end of June when the diary ends, there
are entries which detail Tchaikovsky's sheer slogging hard
labour at orchestrating the ballet. The entries contain phrases
like *'worked, worked and worked – nothing unusual'* or *'I worked
all day like a madman'*, and at the same time he was obliged to
indicate the markings in the score for his friend the pianist
Alexander Siloti who was undertaking the preparation of a
piano transcription for publication in the autumn.

Tchaikovsky's most revealing comment on his labours during
this period comes in a letter he wrote to Mme von Meck on
July 25th. *'My ballet will be published in November or December.
Siloti is making the pianoforte arrangement. I think, dear friend,
that it will be one of my best works. The subject is so poetical, so
grateful for musical setting, that I have worked at it with all that
enthusiasm and goodwill upon which the value of a composition so
much depends. The orchestration gives me far more trouble than it
used to do; consequently the work goes slowly, but perhaps all the
better. Many of my earlier compositions show traces of hurry and
lack of due reflection.'*

The ballet was put into rehearsal in September, and Tchaikovsky was on hand to assist, and even play the piano – so says Kschessinskaya – at rehearsals. He was equally prepared, as we have seen, to make alterations to the score, even excising the beautiful entr'acte before the Awakening (a lengthy section whose dominant violin part had been intended for the great virtuoso, Leopold Auer). An important alteration was the suppression of two characters in the pas de quatre for Cinderella, Prince Fortuné, Princess Florisse and the Bluebird, which, to make a better vehicle for Cecchetti's virtuosity, was set as the *pas de deux* we know today. (Cecchetti's mimic skill was displayed in the role of Carabosse.) One other change has become famous: that of the Panorama music. Petipa's notes read: '*The duration of the music depends on the length of the panorama*'; when the vast roll of the Panorama's painted canvas was unwound, so that the audience might see the fantastic world of Perrault's tales unfolding before their eyes, it was found that there were several yards of canvas without accompaniment. To cut the canvas was unthinkable, so Tchaikovsky very obligingly wrote the extra music needed, which became known as the 'Yard Music'.

The actual first performance was on Tuesday, 2nd January, 1890, o.s. taking the form of a répétition générale in the presence of the Emperor Alexander III and the whole Court.

The reception was far from the triumph Tchaikovsky might have expected. His diary for January 2nd and January 3rd records, baldly, the events:

'*Jan 2. Rehearsal of the ballet with the Emperor present. "Very nice"!!! His Majesty treated me very haughtily. God bless him. Jan 3. First performance of the ballet.*'

That is all. The ballet's reception by the critics was as dispiriting as the Tsar's comment. Stasov referred to Vsevolozhsky as '*that insipid Frenchman*' who thought of nothing but French operettas and '*Tchaikovsky's music for them*'. Some found the work '*much too serious*', or dismissed the ballet as '*not a ballet at all, but a fairy tale, a whole divertissement*' or thought Tchaikovsky's music was '*for the concert hall, serious and heavy*'.

Despite this carping, the ballet swiftly won its public. In November, 1892 it had achieved fifty performances, an occasion marked by the ballet's artists giving a crown to Tchaikovsky on stage at the Maryinski, and Nicolai Legat states that by 1914 the work had reached nearly 200 performances.

Tchaikovsky in particular won devotees for the ballet: his score, Bakst tells us, was exciting admiration in Siloti's transcription even before the première, and its effect on a group of young artists and writers was to have a profound influence on ballet itself. The 'Neva Pickwickians', a band of young artists and intellectuals, led by Benois, with Nouvel, Bakst, Filosofov, and eventually their most junior member, Diaghilev, were all enthusiasts for the work. During one Carnival week, Benois and Nouvel managed to see *The Sleeping Beauty* six times, and this inspiration was to reach an extraordinary fruition in the Diaghilev Ballets Russes movement of twenty years later. Benois even remarks that had it not been for *The Sleeping Beauty* it is much more difficult to envisage the birth of the Ballets Russes.

But the ultimate triumph of *The Sleeping Beauty* is as much due to Vsevolozhsky as to Tchaikovsky and Petipa. Vsevolozhsky aimed at the creation of a *Gesamtkunstwerk*, and in the original staging it must seem that he succeeded. He intended the ballet to show a fascinating contrast in historical styles in its two halves: he placed the Prologue and First Act in the middle of the sixteenth century, which was to be designed in a fantastically stylized manner, while the Awakening and Wedding were to be seen in an historically accurate evocation of the golden years of the young Louis XIV.

Of course, *Beauty* is markedly a work of its time and place, one of the highest theatrical achievements of the westward-looking culture of Imperial St Petersburg, reflecting the aristocratic spirit of the Court and the pomp, luxury and opulent grandeur of its ultimate master, the Emperor, who made up the Imperial Theatres' annual deficit of two million gold roubles (£200,000) from his privy purse.

It is no accident that the finale of *The Sleeping Beauty* is a hymn to the monarchic ideal as seen in its most glorious and ab-solute form: Petipa's apotheosis showed '*Apollo, in the costume of Louis XIV, lighted by the sun's rays and surrounded by fairies*'. The style and grandiose decoration of the ballet (for which silks and velvets were imported from Lyons) reflected Vsevolozhsky's own taste very clearly, since he designed all the costumes and suggested the type of setting. But as organizer of the Court entertainments – in which, perhaps, he saw himself as the equivalent of Louis XIV's *maître des menus plaisirs du roy* – he showed considerable elegance, and a supreme skill for getting the best out of people in the nicest way. Tactful, persuasive, '*a great charmer*' according to Benois, he inspired real affection, and as we have seen from his efforts on Tchai-kovsky's behalf and in his ideals for the development of the Imperial Ballet itself, possessed a strong artistic conscience.

Petipa, who dedicated his memoirs to him, wrote glowingly of his gifts: '*During the long years of Vsevolozhsky's manage-ment, all the artists, without exception, adored their noble, kind, cultured director. This kindest of men was a real courtier, in the best sense of the word.*'

That *The Sleeping Beauty* so far transcends the limitations of its form – and even of the world that created it – is in no small measure due to Vsevolozhsky. His personal involvement in the work, which went far beyond designing the costumes and devising the scenario, resulted in a masterpiece that is not only a telling portrait of a vanished world, but also a tribute to Petipa's 'noble, kind and cultured' master.

But let the last word be Tchaikovsky's. Writing to his publisher, Jurgenson, he said '*I dedicate this ballet to Vsevo-lozhsky. Do not forget to put this on the title page in large letters. He is extremely proud of the dedication.*'

The Sleeping Beauty was first seen in the West in 1921. In that year Diaghilev was without a choreographer, and so he decided to show his European audiences something of the splendour of the Imperial Ballet. *The Sleeping Beauty* was thus staged by Nicholas Sergueyev, who had been régisseur at the Maryinski Theatre from 1904–1917. He used the priceless Stepanov notations in which most of the St Petersburg repertory was recorded and which he had brought with him when he left Russia. The ballet was decorated in superb style by Léon Bakst; the finest St Petersburg ballerinas – Spessivtseva, Trefilova, Egorova – were seen as Aurora; Lopokova was first Lilac Fairy and later danced Aurora; Vladimirov was the Prince; and Brianza, the first Aurora, was lured out of retirement to dance Carabosse (though Diaghilev had at first tried to persuade her to dance Aurora again). The production opened at the Alhambra Theatre, London, on 21st November, 1921, but the audience were incapable of responding to its magnificence of music, design and dancing. After 105 performances, it was withdrawn, at enormous loss, never to be revived in full by Diaghilev again.

The Royal Ballet gave their first performance at Sadler's Wells Theatre, London, on 2nd February, 1939, with Margot Fonteyn and Robert Helpmann in the leading roles. With this production the company also re-opened the Royal Opera House, Covent Garden, after the war, on 20th February, 1946, and it has been associated ever since with some of the company's most triumphant moments – notably the first New York appearance in 1949.

LEV IVANOV (1834–1901)

The Nutcracker

A ballet in two acts. Choreography: Lev Ivanov. Libretto: Marius Petipa. Music: Tchaikovsky. Décor: Botcharov and Ivanov. First performed Maryinski Theatre, St Petersburg, 17th December, 1892 with Antonietta dell' Era as the Sugar Plum Fairy.

Act I:

The President Stahlbaum is giving a Christmas party for his son and daughter, Clara and Fritz. The guests arrive and dance, and the children are given presents from the Christmas tree; suddenly, mysterious chords announce the arrival of

another guest. Herr Drosselmeyer, an eccentric old gentleman.
He produces four clockwork toys: a Vivandière and a soldier;
and Harlequin and Columbine, who dance for the children.
Then Drosselmeyer brings out a special present for Clara – a
Nutcracker. She is enchanted with it, but her brother interrupts
the girls' games with their dolls by leading on his young companions in a mock cavalry charge in which they all brandish the
swords and toys that they have been given. Jealous of the Nutcracker, he snatches it from Clara and breaks it; Clara is disconsolate, but Drosselmeyer repairs it, and the guests all join in
a final *Grossvatertanz*, before the over-tired children and their
parents take their leave. The Stahlbaums now retire for the
night with their children, but Clara cannot sleep for thinking of
her Nutcracker whom she has left in the drawing room. She
comes down to fetch it, but as she clasps it to her, midnight
sounds. Drosselmeyer seems to be peering from the clock, and
suddenly the room is invaded with mice. There follows a
battle between the mice and the toy soldiers who have magically
come to life; Clara's Nutcracker is their commander, and, as he
is about to be attacked by the king of the mice, Clara throws
her shoe and fells the mouse-King. This devoted act causes the
Nutcracker to be transformed into a Prince and he invites
Clara to accompany him on a journey to the Kingdom of
Sweets.

Scene II:

Their way to the country of sweets lies through an enchanted
snow-covered forest where they see a swirling, dancing group
of Snowflakes.

Act II:

Clara and the Prince arrive at the Kingdom of Sweets, and
are greeted by the Sugar Plum Fairy. The Prince tells of
Clara's bravery, and in her honour a grand divertissement is
presented. There are dances by Chocolate – *Danse Espagnole;*
Coffee – *Danse Arabe*; Tea – *Danse Chinoise*; there is a Trepak
(a Russian dance); Mère Gigogne appears with her troupe of
children peeping from under her skirts; there is a *Danse des*

Mirlitons, a grand *pas de deux* by the Sugar Plum Fairy and her Cavalier and a final Valse des Fleurs, and the ballet ends with an apotheosis.

In February 1891, Tchaikovsky received a commission from the Imperial Theatres to write a double bill for the Maryinski; this was to comprise the one-act opera *Iolanthe*, and the two-act ballet *Casse Noisette*. The Director of the Imperial Theatres, I. A. Vsevolozhsky had already decided on the theme for the ballet: a story by Alexandre Dumas (père) based on E. T. A. Hoffman's tale of the *Nutcracker and the Mouse King*. Marius Petipa was to create the choreography and, in March, Tchaikovsky received the usual immensely detailed plan of the stage action which was to serve as a working plan for the score. This scenario had caused Petipa some difficulty; Vsevolozhsky had rejected a first draft, but Petipa's notes, preserved in Russia, comment at the end of the second draft: 'j'ai affranchi, j'ai écrit cela, c'est très bon.' Très bon it certainly is not; the dramatic weakness of the plot is plain for all to see. Tchaikovsky was impelled to write that he 'liked the plot of *The Nutcracker* very little', and he found that the second act was particularly feeble: 'I feel a complete impossibility to reproduce musically the *Konfiturenberg* (The Kingdom of Sweets).' Even when he had completed the score he was still seized with doubts (and who should blame him?). 'The ballet is infinitely worse than *The Sleeping Beauty*.' What Petipa would have made choreographically of the score we shall never know, for shortly before rehearsals were due to begin he fell ill, and the task of creating the choreography went naturally to the second ballet master, Lev Ivanov. It was too late for him to make any changes in either libretto or in style of staging; his task, as so often throughout his career, was to do the best he could. Only in the Snowflakes scene, in which Tchaikovsky's genius had been given its head, and where there were none of the detailed requirements that abounded in the rest of the ballet, did music and choreography meet to create something very beautiful. It became the most admired section of the ballet, surviving in a slightly altered form in the Sergueyev staging for the Royal

Ballet in 1934. With the *grand pas de deux* of the second act, this is all that remained of the original choreography, but it insisted upon the merits of Ivanov as a creator.

The ballet was a failure. Despite the splendour of its staging, 'it can under no circumstances be called a ballet' wrote one paper. 'The production of such "spectacles" on our stage is an insult of sorts . . . this may soon and easily lead to the ruin of our ballet troupe' wrote another. Abuse was heaped on the ballet, and certainly it is a hugely-flawed piece. Its faults include a total absence of logical plot; a heroine – or no heroine if you prefer – who is a child; the appearance of the ballerina to dance one *pas de deux* in the second act; a profusion of *divertissement*, and a dramatic action in the first act that is hardly compelling. Its merits (such as they are) are of a nostalgic kind; we can accept the ballet as a look back at the magic world of childhood at a time more innocent than our own. It might be made to work as a magical fantasy, rather after the fashion of *L'Enfant et les Sortilèges*; certainly the music might sustain this.

Tchaikovsky's score has great moments, and is never less than marvellously assured, but it lacks both the splendour and opulence of *Beauty* and the elegiac tragedy of *Swan Lake*.

Despite the failure of the work, it is (as we know to our cost) impossible to keep a good Tchaikovsky score down. The ballet has been constantly re-staged, both in Russia (by Vainonen) and in Europe. Festival Ballet mounted a version early in their existence, and later invited Alexandre Benois to supervise and decorate a staging which has remained remarkably true in essence (though not in choreography) to the original. Sergueyev staged the ballet for the Sadler's Wells Company in 1934 and it did yeoman service before the war and gave Markova a role which she danced to perfection. After the war it was not revived – though Sir Frederick Ashton supervised a staging of the second act for the Sadler's Wells Theatre Ballet; and in 1968 Rudolf Nureyev also mounted a version. This, with designs by Nicholas Georgiadis, was first seen at Covent Garden (it had earlier been given in Sweden), on 29th February,

1968. Entirely re-choreographed by Nureyev, the ballet offered a complete re-thinking of the dramatic structure in an attempt to give cohesion to the piece. With an intrigue that is best described as sub-Freudian, the ballet starts conventionally enough with the party, but after receiving the Nutcracker doll, Clara falls asleep in mid-party and dreams of the battle of mice, now aggrandized into bloated and repellently frightening rats; she rescues the Nutcracker who reveals himself as a Prince and they journey through the kingdom of snow. But once arrived at the second act, we find Clara attacked by bats (who turn out to be members of her family) and Drosselmeyer reappears to reveal himself as the Nutcracker Prince. The *divertissement* is given by the dolls from Clara's toy theatre: it comprises the Spanish dance, Russian dance, a dance for three Chinese acrobats, a porcelain *pas de trois* for a man and two girls (to the Mirliton's music) and a singularly unconvincing domestic scene for the *Danse Arabe*, after which Clara and Prince Drosselmeyer (what else is one to call him?) dance the *grand pas de deux*, and there follows the *Valse des Fleurs*. Suddenly we are back at the party; Clara awakes from her sleep, the guests depart and Clara rushes to the door of the house to watch Drosselmeyer departing into the snowy night. Though Nureyev's attempt to provide a serious role for a principal male and female dancer and give the ballet dramatic shape is interesting, the piece works rather less well than do the uncomplicated charms of the 'traditional' Festival Ballet staging; and the new choreography is markedly unable to sustain our attention. Other productions proliferate.

Swan Lake

A ballet in four acts. Music: Tchaikovsky. Choreography: Julius Reisinger. Libretto: V. P. Begichev and V. I. Geltser. First performed Imperial Theatre, Moscow, 4th March, 1877. Act II, Choreography: Lev Ivanov. First performed Maryinski Theatre, St Petersburg, 29th February, 1894; the whole ballet – Act I and Act III, Petipa; Act II and Act IV, Ivanov, 15th January, 1895. Pierina Legnani as Odette-Odile.

ACT I:

It is Prince Siegfried's birthday and in the garden of his palace he is celebrating with his friends, with Benno, his attendant, and with Wolfgang, his tutor. Peasant boys and girls are also present, and two girls and a boy who dance a *pas de trois*. Siegfried's mother enters with her attendants; she chides her son for revelling, and announces that at a ball the next day a group of young and eligible girls will be presented; from among them he must choose a bride. Despite Siegfried's protestation, his mother is firm. She leaves, and wine flows again. Wolfgang becomes drunk and tries to dance with a peasant girl, and the assembled peasants start a general dance. Siegfried is oppressed by his mother's news and, as dusk falls and the guests leave, he seems lost in thought. Suddenly Benno sees a flight of swans, and he urges the Prince to come hunting by night with his companions. Eagerly Siegfried agrees; Wolfgang is left alone and the hunting party departs.

ACT II: Beside a lake.

As the hunters enter they decide to watch for the swans here. Siegfried orders them to leave him so that he may watch alone, and suddenly he is amazed to see a swan landing on the lake and immediately change into a beautiful girl wearing a crown. Siegfried approaches her; terrified she tries to flee, but he reassures her that he means no harm and he already seems attracted to her beauty. She tells him that she is an enchanted Princess, queen of the swan-maidens whom the enchanter, von Rothbart, has bewitched. The lake is made of her mother's tears. She can never be released from the enchantment that turns her into a swan during the daylight hours unless a man falls in love with her and swears eternal fidelity. Siegfried, now obsessed with her beauty, promises to love her, but at this moment von Rothbart appears. Odette pleads with the magician, while Siegfried reaches for his crossbow and attempts to shoot him; Odette rushes toward Siegfried and prevents him from shooting. They leave the lake-side as the swan-maidens appear and dance. Suddenly Benno returns. He is dazzled by the sight of these white figures whom he takes for swans; he calls to his companions who enter, but just as they are about to shoot, Siegfried runs in, ordering them to put down their bows, while Odette flutters protectively in front of her maidens. As the swan-maidens dance, and Odette moves away, Siegfried turns to search for her; he fears she may have flown away, but she appears and they dance an intense and lyric duet which tells of their ever-growing love. As they leave, four cygnets enter to perform a celebrated quartet, and then Odette enters to dance a solo. There follows a general dance, and as day breaks the maidens must return to their swan form again. Odette takes an impassioned farewell of Siegfried who is left staring in wonderment at the sky where the swans have disappeared.

Act III: The Ballroom of Siegfried's Castle.

The guests are assembling to celebrate the coming betrothal of the Prince. The Queen Mother arrives with Siegfried, and six eligible girls are presented to him. He dances with each, but his mind is filled with thoughts of Odette, so that at the end of the dance he refuses to choose a bride. The Queen Mother's angry remonstrances are interrupted by the sound of trumpets which announce the belated arrival of an unexpected guest. The orchestra sounds the swan theme in ominous tones, and suddenly von Rothbart appears, disguised as a nobleman, bringing with him his daughter Odile, who has assumed the face and form of Odette. (Although originally the roles of Odette and Odile were danced by two ballerine, Legnani instituted the continuing tradition of a single ballerina interpreting both roles.) The enraptured Siegfried rushes to her and leads her away, while a *divertissement* of national dances – Spanish, Neapolitan, Hungarian and Polish – entertain the guests. As these dances end, Odile and Siegfried enter to dance the great *pas de deux* in which the enchantress dazzles and tricks the young Prince who is exultant with happiness. The duet is filled with virtuosity – in its coda, Legnani introduced her favourite trick of multiple fouettés, 32 in all, which she performed with incredible ease and these have since been retained by almost all subsequent interpreters – but it is also a scene of high drama. As the *entrée* proceeds, the sorrowing figure of Odette appears outside the castle windows, seeking to warn Siegfried, but von Rothbart casts a spell over the assembled guests so that they shall not notice this, and Odile mockingly echoes the swan movements of Odette which further bemuse and delight Siegfried. At the conclusion of the duet Siegfried asks for the hand of Odile: von Rothbart demands that he swear eternal fidelity to Odile, which Siegfried does. At once von Rothbart and Odile reveal their true nature. With peals of mocking laughter they jeer at the Prince and exit amid clouds of sulphurous smoke, while Siegfried rushes to his mother, realizing that he has broken his vow, and then hastens to the lake-side in an endeavour to find Odette.

ACT IV: The lake-side, later that night.

The swan-maidens are mourning their queen's departure. A moment later she returns, heart-broken at what seems the stupidity of Siegfried and his lack of faith. Von Rothbart summons up a storm to try to prevent Siegfried reaching the swans, but he appears in the forest, seeking desperately for his love. He discovers Odette amid her swans, and begs forgiveness. In a last elegiac *pas de deux* they re-affirm their love and Odette states that the only possible means of escaping from her enchantment is to kill herself in the lake. Despite Siegfried's pleas she makes as if to throw herself into the waters. He restrains her, then agrees to join her in death – thus their love shall be consummated and they will be united. Von Rothbart enters, struggling with Siegfried for possession of the Swan Queen, but the strength and determination of the two lovers defeat him. As they plunge into the lake to their death, von Rothbart's power fades and he dies, while the swan-maidens, now restored to their human form, watch an apotheosis in which Siegfried and Odette are reunited in a kingdom of eternal happiness beneath the waves.

The history of *Swan Lake* is the history of the most popular ballet in the world – a popularity sustained partly by the magnificence of Tchaikovsky's score, with its irresistible

melancholy and melodic riches, and partly by the splendour of
the work of Ivanov and Petipa. Yet its initial production might
have seemed to have doomed it to oblivion. Tchaikovsky's
score was originally written for the Bolshoi Theatre, Moscow,
where it was choreographed by an entirely inadequate ballet
master, Julius Reisinger, for the benefit performance of an
undistinguished ballerina called Karpakova. The score was
found to be too 'difficult' and alterations and interpolations by
both ballerina and conductor guaranteed that the ballet as performed must have been singularly unlike what Tchaikovsky
intended. In 1880, and again in 1882, a rather more able
choreographer, Joseph Hansen, staged versions of the ballet,
but it still failed to keep any permanent place in the repertory.
It was not until 1893 that St Petersburg and the Maryinski
Theatre enter the story. In 1890, *The Sleeping Beauty* had been
staged and had won an enthusiastic audience after an initial
coolness; in 1892 *Casse Noisette* had had a mixed reception, but
Tchaikovsky's death in 1893 had occasioned an upsurge of
interest in his theatre works, and in 1894 an evening devoted to
the memory of the composer was given at the Maryinski. It included the second (lake-side) act of *Swan Lake* in a choreography
by Lev Ivanov. The role of Odette was taken by the visiting
Italian virtuoso ballerina Pierina Legnani, and the performance
was a great success. Inspired by this, Marius Petipa decided to
stage the entire ballet; he asked Riccardo Drigo, conductor at
the Maryinski, to clean up the score, restoring numbers that
had been excised in Moscow, but also concocting a couple of
variations from some salon pieces by Tchaikovsky, and on
15th January, 1895, the full length ballet was given at the
Maryinski with Legnani in the double role, and Paul Gerdt as
Siegfried. The ballet was a huge success and started on its
career – that seemingly interminable series of incarnations
which have, alas, brought it to nearly every ballet company in
the world, whether or not they have forces sufficient to dance it.
Inevitably, it has been re-staged, re-thought, re-choreographed, punched, pulled, twisted and generally mangled in the
years since the Maryinski première. In Russia, the most
significant stagings were by Alexander Gorsky, who even dur-

ing the life of Petipa (when the old master was in retirement) had started the vulgarizing and humanizing of Petipa's classically perfect creations. Gorsky made no less than five productions in Russia. Later Agrippina Vaganova (the great teacher and founder of the Soviet ballet school) also produced a version in 1935. A significant and influential staging was later made for the Stanislavsky Theatre in Moscow by Vladimir Bourmeister in 1953, in which he sought to return to the ballet as originally conceived by Tchaikovsky. This production, later given at the Paris Opéra and revised when partially staged for Festival Ballet, had many innovations: among them a prologue showed Odette's abduction and the national *divertissement* of Act III was given as if the dancers were in the magical train of von Rothbart. In another staging for Festival Ballet, reproduced from an earlier version he made for the Teatro Colon, Buenos Aires, Jack Carter returned even more whole-heartedly to Tchaikovsky; re-placing musical numbers that had been given in different sequence, and using two ballerinas for the roles of Odette and Odile – very necessary since in his staging they meet at the Act III ball – and also introducing the whole of the *grand pas des fiancées* from the score. But the most rewarding and most 'authentic' version remains that staged by Nicolai Sergueyev for the Sadler's Wells Ballet at Sadler's Wells Theatre on 29th November, 1934. When Sergueyev fled Russia after the Revolution he brought with him a collection of notebooks in which he had written down all the current Maryinski repertory. From these notebooks stem all the classical stagings of the old Imperial Russian repertory in the West. His *Swan Lake* for the Sadler's Wells Ballet was, and remains (in the version now maintained by the Royal Ballet Touring Company) the most authentic version in the West. As every passing year brings new and more frolicsome stagings from companies all over the world, the tremendous merits of this original become more and more apparent. In 1964, the Royal Ballet at Covent Garden acquired a new version by Robert Helpmann with additional choreography by Ashton (among others) and this is still maintained at the Royal Opera House. Elsewhere in the world new *Swan Lakes* proliferate.

But what is *Swan Lake?* Apart from being the most performed ballet in the world, it is also one of the most misunderstood and the most misinterpreted. The perennial attraction of
Tchaikovsky's score lies in its melancholy as well as in the
profusion of melody; the story looks back to the simpler
Romantic forms of the 1840s rather than following the complicated and usually quite idiotic stories that were needed to sustain
the whole complicated paraphernalia of Petipa's spectacular
creations. It is a story that offers the great Romantic dilemma
of impossible love finding its resolution only in death – and
though we can say that *La Bayadère* or *Le Roi Candaule*
also offer a similar debased romanticism, *Swan Lake* has the
advantage of a grand simplicity that recalls *Giselle* or *La
Sylphide*. It also provides our only serious view of a choreographer who has always been overshadowed by his master,
Petipa – Lev Ivanov. Soviet scholarship has done much in
recent years to try to rescue the reputation of this sad figure.
Born in 1834, he became a pupil of Jean Petipa (Marius' father),
at the St Petersburg school, entered the company in 1850, and
spent the remainder of his life as dancer, mime and teacher in
the theatre. He possessed an extraordinary musical talent (he
could reproduce music after hearing it once) and this was to
stand him in good stead later on. But he lacked ambition and
drive: he never tried to forward his career either as choreographer or as composer (he wrote interpolated solos for certain
ballets). After his appointment as régisseur, in 1882, he re-
staged many of the old ballets, and three years later became
second ballet master. He was responsible for the ballets in
operas: he mounted the Polovtsian dances in *Prince Igor* (which
were given – in Sergueyev's reconstruction from notation – by
International Ballet just after the 1945 war) and they are plainly
the basis on which Fokine made his version. Ivanov's first long
ballet was *The Haarlem Tulip* in 1887; the score was by the
Baron Fittingov-Schell, and it has been suggested that
Ivanov's inspiration was entirely weighed down by the score.
His first important work came with *Casse Noisette* (*q.v.*).

This experience contributed to his success with *Swan Lake*,
in which we can see his genius completely at one with that of a

composer of markedly similar temperament. It is interesting to consider how Petipa, who had all those qualities of experience and cut and dried matter-of-fact practicality, could work with the superabundant emotionalism, the personal neuroses of Tchaikovsky. All the easier, then, to see what emotional sympathy Ivanov must have felt when faced with the melancholy of *Swan Lake*, Act II. The result is a thoroughly original conception of what the classical ballet should do. Ivanov offers the complete opposite to what was the standard procedure of Petipa's ballets. He was working quite freely – there were none of the detailed notes (see *The Sleeping Beauty*) that Petipa provided for his composer and with which he prepared every moment of the stage action before coming into the rehearsal room. The music spoke to Ivanov and he proceeded to find a marvellous realization of it. With Petipa by this time – though not earlier (see *La Bayadère*) – the formal structure of such an act was set hard and fast: the *pas de deux* would unfold against the rigid patterns of the *corps de ballet*. How different Ivanov's conception: his *pas de deux* remains central, but there is constant participation in its emotional structure by the *corps de ballet*. It is entirely dependent in its shape on the shape of the music; technical proficiency of course is called for, but instead of virtuosity there is emotion; instead of the tight, bright fireworks of the French master, there is the broadly-spaced, very Russian flowing of arabesques, characteristic poses of head and arms that remind us constantly of Odette's swan nature by day. It is a masterly conception, not least in the way the *corps de ballet* are called on to enhance the central duet – in a marked advance on the originality of *La Bayadère*, or on *Giselle* Act II, both of which contain similar structural devices.

The staging of Act II was a success, and Vsevolozhsky (or possibly Petipa) decided on the staging of the whole ballet. Petipa's notes here are far less full than for *Beauty* or *Casse*; they state quite simply 'that the second scene has already been done', and we are assured that the fourth act is also by Ivanov. The rest of the task (Acts I and III) may have been shared between the two, as certain Soviet authorities state; certainly their form bespeaks the usual Petipa formula of general dances, brilliant solos and *divertissement*.

Whatever the division of labour, though, the ballet as staged at the Maryinski was still a typical formal display such as Petipa had been creating for nearly 40 years: its score was superior to most, its drama more clean-cut than many others, but it was still no novelty. It was, however, a beautifully and soundly constructed piece, and (as we know it from the Sergueyev staging) totally effective in the theatre. This is exactly what none of the later recensions, alterations, rethinkings and general assaults on the work, has ever been, in our experience. Those versions that have sought to show us 'the ballet that Tchaikovsky intended' have been markedly less successful. We are forced to the inescapable conclusion that the genius and long experience of Petipa were infinitely more sure in theatre matters than the romantic visions Tchaikovsky had hoped to see.

Raymonda

A ballet in three acts and four scenes. Choreography: M. Petipa. Music: Glazunov. Décor: Allegri, Lambini, Ivanov. First performed Maryinski Theatre, St Petersburg, 19th January, 1898, with Legnani as Raymonda.

ACT I, *Scene I*:

The libretto, largely invented by Lydia Pashkova – a society authoress – has always been the downfall of *Raymonda*; it is a farrago whose complications and inadequacies are barely comprehensible. The scene is medieval Provence at the château de Doris where we meet the Comtesse Sybille, and her niece Raymonda. On Raymonda's birthday the Comtesse chides various girls for their idleness, and tells them about the statue of the Comtesse de Doris, who appears as a ghostly White Lady to warn the family when there is any danger. A messenger appears with a letter from Raymonda's fiancé, Jean de Brienne, announcing his imminent return from the Crusades, and Raymonda makes her first entrance to read the letter. Jean will be back tomorrow, and everyone hastens to prepare a worthy reception. Raymonda plays the lute, but is overcome by a mysterious sleep; the ghost of the White Lady appears to her and leads her on to the terrace.

Scene II:

Through mists, a vision of Jean de Brienne appears; Raymonda rushes to him and they dance a grand adage. There follows a *divertissement* for Jean's attendants and assorted sprites, but the White Lady shows Raymonda another figure, that of the Saracen Chief Abdérâme, who declares his love for her, which she rejects in horror. Elves and goblins appear and dance and Raymonda faints; as dawn breaks her attendants find her and take her into the castle.

Act II:

In the courtyard everything has been prepared to welcome Jean. Guests arrive from neighbouring castles, and trumpets announce the arrival of Abdérâme and his Saracen knights. Raymonda shudders with horror as she recognizes the figure of her vision: Sybille calms Raymonda, but Abdérâme now speaks of his love and becomes more and more pressing in his declarations (*grand pas d'action*). Abdérâme presents his suite of Arabs, Saracens and Spaniards who dance for Raymonda and pour out quantities of wine for the guests; while the entire assembly is thus occupied, Abdérâme prepares to abduct Raymonda, but Jean de Brienne appears, together with King Andrew II of Hungary. Jean immediately rescues Raymonda and a general mêlée ensues. King Andrew orders Jean and Abdérâme to settle their dispute in single combat. Raymonda gives her scarf to Jean and, furious at this, Abdérâme attacks Jean fiercely, but the White Lady appears and protects Jean, who kills Abdérâme. The Saracen is carried away by his attendants, while King Andrew joins the hands of Jean and Raymonda amid general rejoicing.

Act III:

King Andrew and the now happily-married couple watch a

grand Hungarian *divertissement* given in their honour; after
numerous dances it ends with a final *galop* and an apotheosis
showing a brilliant tourney.

Idiotic though this scenario is, the ballet as we know it is a
glorious work. It boasts a magical score by Glazunov, filled
with melody, colour and grand effects which inspired the
eighty-year-old Petipa to produce his last masterpiece. If there
seems something autumnally golden about the beauties of
Glazunov's score – and the ballet was the last great work produced by the Maryinski Theatre before the Revolution –
Petipa's choreography, as we know it from Rudolf Nureyev's
versions for the Royal Ballet and Australian Ballet, is dazzling.
The ballet has been maintained in the repertories of both the
Kirov and Bolshoi companies, though neither, alas, has yet
brought it to London. The Royal Ballet Touring Section presented a three-act version by Rudolf Nureyev, after Petipa, at
the Spoleto Festival in July, 1964. This was the version,
slightly amended, which he staged for the Australian Ballet and
which was seen in London in December, 1965 with Fonteyn,
Fifield and Doreen Wells as Raymonda, and Nureyev and
Garth Welch as Jean. The Royal Ballet Touring Section (and
later the larger company) now present only an amplified version of Nureyev's third act.

Chapter Five

Diaghilev's Ballets Russes

MICHEL FOKINE (1880–1942)

Trained at the Imperial Ballet School of the Maryinski Theatre, St Petersburg, Fokine graduated in 1898 and achieved the rare distinction of entering the Imperial Ballet directly as a soloist. He began teaching in 1902, became a first soloist in 1904, and staged his first ballets the following year, *Acis and Galatea* for a pupil's performance and *Le Cygne* for Anna Pavlova. His first ballet for the Imperial Theatre was *Le Pavillon d'Armide* in 1907.

Had he not been a choreographer, Fokine would have lived in history as an outstanding dancer. His achievements in the one art have tended to overshadow his greatness in the other. And reasonably enough. As a choreographer he is the most influential figure of the first half of the twentieth century, matching Noverre in the importance of his reforms and providing a reference point for all his successors. The company he entered at the age of 18 was fossilized in the precepts which Petipa had evolved through his long reign. This was the year of *Raymonda*, illustrating in the confusion of its story (*q.v.*) and the quality of its dances the formula against which Fokine rebelled. Not the meaning of a ballet but its prima ballerina was what mattered in this formula; not the story, but the set dances predetermined in their order and designed to show off the ballerina's virtuosity. Whatever the subject matter of a ballet the dances would be always *à pointe* with the *danseuses* clad always in variations of the conventional ballet tutu. The music, composed to the dictates of the choreographer, would probably be a pastiche prepared to its own formula, with numbers interpolated or changed at the ballerina's whim. And in the same way the set designer would have worked independently without reference to costume designer or choreographer.

Deeply influenced by the lofty qualities of Romantic Ballet, with its emphasis on expression, and by a personal passion for art which carried him into museums and galleries to study the noblest works of the past, Fokine formulated his ideas even before creating his first ballets. 'Dancing should be expressive', he wrote in a note submitted to the management of the Imperial Theatres with the scenario of *Acis and Galatea*. 'It should not degenerate into mere gymnastics. It should reflect the feelings of the character portrayed. Above all, it should be right for the place and period indicated by the subject. The dance panto-mime and gestures should not be of the conventional style . . . but should be of a kind that best fits the style of the period. The costumes also should not be established ballet style, but be consistent with the plot. . . .

'The ballet must be uninterrupted – a complete artistic creation and not a series of separate numbers. In the interests of retaining the scenic illusion the action must not be inter-rupted with applause and its acknowledgement by the artists.

'The music should . . . express the story of the ballet and, primarily, its emotional content. . . . Instead of the traditional dualism, music-dancing, complete and harmonious artistic unity of the three elements, music, painting and movement. . . .' Such were the principles of the choreographic revolution he effected in the next ten years, principles evolved before meet-ing Diaghilev and before the visit of Isadora Duncan to St Petersburg in 1905, supposed by many to have had a decisive influence on Fokine's thinking.

This thinking in search of change was paralleled by a similar movement of painters led by Alexandre Benois and ex-pressed through the review, *Mir Isskustva*, edited by Diaghilev. The two movements of artistic reform, the dancers led by Fokine and the painters led by Benois, came together during the creation of *Le Pavillon d'Armide* for which Benois created the décor and wrote the libretto. Benois introduced Fokine to Diaghilev who made of the two movements a single force, the *Ballets Russes*.

Le Cygne (The Dying Swan)

Solo dance. Choreography: Fokine. Music: Saint-Saëns (from 'Le Carnaval des Animaux'). Costume: Bakst. First performed Hall of Nobles, St Petersburg, 1905.

Almost an improvisation, composed in only a few minutes for a concert at which Pavlova was to dance, *Le Cygne* was immortalized by her to become her symbol throughout the world, significant only as long as she danced it. Based largely on a single step, the *pas de bourrée couru*, it requires, said Fokine, 'a high degree of technical perfection. . . . But the object of the dance is not a demonstration of technique, nor a demonstration in surmounting difficulties. Indeed, the perfection of technique serves only as the means of creating a poetic image, a symbol of the perpetual longing for life by all mortals. It is a dance of the entire body, and not the legs alone, such as was the object of the old ballet. This dance aims, not so much at the eyes of the spectator, as at his soul, at his emotions.'

Through her dancing, of which *Le Cygne* is the most famous example, Pavlova became a missionary for ballet. More than any single person she made the world conscious of the art and its dancers. Her dancing was light, graceful and simple, illuminated always by her own indefinable genius which made her the most famous ballerina of the age. If, therefore, Fokine and Diaghilev and the choreographers who followed Fokine refashioned ballet to carry it into the twentieth century, it was Pavlova who created the other essential, a mass audience able to support what Diaghilev's wealthy backers initially brought into being. Diaghilev's work would have been incomplete without her missionary journeys, as her work would have been incomplete without him.

Les Sylphides (Chopiniana)

Ballet in one act. Choreography: Fokine. Music: Chopin; orchestration: Glazounov and Keller. Scenery and costumes: Benois. First performed at an examination performance, Maryinski

*Theatre, St Petersburg, 20th March, 1908; then in the theatre
proper, 4th March, 1909. First performed Ballets Russes,
Western Europe: Théâtre du Châtelet, Paris, 2nd June, 1909.*

The Dances

Prelude, op. 28, No. 7		*Overture*
Nocturne, op. 32, No. 2	*ensemble*	*The Company*
Valse, op. 70, No. 1	*solo*	*première danseuse*
Mazurka, op. 33, No. 2	*solo*	*danseuse étoile*
Mazurka, op. 67, No. 3	*solo*	*premier danseur*
Prelude, op. 28, No. 7	*solo*	*première danseuse*
Valse, op. 64, No. 2	*pas de deux*	*danseuse étoile and premier danseur*
Valse, op. 18	*ensemble*	*The Company*

The ballet was titled *Chopiniana* for its first Maryinski per-
formance and remains so titled still in Russia. It was renamed
Les Sylphides for its first performance in Paris by the Ballets
Russes.

Scene: A forest glade.

On one side the grey ruins of a monastery, on the other
leafless trees with, in the background, the faint outline of a
tomb. It is night. The moon throws patches of silvery light.

When the curtain rises, the *corps de ballet* and four principals
(one *danseuse étoile*, one *premier danseur*, and two *premières
danseuses*) are grouped in a semi-circle against the forest background. The *danseuses* wear the traditional white ballet skirts
of the Taglioni period. When they move the effect is of mist
dissolving and reforming. *Les Sylphides* is composed in the
manner of the pure romantic ballet as a series of four *variations*
and a *pas de deux* framed in two ensembles. The mood is
spiritual, tinged with sadness, except for the more animated
concluding ensemble. The total effect is poetry for whose proper
performance purity of style is essential without any form of
excess or exaggeration.

Although descended from storyless *divertissements* like the
Pas de Quatre of 1845, *Les Sylphides* introduced what was
essentially a new *genre*, the ballet of mood with no narrative

structure whatever and no clearly defined characters. Its inspiration was the romantic ballet and the title by which it is known in Western Europe was suggested by Benois from the original *La Sylphide*. Thus it expresses in the purest form the essence of that neo-romantic revolution (or renaissance of romanticism – as you wish) which lies at the heart of the reforms initiated by Fokine.

Fourteen years after *Swan Lake*, *Les Sylphides* carried further the search for a more expressive movement which Ivanov had initiated in his lake-side scene. The dance style of *Les Sylphides* is quite different from that of a Petipa ballet. In technique, no virtuoso double turns and pirouettes; in partnering, a genuine equality between man and woman based on music; in the patterns and lines of the choreography, a more rounded lyrical quality than the classical lines of Petipa's time, and seeming to flow out of the music. The great achievement of *Les Sylphides*, in fact, is its musicality. Fokine wanted it to be 'the personification of a poetic vision'. This is what his original cast led by Pavlova, Karsavina, Baldina and Nijinski sought to interpret.

Polovtsian Dances from 'Prince Igor'

Ballet in one act. Choreography: Fokine. Music: Alexander Borodin. Scenery and costumes: Nicholas Roehrich. First performed Ballets Russes, Théâtre du Châtelet, Paris, 18th May, 1909.

Scene: A Polovtsian Camp at dawn.

The outline of tents with, in the distance, hills in the smoke of dying camp fires. The whole lit by the glow of embers.

The second act of Borodin's *Prince Igor* is set in the Camp of the Polovtsi, a Tartar tribe occupying the plains of the Don, where Prince Igor and his son, Vladimir, have been taken prisoner. Instead of treating the two princes as captives, Khan Kontchak of the Polovtsi seeks to dispel Igor's depression by giving a banquet in their honour, followed by dances in which the warriors, their women folk and slaves take part.

When the opera was first given at the Maryinski Theatre on 4th November, 1890 these dances were arranged by Lev Ivanov, but when Diaghilev decided to include extracts from the second act in his first Paris season with Chaliapine as Prince Igor, he asked Fokine to stage a new version of the dances. The result was one of the outstanding successes of the season and a work rightly acclaimed as a masterpiece. Nothing could be more different from the traditions of Petipa, nor indicative of Fokine's genius as a choreographer.

Fokine himself considered the Polovtsian dances one of the most important of all his works, illustrating much more than *Les Sylphides* the expressive power of group dance and therefore the importance of the *corps de ballet*. Marvellous as was the architecture of Petipa's use of the *corps de ballet*, it rarely *danced* in the sense that principals and soloists danced. Fokine, on the other hand, disposed his *corps* as a collective whole, or as groups of individuals – in both uses demanding great dance ability. The Polovtsian dances are a supreme example of this choreographic revolution in the use and standing of the *corps de ballet*. No one thereafter could ever argue that the *corps'* main value was only to provide a background or framework for the principal dancers. Here the importance of the work lies in the ensemble; the *corps* are the ballet, putting into practice also Fokine's theories of appropriate steps and gestures to depict period and place. It is a character ballet in which the movements of oriental slaves are contrasted with a wide range of primitive and barbaric movements for the warriors and their chief. In the role of the chief on that historic opening night, Adolphe Bolm achieved a success greater than Nijinski's in *Les Sylphides*. If anyone can claim the right to have restored by his dancing the position of the male dancer in the west, it is Bolm.

Le Carnaval

   Ballet-pantomime in one act. Libretto and choreography: Fokine. Music: Schumann; orchestration, Rimsky-Korsakov. Scenery and costumes: Léon Bakst. First performed Pavlov Hall,

St Petersburg, 1910; *first performed Western Europe: Ballets Russes, Theater des Westens, Berlin*, 20*th May*, 1910.

Characters:

Columbine	Papillon	Eusebius
Chiarina	Harlequin	Pantalon
Estrella	Pierrot	Florestan
	Waltzers, Philistines	

Scene: The ante-chamber of a ballroom, its only furniture two small striped settees.

Columbine, Harlequin, Pantalon, the wistful Pierrot, and other characters from *Commedia dell'arte*, intrigue, frolic and suffer with the characters of Schumann's youthful imagination in a succession of dances and situations linked by the antics of Harlequin.

No great success with the Parisian public who saw it a month after Berlin in 1910, *Le Carnaval* became beloved elsewhere and is recognized as one of Fokine's more important works. It is another exercise in his romantic revival, another restoration of the male dancer through the roles of Harlequin, Pierrot and Pantalon, first danced respectively by Nijinski, Bolm, and Cecchetti (with Karsavina as Columbine), another ballet of contrasting moods evoked through dances which extend the range and forms of the *pas de deux, pas de trois*, and *pas seul* which it uses. The elusive combination of gaiety, sadness and precise timing required for the total effect is extremely difficult to achieve and a reason why satisfactory performances of this ballet have very rarely been seen since the end of the Diaghilev Ballet.

L'Oiseau de Feu (The Firebird)

Ballet in one act and two scenes. Libretto and choreography: Fokine. Music: Stravinsky. Scenery and costumes: Golovine, with the original Firebird costume by Bakst. First performed Ballets Russes, Paris Opéra, 25*th June*, 1910. *Revived with new designs by Natalia Gontcharova, Lyceum Theatre, London*, 1926.

In a dark garden a tree glows, its branches laden with golden fruit. As the scene lightens, a bird, gleaming with orange radiance, flashes across the background of foliage and is gone. Dimly one sees Ivan Tsarevitch in hunting dress climb a high wall to the right and drop into the garden. The bird appears again. Ivan aims with his cross-bow and misses. The third time she appears, attracted by the gleaming fruit of the tree, he catches her in his arms. She struggles until exhausted then offers him a golden feather for ransom, provided he allows her to go free. She promises that if he is in trouble and waves the feather she will come to his aid. She flies off and Ivan is about to leave when twelve girls appear through the gates of the garden. Ivan watches from the shadows as the girls are joined by another, more richly dressed. They shake down the golden apples from the tree, throwing them from one to the other until Ivan is discovered. The Princess warns him to leave at once since he is trespassing on the land of the magician, Köstchei, who will turn him to stone. But Ivan already loves the Princess and wishes to stay.

Suddenly a discordant trumpet sounds, the maidens run through the gate, which closes after them, and Ivan is left in darkness unable to find his way out. He runs to the gates and shakes them. They fly open and disappear; the forest blazes with light, and a motley horde of demons and goblins seize the Prince to await the coming of Köstchei. The maidens appear, then more guards, finally the magician, who tries to cast a spell on Ivan. But Ivan remembers the golden feather and waves it aloft. The Firebird appears, scatters the demons and compels everyone to dance until, exhausted, she puts them to sleep. She bids Ivan search in the roots of a hollow tree. He draws out a casket containing an enormous egg. Köstchei trembles, for it contains his soul. Ivan Tsarevitch dashes the egg to the ground where it breaks. There is a dreadful crash and darkness falls.

When the stage lightens Köstchei, his court and the Firebird have vanished. The Princess appears with nobles and ladies freed from Köstchei's enchantment. Then follows a procession of knights, priests and pages who invest Ivan with sceptre, crown and ermine robe to proclaim him their deliverer and sovereign lord.

When Diaghilev returned from the success of his first Paris season in 1909, it was already agreed to present another season the following year with new ballets. One of these would certainly be *L'Oiseau de Feu* since the ballet was already in hand and only delayed by the dilatoriness of Liadov, Diaghilev's first choice as composer. The commission was transferred to Stravinsky, then aged 28, who set to work at once with Fokine.

The libretto had been prepared by Fokine and Grigoriev, Diaghilev's *régisseur*, collating several Russian fairy-tales. The result of this first and closest collaboration between Fokine and Stravinsky became one of the seminal works of modern ballet, changing ballet music for ever and anticipating in style their finest work, *Petrushka*.

The Firebird is chiefly important because it revealed so clearly the nature of the revolution represented by the Ballets Russes. Not just a choreographic revolution, nor a revolution in scenic design, but a profound change in the whole direction of ballet. It rested upon a new conception of music for choreography and a new partnership between composer, choreographer and designer. 'Becoming free,' said Fokine, 'the music grew richer and enriched the dance itself.' Beyond this the ballet again illustrates the gradual fulfilment of the principles Fokine had already put forward before joining Diaghilev: scenery and costumes to realize and recreate exactly the mood and characters of a story; choreography pursuing the same purpose. Hence the Firebird's special role and powers are illustrated in her dancing, the only role created *à pointe*. The Princesses are given dances of elegant style on *demi-pointe* to emphasize their captive state as well as their gentleness. The demons and monsters have heavy character steps. Above all, an atmosphere of mysterious and threatening enchantment is produced by the perfect fusion of music, décor and choreography.

Schéhérazade

Choreographic drama in one act. Libretto: Alexandre Benois.

Choreography: Fokine. Music: Rimsky-Korsakov. Scenery and costumes: Léon Bakst. First performed Ballets Russes, Paris Opéra, 4th June, 1910.

Shahryar, King of India and China, is seated in his harem with his favourite wife Zobeida on his left hand and his brother Shah Zeman on his right. Shahryar is in angry mood because his brother has hinted that his wives are unfaithful. To test the harem, Shahryar departs on a hunting expedition.

As soon as he is gone the wives adorn themselves with jewels and bribe the Chief Eunuch to open two of three blue doors at the back of the room where live the male slaves. The Chief Eunuch is about to depart when Zobeida demands that the third door, too, shall be opened. Deaf to his warning and entreaties she insists and bribes him. There is a flash of gold and a negro leaps from the open door to Zobeida's side. Together they fall upon the divan.

Immediately young men, musicians and servants bring in food, wine and music. They dance, led by the Golden Slave, joined by Zobeida. Into the midst of this orgy Shahryar returns. The slaves and women seek blindly to escape only to be cut down by Shahryar's soldiers. The Chief Eunuch is strangled; Shahryar himself destroys the gold-clad negro. There remains Zobeida. Proudly, she confronts the Shah, then, preferring death to public dishonour, snatches a dagger and takes her own life.

Schéhérazade is based on the first tale in the book of *The Thousand and One Nights*. Although creating a tremendous impression through the performance of its principal artists with Ida Rubinstein as Zobeida, Cecchetti as the Chief Eunuch and, above all, Nijinski as the Golden Slave, the honours must go chiefly to Bakst's décor. Its skilful juxtaposition of violent, glowing colour with cunning use of perspective created exactly the atmosphere of sensuality and passion which the theme required. What *L'Oiseau de Feu* did for music, *Schéhérazade* did for décor, demonstrating the essential contribution of a painter's imagination to the creation of ballet. So successful were Bakst's designs that they influenced Parisian fashions at once and continued to influence interior decoration for many years thereafter.

Fokine's choreography, based on a study of Persian miniatures, was economical and dramatic, realizing in movement every feeling and thought of the characters. Even so, the ballet required artists of the quality of its original performers to interpret the subtleties of Fokine's style, and achieve a proper suspension of disbelief. Consequently, it is a work by which to remember the Russian Ballet rather than to revive today. No revival has managed to achieve more than a bogus orientalism, crude, feeble and very far from the power of the original.

Petrushka

Burlesque ballet in one act and four tableaux. Libretto: Stravinsky and Benois. Choreography: Fokine. Music: Stravinsky. Scenery and costumes: Benois. First performed Ballets Russes, Théâtre du Châtelet, Paris, 13th June, 1911.

Scene I: Admiralty Square, St Petersburg in 1830. The Butterweek Fair.

Hawkers, gypsies, dancing girls, showmen of all kinds and their customers fill the square. One showman dressed as a magician calls attention to his curtained booth by a drum roll. He displays to the crowd three puppets; the pretty, doll-like Ballerina, the sad-faced insignificant Petrushka and the splendid, but foolish Moor. At a touch of his wand he seems to bring them to life. They dance, then chase each other round the square.

Scene II: Petrushka's cell inside the Booth.

Petrushka bemoans his fate, his hopeless love for the ballerina, his subservience to his master the Showman, his suffering inside his puppet's body. The Ballerina visits him but in his agitation he frightens her away.

Scene III: The Moor's Cell.

The Moor plays idly with a coconut. Stupid and coarse he

thinks only of his material needs. The Ballerina visits him and exerts her charms to rouse his interest. Finally, she succeeds but in the midst of their duet Petrushka forces his way into the cell. The Moor attacks him, stamps on him and kicks him out.

Scene IV: The Fair.

The fair is at its height. Suddenly the crowd becomes aware of tumult behind the curtains of the showman's booth. Out runs Petrushka, pursued by the Moor and the Ballerina. Cut down by the Moor's scimitar, Petrushka dies in the snow. The crowd, horrified by the tragedy, angrily summon the Showman, but he picks up the body and reveals it as only a puppet of cloth and sawdust. The crowd drifts away and the Showman turns for home, dragging the puppet behind him. Suddenly he hears a cry. Above the booth appears the ghost of Petrushka, defying him for the last time. Terrified, the Showman runs from the scene as the figure of Petrushka falls inanimate once more over the edge of the booth.

Of all the master works created by the Diaghilev Ballet, *Petrushka* is generally considered the greatest because it is the supreme example of a perfect collaboration. Alexandre Benois recreated the Butterweek Fair from childhood memories of St Petersburg, stimulated by Stravinsky's short piece, *Petrushka's Cry*, which had first roused Diaghilev's interest in the theme.

The scenario achieves an exceptional continuity through the device of a plot within a plot. To match it, Stravinsky composed music within music: first, national dances and traditional dances for the people at the fair, marvellously enriched with background accompaniment; second, music for the principal characters describing not only their external characteristics but also their inner feelings. Thus the music contributed incident, character, psychological interpretation, atmosphere and narrative continuity through a variety of rhythm and sound colour which startled dancers and musicians when first they heard it.

Petrushka also shows very vividly the motivating principle of

Fokine's revolution. He sought to make ballet a powerful art in its own right, not just spectacular entertainment. To do this he used images and symbols like poetry: Petrushka, the down-trodden; the Ballerina, symbol of empty womanhood; the Moor personifying all smug, self-satisfied people. Hence the strength of this ballet is also the strength of Diaghilev's own work as an impresario/artistic director, a perfect fusion of music, design and dancing to communicate meaning.

The process can be shown through Petrushka himself. Benois creates his outer form in the costume and grotesque make-up of the puppet. The torment of his inner personality is revealed in Stravinsky's music. His relations and conflict with the outside world are portrayed in the choreography. Fokine uses a turned-out second position, for instance, to depict the extrovert Moor; a turned-in position to depict poor, introvert Petrushka, in love with the Ballerina, knowing always he is despised. Against these main streams of movement Fokine allows every individual in his *corps de ballet* to create the seething life of the fair. Nothing in the dancing is virtuoso, everything is expressive, the principles of romanticism translated into character ballet.

Le Spectre de la Rose

Choreographic tableau in one act. Libretto: Jean-Louis Vaudoyer, after Théophile Gautier. Choreography: Fokine. Music: Weber ('The Invitation to the Waltz'; orchestration, Berlioz). Scenery and costumes: Léon Bakst. First performed Ballets Russes, Théâtre de Monte Carlo, 19th April, 1911.

Scene: A young girl's bedroom, painted white, its windows open to the summer night. She returns from a ball, holding to her lips a rose, breathing its scent. Dreamily, she removes her cloak, sinks into a chair and falls asleep. Suddenly a spirit, half-youth, half-rose, floats into the room through the open window. Like a petal blown by the wind he dances, seeming hardly to touch the ground. As he dances he bends over the sleeper and draws her into the dance. But the dream cannot last. He leads her back to her chair, brushes her lightly with his lips and is gone. Her eyes open, and she stoops to retrieve the rose whose scent recalls her dream.

This composition in the style of the romantic ballet illustrates exactly Fokine's contention that the technique of the classical ballet should be used only where it is appropriate. *Le Spectre de la Rose* is a classical *pas de deux* with Nijinski's wonderful elevation and dancing used in leaps and bounds to evoke an ethereal being, the spirit of the rose, rather than to display an extraordinary technique. 'In no circumstances,' observed Fokine, 'is he a "cavalier", a ballerina's partner. The arm positions in this ballet are the opposite of the "correct" arm positions of the old ballet. The arms live, speak, sing and do not "execute positions".'

Thus the basis of the choreography is purely classical for the legs. To this Fokine added movements in a contrasting romantic idiom for the shoulders, head and arms, to establish a dance style which suggested the product of a young girl's romantic imagination. What made the role of the Rose one of supreme virtuosity was the contrast of Nijinski's great elevation with these ethereal qualities, just as the young girl's dreamy dance, eyes closed, was not only a contrast with the spirit but required the exceptional acting ability which was one of Karsavina's greatest attributes. Hence this work of atmosphere, simplicity and great poetic integrity became so linked with the two artists who gave it life that it should – like Pavlova's *Le Cygne* – be left with them, uncopied by others, a memory.

VASLAV NIJINSKI (1890–1950)

Born in Kiev, of Polish parentage, Nijinski was the child of travelling dancers. It was natural he should be entered for the Imperial Ballet School in St Petersburg at the age of 10, in 1900. From the first he displayed rare gifts for dancing and mime. Studying under Legat, Gerdt, Oboukhov and Cecchetti he was first noticed in 1905, when he danced a faun in a

student performance of Fokine's *Acis and Galatea*. He then
created a great impression at his official debut three years later
in Mozart's *Don Giovanni* – after having already created the
part of the slave in Fokine's *Le Pavillon d'Armide*.

Since it was through *Le Pavillon d'Armide* that Benois
brought together Fokine and Diaghilev, it could not be long
before Nijinski made the acquaintance of Diaghilev. Thus
that personal and professional partnership was launched which
made their names inseparable in the history of the theatre. No
other dancer, except Taglioni and Pavlova, has become so
legendary during and after his lifetime; no other male dancer
of his generation could match him in the range of his powers
though some, like Bolm, might make more impression in a
particular direction. His astonishing *ballon*, elevation, beats,
and quality of movement were unsurpassed, providing Fokine
with the matchless material from which he fashioned the
Golden Slave, Harlequin, the poet of *Les Sylphides*, Petrushka
and the Spectre of the Rose. Most especially, Nijinski had the
gift of merging himself completely in all his roles. 'The fact
that Nijinski's metamorphosis was predominantly sub-
conscious,' wrote Benois of this phenomenon, 'is, in my
opinion, the very proof of his genius.'

This was the being whom Diaghilev sought to make into a
choreographer – and not just for reasons of personal affection.
Changes, only possible through a new choreographer, were
necessary in the Ballets Russes. Through ballets like *Les
Sylphides*, *The Firebird*, *Petrushka* and *Le Carnaval*, created
for Diaghilev over four seasons in Paris and London, Fokine
had carried choreography into the twentieth century and re-
established the male dancer and ballet as an art in Western
Europe. All choreography since then looks back to him.

But Fokine's reforms had been carried out entirely within
the context of a wholly Russian company drawing its resources
from the Maryinski Theatre in St Petersburg. By 1912, not
only were these reforms complete, it was clear the company
must draw upon additional resources to retain its leadership in
the arts. It could not continue to offer the work of only one
choreographer, however great. Yet when Diaghilev presented

Nijinski's *L'Après-midi d'un Faune* it produced inevitably a break with Fokine. And *Faune* was itself preliminary to other things – *Le Sacre du Printemps* and *Jeux*, and then a more profound break with Russia, when war and Russian revolution accelerated a trend already apparent. From 1914 onwards, the history of the Diaghilev Ballet merges more and more with the culture of Western Europe, especially France, so that it becomes no longer Russian, but Franco-Russian. *L'Après-midi d'un Faune* was the first step in this direction.

L'Après-midi d'un Faune

Choreographic tableau in one act. Libretto and choreography: Nijinski. Music: Claude Debussy. Scenery and costumes: Bakst. First performed Ballet Russes, Théâtre du Châtelet, Paris, 29th May, 1912.

From a hillside one summer afternoon, a faun sees seven nymphs in the valley below. Filled with curiosity he descends from his hill, but they run away. Soon, they return and the faun tries to woo them. Again they run away – except one who is half frightened, half attracted to him. They touch, then fear overcomes her too, and she escapes, leaving behind her scarf. For a moment she hesitates, hoping to retrieve the scarf, but caution prevails and she follows her companions. Filled with sadness, the faun takes the scarf in his arms and returns to his hillside. He kisses it, places it upon the ground and lies upon it.

Nijinski sought to represent in this ballet the solitary passion of a faun for a nymph in the pastoral setting of ancient Greece, using movements inspired by ancient Greek friezes. He and his designer, Léon Bakst, tried to keep the two-dimensional quality of a frieze through a special style of movement, bodies facing the audience, heads and limbs in profile (see Plate 14). Further to preserve the impression of a two-dimensional surface, the dancers moved only in straight lines, from side to side of the stage at different speeds and sometimes on different planes, the faces expressionless, the arms angular.

It was not easy for classically trained dancers, accustomed always to the turnout of the legs, to achieve the naturalistic, turned-in movements Nijinski wanted. Moreover Debussy's silvery music, though exactly right for the ballet, was employed simply as an accompaniment, for atmosphere, rather than to give the kind of guidance and support dancers usually expect from music. Therefore this brief, twelve-minute ballet needed 120 rehearsals before it was finished, not to speak of a visit to Greece and intense research in museums. The result was something which seemed to break with all the classical traditions of the Ballets Russes – yet the choreographer needed very good classically trained dancers in order to succeed.

Thus the new ideas and new lines of Nijinski's *Faune* signalled the beginning of a new period for the Ballets Russes. The 'new ballet' of Fokine, and the classical vocabulary itself, became a base for further exploration. Fokine, of course, remained in the wings and returned briefly as choreographer in 1914 – so that the new period did not begin seriously until the appointment of Massine as choreographer in 1915. But the sound of the flute, with which *Faune* begins, did indeed announce a new era. Diaghilev had discovered for himself Dalcroze and eurhythmics some time around 1910. Interested in these ideas, he took Nijinski to see Dalcroze at Hellerau near Dresden, when the libretto of *Faune* was already sketched out. The ideas appealed to a young man, aged 20, who sought to react against academic constraints and was feeling his way towards a new kind of choreographic expression and perhaps a new kind of dance language. Especially, it seems, he wished to prove that movement, any movement however apparently heavy and ugly, could become beautiful if it was placed to express some idea or emotion.

Fokine, of course, had sought the same ends and also used the profile position in his creation of the Venusberg scene from the opera *Tannhäuser* at the Maryinski the previous year, but this does not diminish Nijinski's further exploration of what Fokine began. He continued it with less success in *Jeux* at the Théâtre des Champs-Elysées on May 15th the following year, and then two weeks later in *Le Sacre du Printemps*. *Jeux* is only notable now because it introduced the first contemporary theme of modern times and was the first time dancers had appeared on stage in contemporary dress. *Sacre*, on the other hand, with its complicated score by Stravinsky and its vision of pagan Russia, was exactly suited to the *terre à terre* ideas of Jacques Dalcroze. Hence Dalcroze was asked to delegate an adviser to Nijinski. He sent Marie Rambert. Partly from Dalcroze arose the turned-in feet, earth-bound, heavy movements and groups of massed dancers which characterized Nijinski's rites – and shocked his Parisian audience.

It is difficult today to recapture the curiously exotic atmosphere of the Ballets Russes with its almost desperate search for the new and *avant-garde*. *Sacre* was one result; *Faune* another, indeed the only remaining example, since it alone continues to be performed under the guidance of Marie Rambert in the repertory of her company. The costumes by Bakst established the atmosphere of sultry passion as richly as the larger *Schéhérazade*, and with the same instant impact. The total result was a work whose direction was followed by no one else, as Nijinski too has had no successor. His career lasted a brief ten years; that of the Ballets Russes only twenty; but both remain an influence throughout this century.

LEONIDE MASSINE (b. 1894)

Born in Moscow, Leonide Massine studied at the Imperial Ballet School there, and joined the Bolshoi Company in 1912. His interest was in acting as well as dancing and he had even considered giving up dancing in favour of acting when, in 1913, Diaghilev came to Moscow in search of a dancer to take the leading role in the projected *Légende de Joseph*, which was to have starred (and been choreographed by) Nijinski. But Diaghilev had broken with Nijinski, following his marriage, so the young Massine was promptly offered the role of Joseph, and set to work with Maestro Cecchetti, then ballet master to the Diaghilev Company. *La Légende de Joseph* had its first performance in May, 1914, but the declaration of war later that summer brought an end to the first great Russian period of the Diaghilev ballet. Massine stayed with the nucleus of artists that surrounded Diaghilev in Switzerland, being educated in the usual Diaghilev manner by visits to galleries and close contact with creative artists and musicians, as well as working with Cecchetti; inevitably Diaghilev was grooming him for choreography and in 1915 he staged his first ballet, *Soleil de Nuit*. It was a success and initiated the long sequence of ballets that extend up to this day, a total output of ballets and dances numbering more than a hundred. As a dancer he demonstrated throughout his life a tremendous skill in character roles and many of his ballets reflect this same quality – though he also had a sensational success in the 1930s creating symphonic ballets. His first, *Les Présages*, in 1933 used Tchaikovsky's Fifth Symphony; there followed *Choreartium* (1933) to Brahms' Fourth Symphony and *La Symphonie Fantastique* to Berlioz' work of the same name. In 1938 he used Beethoven's Seventh Symphony for *Septième Symphonie* and he made one last essay – *Rouge et Noir* – in 1939 to Shostakovich's First Symphony. He is best known today, though, for the early ballets that did so much to enhance post-war Diaghilev seasons: *The Good-Humoured Ladies* (1917), *La Boutique Fantasque* (1919), *Le Tricorne* (1919), together with *Le Beau Danube* (1933) and *Mam'zelle Angot* (1943). A man of very considerable intellectual gifts, Massine has experimented with a notably adventurous spirit in ballet, as with his symphonic works. His *Parade* (1917) was a Cubist manifesto, and in America in the 1940s he collaborated with Salvador Dali in producing a series of surrealist-inspired ballets: *Mad Tristan* (1944), *Labyrinth* (to Schubert's great C Major Symphony) (1941) and *Bacchanal* (1939), which had a *succès de scandale* but little other reported merit. (*Mad Tristan* turned up in the De Cuevas repertory in London after the war, and was hugely enjoyable for all the wrong reasons.) But those ballets of Massine's that now seem most likely to survive are the early masterpieces of the Diaghilev era. Here he introduced to the Ballets Russes the dramatic tradition of the Moscow company from which he came, basing himself not on the classical canon direct, but rather on that canon as modified by Fokine. Building on what Fokine began, he developed enormously the character ballet and character dancing through a personal language which drew particularly on national sources, and extended the use of the *corps de ballet* through his orchestration of mass movement on stage.

La Boutique Fantasque

A ballet in one act. Choreography: Massine. Music: Rossini, arranged Respighi. Décor: Derain. First performed Ballets Russes, Alhambra Theatre, London, 5th May, 1919, with Massine and Lopokova as the Can-can Dancers.

Curtain rise reveals a toy-shop, through whose windows we can glimpse a Mediterranean harbour. The shopkeeper and his assistant enter; a street urchin dashes in and tries to steal something but is speedily ejected, and now the customers start to arrive. First are two English old maids, then an American husband and wife with their son and daughter, and next a Russian family wilting in the heat, with father carrying one daughter, three more girls in tow, plus mother and son. All these visitors are delighted with the variety of toys that are displayed: two dolls on a stand, a pair of Tarantella dancers, a quartet of court cards, a snob, a melon seller, a Cossack chief, his five soldiers and a Cossack girl, two dancing poodles, and finally a pair of Can-can dancers. These last win everyone's hearts, the Russian father is pestered to buy the girl; the American father must then buy the man for his children. The two dolls are packed up, the customers pay and leave, with a promise that the dolls shall be delivered in the morning. The shop is closed for the night, and as in every well-regulated fantastic toy-shop, the dolls promptly come to life. They are filled with sadness that the two Can-can dancers are to be separated; this must not be! The two Can-can lovers decide to flee, and take a fond farewell of their companions, who aid their flight. In the morning the shopkeeper and his assistant open the shop; soon their customers of the previous day arrive demanding to know why the two dolls have not been delivered

as promised. The shopkeeper reassures them and shows them
the two parcels ready; but on examining them, the dolls are
found to have flown. The irate customers turn on the shopkeeper, but before they can do much damage all the dolls
return to life and chase the terrified customers and the shopkeeper out into the street.

The ever-popular idea of dolls coming to life (source of a
number of ballets from *Coppélia* onwards) is given an irresistible
charm in *Boutique*, not least because of the skill with which
Ottorino Respighi orchestrated a series of unpublished piano
works by Rossini with merry titles, like *Four Hors d'Oeuvre*,
Castor Oil, *Asthmatic Study*, *Ugh! Peas*, and *Abortive Polka*.
Equally attractive are the designs by André Derain, still
appealing even after fifty years . . . but then so is the ballet.
Unlike many works of this period, *Boutique* can still (with
loving, careful performance) retain something of that first
rapture it must once have had so abundantly. The choreography is witty, strongly-made, even more strongly characterized
(with what economy Massine captures the Snob) and the
action combines drama with *divertissement* elements in
marvellous balance. And of course the roles were excellently
created.

Massine and Lopokova were the original Can-can dancers.
When, in 1947, Massine came as guest artist to the Royal Ballet
at Covent Garden, and mounted *Boutique* for them, he danced
the male Can-can dancer again. In the following year Alexandra
Danilova also came to Covent Garden as a guest and we had the
joy of seeing her performance as the Can-can girl in partnership
with Massine. Danilova's beautiful legs, her wit, the sheer
bubbling champagne of her presence on stage set a standard
that no later Royal Ballet performer has yet approached.

Le Tricorne (The Three Cornered Hat)

A ballet in one act. Choreography: Massine. Music: de Falla.
Décor: Picasso. First performed Ballets Russes, Alhambra

*Theatre, London, 22nd July, 1919, with Massine as the Miller
and Karsavina as his Wife.*

The Three Cornered Hat is unique because of the mastery
with which Massine adapted the techniques of Spanish dancing
to the theatre; the steps are all authentic. However, their
organization and arrangement are the fruit of classical choreography. The story tells of a miller and his beautiful wife, who is
the recipient of numerous attentions. A dandy crosses a bridge,
flying a kite, and blows her a kiss. He is soon to be followed by
the Corregidor the (provincial governor – the wearer of the
tricorne) who passes by with his wife and a retinue, and takes a
fancy to the miller's wife. Their procession leaves, but soon the
governor returns, and as the miller is away, he indulges in a
flirtation with the miller's wife. But as they dance, he falls
exhausted to the ground, and the miller returning, joins his wife
in mocking the old man. He exits and the miller, his wife and
their neighbours perform a general dance, which features a
dazzling Farucca from the miller. Suddenly the Alguazils (the
governor's guards) return bearing a warrant for the miller's
arrest, and desolated, the wife watches them lead her husband
away. With the miller out of the way, the Corregidor returns
yet again to complete his supposed conquest of the miller's
lovely wife, but as he dodders after her on to the bridge,
dropping his cloak, she pushes him into the river. As he
struggles out, the miller's wife threatens him with a musket and
then leaves, while the Corregidor, old, cold and suffering,
wraps himself into the miller's huge hooded coat and takes
refuge in the miller's bed to try to warm himself. The miller
enters, escaped from the Alguazils, discovers the Corregidor,
and mocks him by rudely caricaturing him on the wall of the
house. The Alguazils now enter in search of the miller, but they
find instead the dripping figure of the Corregidor in the
miller's coat; they do not recognize him at first, and after mal-
treating him, drag him away; the villagers celebrate the departure of this petty tyrant with a final *jota* in which they toss him
in effigy in a blanket.

During the first world war the relics of the Diaghilev Ballet found refuge in Spain (King Alfonso had for some time been a devotee and important supporter of the Ballets Russes); there Diaghilev heard the incidental music that de Falla had made for a version of Alarcon's story, and he decided that it should be amplified to make a ballet score. Massine was already fascinated by Spanish dancing and took every opportunity to increase his knowledge, notably by employing a young Spanish gypsy boy, Felix, to teach him. The tragedy surrounding Felix's name is open to interpretation, but what we know for a fact is that he believed he was to create the role of the miller. When in London, he discovered that Massine was himself dancing the role, his mind, already unstable, became deranged; he was found dancing before the altar of a church in London in May 1919, was admitted to a mental home, and died there some twenty-two years later.

Tricorne was a triumph from the very first; the glorious de Falla score, which, like the choreography, takes folk art and makes it viable for the theatre (rarest of feats) is a masterpiece – as, too, the dazzling Picasso set; while Massine's choreography is thrillingly exact in its ability to evoke Spain and sustain the dramatic intrigue and reveal character. It remains a unique work. Despite countless attempts to make other 'Spanish' ballets, to re-use the music, even to cast Spanish dancers in it, Massine's *Tricorne* has never been rivalled – nor even approached in its *genre*.

Mam'zelle Angot

A ballet in one act. Choreography: Massine. Music: Lecocq, orchestration, Gordon Jacob. Décor: Doboujinski. First performed Ballet Theatre, New York Metropolitan Opera House, 10th October, 1943.

The plot of Lecocq's operetta, *La Fille de Madame Angot*, is complicated enough as a romp at the time of the Directoire; shortened to make a ballet and without even the dubious help of words, its intrigue and incessant activity can still fox even the most hardened ballet-goer, who after a couple of dozen viewings is often unable to explain coherently what it is all about. In essence it is the story of Mam'zelle (a vile Americanism) Angot, a market girl betrothed to a barber.

Scene I: A Market.

Mlle Angot falls in love with a political caricaturist, who seemingly returns her love (much to the barber's dismay); but the caricaturist whilst drawing a cartoon of a government official falls for the latter's mistress, an aristocrat, and forgets Mlle Angot. The cartoon offends the official who orders the caricaturist to be taken to prison, and Mlle Angot, in an attempt to escape from marrying the barber, insults the aristocrat and is also carted off to jail.

Scene II: At the government official's house a reception is in progress and the aristocrat is dancing, when the caricaturist enters, fleeing from soldiers. He declares his love for the aristocrat, but suddenly the soldiers are announced and though he hides, posing as a statue, the soldiers find him. Mlle Angot, who has come to explain her behaviour to the aristocrat, enters; their meeting reveals that they are old school friends, and anger dissolves into happy reunion. The barber enters in search of Mlle Angot.

Scene III: The Carnival.

Mlle Angot has plotted a meeting between the caricaturist and the aristocrat at a carnival, and she exposes their intrigue to the government official. They all mock him, and Mlle Angot decides that she is really in love with the barber. General rejoicing!

If, after you have read this scenario, you are confused, there is no need to feel alarm; the ballet is incomprehensible in its later development. Ballerina after ballerina, as Angot, has industriously mimed, torn up letters, and cut a dozen merry capers without elucidating this operatic tangle. And it doesn't really matter; what does matter are Lecocq's charming tunes, the pretty Derain sets, and the opportunities given the principal dancers. Massine restaged the ballet for the Royal Ballet in November, 1947 (when it gained its designs by Derain) and its busy joviality has kept it in the repertory regularly ever since. Alexander Grant won golden opinions as the barber – particularly when he expresses grief as Mlle Angot dances with the caricaturist in the first scene; and in the tiny role of the Chief of Police, Stanley Holden has reduced many an audience to helpless laughter with his capers . . . notably a terrible tendency to get his thumbs stuck in the armholes of his waistcoat while ogling the pretty girls in the second scene reception.

BRONISLAVA NIJINSKA (b. 1891)

Sister of Vaslav Nijinski, Bronislava Nijinska was a pupil at the Imperial School in St Petersburg and graduated into the Maryinski Company, whence she joined Diaghilev for his first season, dancing subsequently with him for several years. She spent the war years in Russia, but came to the West in 1921 to participate in staging *The Sleeping Beauty* for Diaghilev. Her gifts suggested to Diaghilev that here was a choreographer able to replace Massine, who had left the company for the first time in 1921. (He was to return later.) After the disaster of *The Sleeping Beauty* in London, Nijinska made her first ballet for Diaghilev, *Le Renard*, which was a success, and she followed it with *Les Noces* (1923), *Les Biches* (1924), *Les Facheux* (1924), *Les Tentations de la Bergère* (1924). She then left Diaghilev, returning in 1926 to stage *Romeo and Juliet*, and thereafter worked in Buenos Aires, and with the Ida Rubinstein Ballet in Paris. Here Frederick Ashton became a member of the company and eagerly watched her rehearsals as well as appearing in many of her ballets. She worked later for De Basil and then settled in the USA, afterwards staging ballets for the De Cuevas Company. In 1963, on assuming Directorship of the Royal Ballet, Ashton decided to pay a tribute to Nijinska and acknowledge her influence by staging two of her greatest works: *Les Noces* and *Les Biches*.

Les Noces

A ballet in one act. Choreography: Nijinska. Words and music: Stravinsky. Décor: Natalia Goncharova. First performed Ballets Russes, Paris, 14th June, 1923.

Les Noces has four scenes:
Scene   I: The Blessing of the Bride.
Scene II: The Blessing of the Groom.
Scene III: The Bride's Departure from her Parents' home.
Scene IV: The Wedding Feast.

Stravinsky originally conceived the idea of a *divertissement* based on the traditional ceremonies of Russian peasant weddings in 1914, and he made an abstraction of those elements of liturgy and folk-experience that are their basis. He saw the work as a masquerade ('Very reluctantly', as he notes in his memoirs, he 'agreed to Diaghilev's staging which did not correspond to my original plan') with singers, musicians and dancers mingled on stage. But Nijinska sought to lay bare the ritualistic elements underlying peasant ceremonies, and aided by the stark simplicity of Goncharova's final setting and costumes (earthy browns and black and white) she made a ballet that reached the very essence of peasant life. The Bride and Groom are two central ikon-figures at the heart of the dancing; in the first scene the Bride is blessed by her parents as her friends dress her long plaits; the dancing is solemn, apparently simple, and there is a use of point work that stresses the abstract quality of the whole concept. There follows a tremendous contrast with the second scene, The Blessing of the Groom, who is surrounded by a stamping whirlwind of his friends while he stands still. After he has been blessed by his parents, we return to the Bride's house; her plaits are wound round her, the groom's friends come to escort her to church and as she leaves, her mother mourns her departure. In the final scene, the bridal party are seen on a raised inner stage while below them there are the joyous festivities of the guests: the women are meekly lyrical, the men stamp and pound the earth with huge energy, and two soloists (a man and a girl) are called upon to sum up certain moments of the work in what are, in effect, variations. The Bride and Groom move into a bedroom that can just be seen at the side of the inner stage, the door is closed, a curtain is pulled to hide the whole of the inner stage while down below the guests form a final pyramid shape (an architectural theme in the choreography throughout the work) as the bells ring out in the score.

Small wonder that Diaghilev wept when he first heard the score; this is a deeply nostalgic work, a glance back at the world that died with the Revolution, the Diaghilev Ballet's last look at Holy Russia. The fruit of exile by war and social change, *Les Noces* is the most authentically nationalist of Diaghilev's post-Fokine ballets, and after its creation he was never to look east again, save for the late, unsuccessful flirtation with Soviet ideas in *Le Pas d'Acier*.

In the Royal Ballet's scrupulous staging (first performed Covent Garden, 23rd March, 1966), *Les Noces* compels attention and admiration by the skill of the conception, and by the continued novelty of Nijinska's choreographic inspiration. It is, in the best sense, an abstract ballet. Depersonalized, yet warm with humanity, it catches a whole social attitude, transmutes it into theatrical form, and never loses touch with its roots in human experience. The actual dance language is amazing; everything looks simple, inevitable, but the underlying structure is rhythmically very complicated. Nijinska uses the dancers as blocks of movement, great shapes of corporate activity that contrast a soft, yielding femininity of the women with a thick muscular style for the men. The work has an extraordinary momentum which builds up through a gradual crescendo until the final scene.

Les Biches

A ballet in one act. Choreography: Nijinska. Music: Poulenc. Décor: Marie Laurencin. First performed Ballets Russes, Monte Carlo, 6th January, 1924.

Les Biches is an untranslatable title: literally it means 'Does' (portrayed on the drop curtain) and cocottes have been known to address each other as 'ma biche' – but none of this quite conveys the idea of a young girl ready for adventure. An English staging – by the Markova-Dolin Ballet in 1937 – was called *The House Party*, which at least suggested the setting. Marie Laurencin's décor reveals a pale, airy drawing-room, presumably in the south of France and it is here that the action takes place. In writing about the ballet, Poulenc noted: '*Les Biches* has no real plot, for the good reason that if it had it might well have caused a scandal. In this ballet, as in certain of Watteau's pictures, there is an atmosphere of wantonness which you sense if you are corrupted, but which an innocent-minded girl would not be conscious of. . . . This is a ballet in which you may see nothing at all or into which you may read the worst.' The eight numbers of the score each contains a dramatic idea: first the twelve young girls of the party, pink-clad, partly innocent, partly wanton; then three heroes of the beach, all muscles and bathing suits, who tread a wary and deliberate path among the girls. They show little interest in the ladies at first, but the entry of an ambiguous figure in a blue velvet jerkin, white tights and white gloves, moving self-absorbedly across the stage awakens the interest of one man in particular. (The figure, since it is danced by a girl, is always called 'The Girl in Blue', a piece of nice-mindedness that cannot disguise the fact that the character is in fact a page-boy, and the proclivities of at least one of the bathers are in no doubt at all.) The girls flirt and play with the athletes, and then the bather and the blue-clad girl enter and dance, while the others peer inquisitively over the sofa. Now the Hostess enters, a lady, in Poulenc's words, 'no longer young, but wealthy and elegant', flaunting beads and cigarette holder, who flirts with the two remaining athletes during a rag Mazurka. When they leave, the athlete and the page-boy return to dance the lovely Andantino. Next two girls in grey arrive – two dear friends, like girls from a *Claudine* novel, exchanging a timorous kiss expressive of their *amitié particulière*, before they exit in different directions. The ballet ends with all the characters on stage in a brisk finale.

Les Biches is a delicious piece – the *Les Sylphides* of the twenties in its romanticism – as light and airy in style as the décor and music, and yet exhaling a delicate, pungent air of sensuality. It is an understated *Fête Galante* where things are certainly not as pretty as they seem; mocking, witty, its slightly *faisandé* air is marvellously sustained. It is a triumph of choreographic stylishness; a shimmering soap-bubble that might so easily be burst, but which Nijinska's skill sustains from first to last. How lightly she treats of the passions, how sweetly they are masked under the air of almost febrile gaiety of the party; but how surely the choreography is made. The cunningly different *ports de bras*, the freshness of use of the classic dance, the clarity of texture in the movement all make it a delight. Without this soundness of the choreography it would never have lasted, and still won its audiences as it does today.

Chapter Six

The English

By August 1929, when Diaghilev died in Venice – almost exactly twenty years after he first brought his Russian dancers to Paris – the art of ballet in Western Europe had been enlarged and changed, through three achievements. He had inspired some of the most perfect works of theatre art then seen; he had blazed the trail of the new and the *avant-garde*; and he had inspired, and largely schooled, those who were about to create the national ballets which arose after his death: Balanchine in America; Lifar in France; Ninette de Valois and Marie Rambert in Britain.

De Valois and Rambert were both in different ways members of Diaghilev's company and both had begun to gather dancers around them in Britain some years before Diaghilev died. So they were ready for the scattering of his company and the tremendous reinforcement of their work which this provided in teachers and dancers after 1929.

Rambert's contribution to the Diaghilev Ballet was as an expert in eurhythmics helping Russian dancers to disentangle the complex rhythms of Stravinsky's *Sacre* (see page 90). Attached to his company, she studied under Cecchetti, then opened her own school in London in 1920, six years before de Valois opened the Academy of Choreographic Art which has become today the Royal Ballet School. By 1926 Rambert was giving successful recitals with her pupils (among them Frederick Ashton) and appeared herself in *A Tragedy of Fashion*, Ashton's first choreography and his first collaboration with Sophie Fedorovitch who designed many of his later ballets. Rambert's contribution to her company as a dancer was never significant, but her contribution as a teacher of dancers

and as the moulder of interpretative artists was profoundly
important for the character and quality of early British ballet.
Especially, she employed her gifts in moulding choreographers
and combining their talents with those of suitable musicians
and designers. From this came not only the first ballets of
Ashton, but of Antony Tudor, Andrée Howard, Walter Gore
and, latterly, Norman Morrice. From the same source, too,
have come distinguished principal dancers like John Gilpin
and dancers who have become directors like Peggy van Praagh
of the Sadler's Wells Theatre and Australian Ballets.

Soundly trained by Edouard Espinosa and Cecchetti, de
Valois' contribution to the Ballets Russes was directly as a
dancer. She was accepted into the company in 1923, rose to
soloist by 1925, and in those two years learned much also about
the organization and administration of a great company. When
she left, it was with the stated intention to train dancers and
choreographers for a British repertory ballet.

Her ambition was not so remote from British capacity as
many people then thought, and she had expert support. 'After
the Russians,' said Diaghilev, 'the English have by far the
greatest aptitude; some day in the future they will form their
own school.' The English have always had this aptitude,
alfthough it was long concealed by historical circumstance.
Alter the famous Elizabethan 'dancing English', the court
balet of Elizabeth's successor James I became the most famous
in Europe, its masques by Ben Jonson and Inigo Jones
influencing the development of ballet at the French courts of
Henry IV and Louis XIII. Even after civil war and puritan
repression the interest remained strong enough to sustain a
brilliant group of dancing masters and dancers in the reigns of
Anne and George I. These not only produced Europe's first
ballet d'action, The Loves of Mars and Venus (*q.v.*) but supported Marie Sallé in experiments she could not pursue in France.
Only during the eighteenth century, in fact, did native English
dancers cease to appear regularly in leading roles and the taste
arise for foreign dancers which made London famous in
Europe for its generosity to visiting artists. The climax of this
trend came in the 1840s when London, rather than Paris, was

the creative centre of romantic ballet under Lumley and Perrot. For the rest of the century every important ballerina and choreographer visited London, among them Adeline Genée from Denmark, Edouard Espinosa from France, Enrico Cecchetti from Italy, and the Ballets Russes.

This is the background of English ballet today. It has not sprung up suddenly, like a plant in a desert, but derives from contact with the three great European schools of ballet, all of which happen to be included in de Valois' professional education. The French tradition descends to us through teachers like Espinosa and the Danish ballerina, Adeline Genée. Trained by the successors of Vestris in Copenhagen, Genée was not only the most important dancer in London preceding Diaghilev, but became, with Espinosa, a founder of Britain's Royal Academy of Dancing. The Italian tradition descends through Enrico Cecchetti and the Cecchetti Society, transmitting experience from the Academy at Milan which trained almost all the ballerinas who dominated European stages at the end of the nineteenth century. Lastly, the Russian tradition descends through the Ballets Russes and the Russian teachers and dancers who settled in England after the Russian Revolution.

Out of this background it is fair to acknowledge that the dominant technical influence on English performers has been Italian-Russian, almost all leading British dancers being trained by Cecchetti or his pupils, or by Russian teachers. The dominant influence over choreography, however, is Franco-Russian. Rambert's taste was decisively influenced as much by living in Paris as by her attachment to Diaghilev; both de Valois and Ashton acknowledge the creative influence of Massine and Nijinska, the two principal choreographers of Diaghilev's most Franco-Russian period. To these influences, of course, each choreographer brought personal experience to evolve a personal style.

NINETTE DE VALOIS (b. 1898)

De Valois was not only well grounded academically by Espinosa and Cecchetti, but, at the age of 25, brought to the

Diaghilev company considerable performing experience in pantomime, revues and opera-ballets. After she left Diaghilev in 1925, she deepened this experience, and the contacts of her dancers, through choreography for the Abbey Theatre, Dublin, the Festival Theatre, Cambridge and the Old Vic, as well as giving classes in stage movement to drama students. The influence of this experience, as well as her classical training, appears in the early ballets of the young Vic-Wells Ballet, almost all of which she had to create herself.

Job

A masque for dancing in eight scenes. Libretto: Geoffrey Keynes. Choreography: de Valois. Music: Ralph Vaughan Williams. Scenery and costumes: Gwendolen Raverat. First performed Camargo Society, Cambridge Theatre, London, 5th July, 1931. Entered repertory of Vic-Wells Ballet, 22nd September, 1931. Revived at the Royal Opera House, Covent Garden, with new décor by John Piper, 20th May, 1948.

Scene I: Job in the sunrise of prosperity.

The Godhead (Job's spiritual self) consents that his moral nature be tested by Satan in the furnace of temptation.

Scene II:

Satan, after a triumphal dance, usurps the throne of the Godhead.

Scene III:

Job's sons and daughters are feasting when Satan appears and destroys them.

Scene IV:

Job's peaceful sleep is disturbed by Satan with terrifying visions of War, Pestilence and Famine.

Scene V:

Messengers come to Job with tidings of the destruction of all his possessions and the deaths of his sons and daughters. Troubled by the three Comforters, Job invokes the Godhead only to find Satan upon the throne.

Scene VI: There enters Elihu who is young and beautiful. 'Ye are old and I am very young.' Job perceives his sin. The heavens again open to reveal Job's spiritual self restored to the throne.

Scene VII:
Satan appeals to Job's Godhead, but is cast out.

Scene VIII.
Job, an humbled man, sits in the sunrise of restored prosperity, surrounded by his family upon whom he bestows his blessing.

Nowadays, *Job* has a certain emotional appeal for the regular ballet-goer as the oldest British ballet still extant. Inspired by Blake's drawings, it is nobly conceived, perfectly synthesizes theme and music, dancing and design, is perfectly English and perfectly individual in the work of its composer and choreographer.

It had been hoped originally that *Job* might have been produced by the Ballets Russes, but the subject did not appeal to Diaghilev. It was, he said, 'too English'! So it was natural its possibilities should have appealed to the Camargo Society, formed after Diaghilev's death to continue the production of ballet in England. It is, indeed, English. Its inspiration, through Geoffrey Keynes, comes from the drawings of William Blake; its music is not only the work of the finest English composer of his day, but itself draws on English folk sources; its conception as a masque is in the direct tradition of a theatrical form the English have made very much their own. The fact that it assumed this form partly because Vaughan Williams stipulated no 'toe dancing', which he detested, and therefore insisted it should not be described as a ballet, does not detract from its place in the English tradition.

It was also very appropriate to its moment in the development of an English company. It provided Constant Lambert – later to be the first musical director of Sadler's Wells Ballet and one of the company's architects – with his first big success as a conductor, and in the role of Satan it gave to Anton Dolin, the first important British male dancer, the first, and still one of the greatest, male roles in the English ballet repertory. Particularly, however, *Job* is an ensemble ballet, exactly reflecting the state of English classical dancing in 1931. Except in the one dominant role of Satan (for the one really good male dancer then available) it makes no great technical demands, but chooses rather to challenge its performers on the level of dramatic movement. Thus *Job* revealed the possibilities for serious English ballet and the creative force of de Valois as a choreographer. Although Ashton's *A Tragedy of Fashion* in 1926 had taken the first step towards the possibility of English choreography, with *Job*, in 1931, this choreography, and the English ballet, stepped firmly on stage for the first time.

The Rake's Progress

Ballet in six scenes after William Hogarth. Libretto and music: Gavin Gordon. Choreography: de Valois. Scenery and Costumes: Rex Whistler after Hogarth. First performed Vic-Wells Ballet, Sadler's Wells Theatre, 20th May, 1935.

Scene I: The reception.

Having inherited a fortune, the Rake, in his new house, is surrounded by people anxious to enter his service. He takes lessons in dancing, parts freely with money – and rejects the girl he has betrayed under promise of marriage.

Scene II. The orgy.

In gay, disreputable company, the Rake tastes the joys of wine, women and song.

Scene III: A street.

The Rake, having squandered his patrimony, is about to be

1. Dancers of the Royal Ballet in the Prologue of Petipa's *The Sleeping Beauty*, St Petersburg, 1890, as staged for the Royal Opera House, Covent Garden, 1946

2. Dancers of the Royal Ballet in George Balanchine's *Serenade*, Hartford, USA, 1934, as performed at the Royal Opera House, Covent Garden, 1964

3. Dancers of Ballet Rambert in Glen Tetley's *Embrace Tiger and Return to Mountain*, London, 1968

Apollon   Le Roy

4. Louis XIV as Apollo in *Les Noces de Pelée et de Thétis*, Paris, 1654, with costumes and settings by Giacomo Torelli

5. John Weaver's *The Loves of Mars and Venus*, London, 1717, recreated by Mary Skeaping for *Ballet for All*, London, 1969. *Left to right:* Alison Howard, Oliver Symons, Jacqueline Lansley

6. Noverre's *Medée et Jason*, Stuttgart, 1763, with costumes by Boquet. This print shows a version produced by Gaetano Vestris in London, 1781, designed by Novosielski, with Vestris himself as Jason

7. Filippo Taglioni's *The Return of Springtime*, Stockholm, 1818, recreated by Mary Skeaping for *Ballet for All*, London, 1965. *Left to right*: Ann Dennis, Gail Thomas and Oliver Symons

8. Filippo Taglioni's *La Sylphide*, Paris, 1832, in Chalon's engraving showing Ciceri's decor for Act I with Marie Taglioni as the Sylphide and Joseph Mazilier as James

9. *Giselle* by Jean Coralli and Jules Perrot, Paris, 1841. Giselle is crowned Queen of the Wine Harvest

10. August Bournoville's *Napoli*, Copenhagen, 1842. A Scene from Act III as performed about 1942. *Left to right:* Kirsten Ralov, Knud Henriksen, Inga Gotha, Margot Lander, Leif Ørnberg and Mona Vangsaa

11. Giuseppina Bozzacchi, the first Swanilda, in St Léon's *Coppélia*, Paris, 1870. *Top left:* Act I, scene 1; *top right and bottom left: Act I, scene 2; bottom right:* Act II

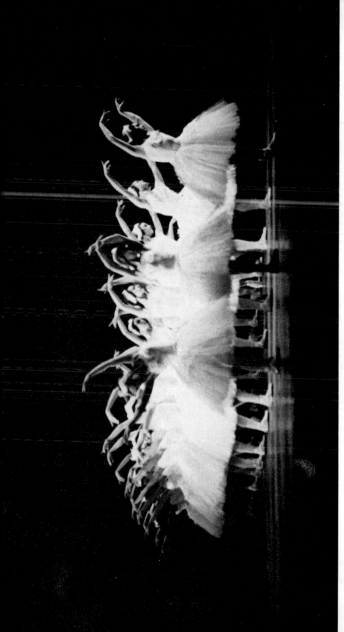

12. Lev Ivanov's Act II of *Swan Lake*, St Petersburg, 1894, as performed by the Royal Ballet at the Royal Opera House, Covent Garden, in a reproduction by Nicholas Sergueyev

13. Michel Fokine's *Petrushka*, Paris, 1911. Scene 2, showing Alexander Benois' decor for Petrushka's cell with Tamara Karsavina as the Ballerina and Vaslav Nijinski as Petrushka

arrested for debt when the betrayed girl pays his creditors with her savings.

Scene IV: A Gaming house.

The Rake attempts to retrieve his position at the gaming-table, only to lose all.

Scene V: Near the prison gates.

The Rake is commited to a debtors' prison, but the girl waits patiently for his release.

Scene VI: The madhouse.

The Rake, ruined in body and mind, dies in a madhouse.

In its blend of dance and mime *The Rake's Progress* continues, in a sense, where *Job* left off. Like *Job* it is a superb piece of theatre craft, strongly native in inspiration, owing nothing to the style of the Russian Ballet. Like *Job* it is intensely English in every element. For his libretto, Gavin Gordon has drawn on one of the finest achievements of the founder of the British school of painting; in his music he has drawn on eighteenth-century English street ballads. Similarly, Rex Whistler, one of the most gifted English theatre designers of the day, has drawn on Hogarth for designs which capture the sober elegance of eighteenth-century London. De Valois' choreography reflects again the developing technical resources of her company and her decision once more to challenge their dramatic ability. The ballet offers a wide range of characterization and moods as well as two technically demanding male roles in the Dancing Master and the Rake, created originally by Harold Turner and Walter Gore. It also shows de Valois' mastery of choreographic construction and her narrative ability. Through movements combining acting and classical dance steps, the minor characters are etched within the manners of their calling and period. The girl's solos, first danced by Alicia Markova, are never solos of technical display in the Petipa manner, but continue the story and develop her character. Being the only innocent and honest person in the ballet she is distinguished from her sordid surroundings by being the only woman to dance on *pointe*. The Rake, too, is depicted choreographically with great economy. In the early scenes as a young *nouveau riche*, the basis of his choreography is classical, with legs turned out. *Port de bras* is exaggerated to show his gaucheness, the palms of the hands turned down and the elbows lifted to establish the eighteenth-century period. As his character deteriorates from brothel to gambling den to madhouse so he loses his classical style and stance. In the madhouse, no academic basis remains at all. The movements become wild, uncontrolled, like an animal.

The three collaborators achieved a magnificent unity of style and their reward has been a work which is now a classic of British choreography and de Valois' masterpiece.

Checkmate

Ballet in one scene with a prologue. Libretto and music: Arthur Bliss. Choreography: de Valois. Scenery and costumes: E. McKnight Kauffer. First performed Vic-Wells Ballet, Théâtre des Champs-Elysées, Paris, 15th June, 1937. First performed Sadler's Wells Theatre, London, 5th October, 1937. Revived and re-designed by McKnight Kauffer, Royal Opera House, Covent Garden, 18th November, 1947.

A brief prologue before a drop curtain shows Love and Death at a chessboard. Love backs the Red Knight to win; Death the Black Queen. The curtain rises on a chessboard setting with an angry-coloured back-cloth on which the red pieces are assembling. First the Pawns, light-hearted pages; then the two Red Knights, fierce and powerful fighters. Two enemy Black Knights enter on a reconnoitring visit of chivalry. They are followed by the entrance of the Black Queen, the most powerful piece on the board. Before her departure she wins the love of the Red Knight, who dances a joyous mazurka. The two Red Bishops enter, their dignified ceremony interrupted by two Red Castles, inhuman and menacing. Finally the Red King and Queen approach. The King, old and feeble, is the weakest piece on the board. The parade of the Red pieces is complete.

The game begins. The enemy Black Pieces attack and 'check' the undefended Red King. His Bishops and his Queen try to defend him, but are defeated. The Red Knight jumps into the arena as champion to fight the Black Queen. He is torn between love and loyalty, hesitates to kill her, and is killed by her.

The Black Queen is now in possession of the board. The Black Pieces force the Red King back to his throne until, at the point of death, he faces his assailants. The Black Queen stabs him; he falls lifeless; it is 'checkmate'.

The figures play out their game as a strong human drama rather than an authentic game of chess, so that the ballet is very much in the dramatic *genre* of *Job* and *The Rake's Progress*, worthy to rank beside them. Bliss's scenario lacks the tightness of their scenarios and his music, though vigorous and exciting in itself, tends to extend crucial scenes beyond the limits of the dancer's physical endurance, thus weakening the dramatic effects. Even so, the ballet makes a powerful piece of theatre, very much reflecting the thirties in the expressionist influences behind McKnight Kauffer's designs and in the growing assurance of the dancing. Heavy technical demands are made now upon the *corps* and a major role is created for a female dancer, unlike the situation in earlier de Valois ballets. Especially it shows once more the craft of its choreographer, with the dual basis of classical technique and national dance on which de Valois' idiom rests. The clean, stabbing *pointe* movements of the red pawns in the opening sequence derive from classical technique. The movements of the black pawns reflect national dance. The *pas de basque* is used again and again; there are traces of Morris and sword dances in the black pawns' staves, and de Valois herself says that some of these movements were inspired also by a Japanese troupe then appearing in London.

FREDERICK ASHTON (b. 1906)

Born in Ecuador, where his father was then in business, Ashton saw Anna Pavlova in Lima in 1917, and the revelation of her dancing set the course for his whole life. He came to school in England and at the age of eighteen entered a business firm in the City of London. But the lure of dancing was too great; he started lessons with Massine (who had opened a school in London), and then went to work with Marie Rambert. While still a student he made his first choreography: *A Tragedy of Fashion or The Scarlet Scissors*, a short ballet in Nigel Playfair's revue *Riverside Nights* at the Lyric, Hammersmith in 1926. He then joined the Ida Rubinstein Company in Paris, where he appeared in several ballets by Bronislava Nijinska, Rubinstein's choreographer, during which time he was able to learn invaluable lessons in the art of making ballets. After a year he returned to Rambert as a dancer and also as a choreographer for the Ballet Club performances, organized by Rambert, which were the cradle of so many English choreographers. He was also to make ballets for the Camargo Society in the early 1930s, including the delectable *Façade* (1931), and for the young Vic-Wells Ballet – for whom he created his first major ballet, *Les Rendezvous* in 1933. In 1935 Ninette de Valois asked him to join the Vic-Wells Ballet permanently as dancer and choreographer, and there began the association which continues to this day.

In the years leading up to the outbreak of war, Ashton composed a series of ballets which were to be of inestimable value in establishing the Vic-Wells (Sadler's Wells) reputation: *Le Baiser de la Fée* (1935); *Apparitions* (1936); *Nocturne* (1936); *Les Patineurs* (1936); *A Wedding Bouquet* (1937); *Horoscope* (1938); as well as three slighter pieces: *Judgement of Paris* (1938); *Harlequin in the Street* (1938); and *Cupid and Psyche* (1939). In 1940 he made *Dante Sonata* and *The Wise Virgins*, but service in the Royal Air Force interrupted his career, and he was only able to make one ballet – *The Quest* (1943) – during a brief leave from his military duties. With peace, and the Sadler's Wells Ballet's move to Covent Garden in 1946, Ashton's creativity was given a fresh stimulus with the need to

produce full-length ballets. He had already made his Covent
Garden debut with *Symphonic Variations* in 1946; he made
two more short ballets – *Les Sirènes* (1946) and *Scènes de Ballet*
(1948) (plus a work for the Sadler's Wells Theatre Ballet in
1947 – *Valses Nobles et Sentimentales*), and then in 1948 he
created *Don Juan*, following it with his first long work:
Cinderella. In 1949 he made *Le Rêve de Léonor* for Roland Petit,
and the following year his first ballet for the New York City
Ballet, *Les Illuminations*. Two works followed in 1951 for the
Royal Ballet, *Tiresias* and *Daphnis and Chloe*, plus a staging of
the Snow Flakes and Kingdom of Sweets scenes from *Nutcracker* for the Sadler's Wells Theatre Ballet. He made a
second ballet – *Picnic at Tintagel* – in 1952 for the New York
City Ballet, and the brief *Vision of Marguerite* for Festival
Ballet in the same year, which also included his second three-
act work – a version of Delibes' *Sylvia* for the Royal Ballet.
The festivities of Coronation Night, 1953, included Ashton's
Homage to the Queen, and his next major creations were
Variations on a Theme of Purcell and *Rinaldo and Armida* given
jointly in January 1955. Four months later he created *Madame
Chrysanthème* at Covent Garden, and then staged his next full-
length work, *Romeo and Juliet* for the Royal Danish Ballet in
May of that year. *La Péri* and *Birthday Offering* (for the 25th
anniversary of the Royal Ballet) followed in 1956; and two years
later he staged *La Valse* for La Scala, Milan, which entered the
Covent Garden repertory in the following year. In 1958 he
composed the three-act *Ondine* for Covent Garden, and in
January, 1960, made the first of his two-act ballets, *La Fille
Mal Gardée*, which was followed the next year by *Les Deux
Pigeons*. In 1961 he staged the Stravinsky/Gide mélodrame,
Persephone, and in 1963 *Marguerite and Armand* as a vehicle
for Fonteyn and Nureyev. For the Shakespeare quater-
centenary celebrations in 1964, he made *The Dream* and at the
Royal Ballet Benevolent Fund Gala in 1965, he staged the brief,
lovely *Monotones I*, to which he added the second *Monotones*
the following year. In 1967 came another ballet for the Royal
Ballet's Touring Section, *Sinfonietta*, and, in 1968, *Jazz
Calendar* at Covent Garden. At the end of that year he pro-

duced his most recent work, *Enigma Variations*, also for the resident Opera House Company.

To write about Sir Frederick Ashton is to write about the history of the Royal Ballet; in Ashton's ballets lie a portrait of the company; their range reflects the range of its dancers, their demands have enriched and ennobled its dancers' style and abilities. As Ashton's genius has developed, so has the Royal Ballet; the mutual stimulus existing between a choreographer and his company, between creator and instrument – and notably with Ashton, between him and Margot Fonteyn (their association having lasted longer and more fruitfully than any other in the history of ballet) – has made for great ballets and a great company.

He is a classical choreographer. That is, the academic dance provides both the stimulus and the material for his creativity which stamps the dance with a clearly personal classicism. In his ballets we sense a temperament that has all the classical virtues of harmony, restraint, control of means, and yet his choreography is full of emotion, poetry, passion, but ordered and refined to maximum effect by his understanding of the academic dance – and, very importantly, by his sensitivity to music. His craftmanship is admirable; his skill in constructing a ballet no less so; and his fluency of invention (particularly in *pas de deux*, of which he is an acknowledged master) is unfailing; his musicality has stimulated the musical understanding of our dancers. These gifts have been of inestimable importance in creating the Royal Ballet and the British school of dancing.

Façade

Ballet in one act. Choreography: Ashton. Music: Walton. Décor: John Armstrong. First performed Camargo Society, Cambridge Theatre, London, 26th April, 931. First performed Ballet Rambert, Mercury Theatre, London, 4th May, 1931. First performed Vic-Wells Ballet, 8th October, 1935.

Façade was originally an entertainment created by Edith

Sitwell, who had written a sequence of poems in which she devised a series of linguistic *tours de force* – dazzling variations in rhythm, sound, and sense. An intensely musical writer, Dame Edith's poems were designed to be recited with a musical accompaniment which high-lighted, pointed, under-lined, the metrical and rhythmic qualities of her verse, and the young composer, William Walton, succeeded in no uncertain terms in achieving just these effects. Sir Osbert Sitwell notes that the title came from a remark made by an indifferent painter who observed of Edith Sitwell: 'Very clever, no doubt . . . but what is she but a façade?' The Sitwells' delight with this judgement is immortalized in the name given to the entertainment, which was first performed in January, 1922. Wittiest of choreographers (and of dancers, as his Ugly Sister in *Cinderella* still proves), Ashton evidently found much to delight him in Walton's parodies, and *Façade* has proved a lasting and endearing view of the dances of the twenties since its first performance in 1931.

It has undergone some slight additions and alterations – and was redesigned in 1940 – but currently it comprises eight numbers: a *Scotch Rhapsody* for two girls and a boy; a *Yodelling Song* for a milk-maid (originally Lydia Lopokova) and three admiring youths in *lederhosen*, which makes wonderfully ingenious use of a stool, and offers a very original mime of milking a cow; a *Polka* (first danced by Markova) in which an elegant and be-boatered lady steps out of her skirt, stands revealed in very natty corsets and dances with delectable *sang-froid*; a *Fox-trot* follows for two couples, the girls in twenties' frocks, the boys in blazers and alarmingly Oxford bags; then comes a *Waltz* for four girls, to be succeeded by a *Popular Song*, danced with a dead-pan precision by two boys; a *Tango Pasadoble* introduces the most oiled and Latin of dagoes and the most inane of debutantes, an irresistibly funny combination of boredom and ineptitude (first danced by Ashton and Lopokova), and the whole company joins in a hectic final *Tarantella*. At one time there were two additional numbers: a *Nocturne Peruvienne* for the Dago alone, in which both Ashton and Helpmann, in the ultimate of pin-striping and diamond rings, were inordinately Spanish and funny, and a *Country Dance* for a Squire, a Yokel and a Country Girl, but these have regrettably been dropped.

Les Patineurs

Ballet in one act. Choreography: Ashton. Music: Meyerbeer arranged Lambert. Décor: W. Chappell. First performed Sadler's Wells Ballet, Vic-Wells Theatre, 16th February, 1937, with Harold Turner as the Blue Skater.

A frozen pond; bare, snowy branches of trees beyond a white trellis hung with Japanese lanterns, and Ashton's charming evocation of skaters as the pretty tunes that Constant Lambert found in *L'Etoile du Nord* and *Le Prophète* ring out. On come the *corps de ballet* in blue and brown, sliding across the ice, to be followed by rather less expert girls; their inexperience is shamingly shown up when a boy in blue comes on and spins, turns and leaps with superb virtuosity. He is joined by two no less expert girls, who indulge in a multiplicity of spins and pirouettes, and we also see a couple in white who dance a lyrical and beautiful adagio. The fun becomes faster and more furious; there are what circus posters always call spills and thrills, and eventually snow starts to fall; the dancers glide away, leaving the blue boy spinning round and round as the curtain falls.

When he made this charming *divertissement* in 1937, Ashton cast Harold Turner, a dancer of splendid technique, as the Blue Skater, and no interpreter since has ever quite matched the panache and bravura that Turner showed in the role. The ballet is compact of delights, and it calls for a very real virtuosity from two girls who have to dash off multitudinous pirouettes and fouettés in a celebrated show-piece. The ballet has lasted surprisingly well in spite of now being something of a period piece in evoking the Sadler's Wells ballet of the thirties.

A Wedding Bouquet

Ballet in one act. Choreography: Ashton. Music and décor:

Lord Berners. Words: Gertrude Stein. First performed Sadler's Wells Ballet, Sadler's Wells Theatre, 27th April, 1937.

The original idea of *A Wedding Bouquet* seems to have come from Lord Berners (1883–1950) a man who stylishly combined the gifts of composer, writer and designer. He was a friend of both Gertrude Stein and Frederick Ashton, and when he came across a play by Miss Stein, *They Must be Wedded to Their Wife*, he realized that it contained the germs of a very amusing ballet. Ashton set to work. Only the beginning of the play was used to provide a dramatic basis for the ballet, and it was Constant Lambert who conceived the idea of giving Miss Stein's description of the play's characters in the ballet's programme. An addition to the cast was Pepé, Miss Stein's Mexican dog, and it was also decided that certain phrases from the play should be spoken from the stage by a narrator, seated at a table, to accompany the action; they do not explain it in any sense, but provide an atmospheric and often amusing commentary on the characters. The ballet is set in provincial (very provincial) France at the turn of the century. We see the maid Webster ('*A name that was spoken*') supervising the preparations for the wedding, and then the guests start to arrive: Josephine, Ernest, Violet, Paul, John, Thérèse, and also poor dotty Julia ('*is known as forlorn*') and her Mexican terrier, Pepé ('*little dogs resemble little girls*'). Meanwhile Violet ('*oh, will you ask him to marry you?*') has made determined advances on Ernest, but is repulsed in no uncertain terms. Josephine is remarkably devoted to Julia ('*not in any other language could this be written differently*') and tries to console her, and Pepé also manages to repulse the attentions of an unwelcome suitor to his mistress – who, as we all realize, has been 'ruined' by the Bridegroom and driven into a Giselle-like madness. Now the bridal party appear; the Bride ('*Charming, Charming, Charming*') is the ultimate in hen-witted vapidity, while the Groom ('*they all speak as if they expected him not to be charming*') has the shifty air of a man realizing that he is about to be confronted with past indiscretions: it seems that most of the ladies present fall into this category. A wedding photograph is taken, and the Groom's evident unease is fully justified when Julia throws herself at him and refuses to be dislodged. Meanwhile Josephine, overcome by it all, has been sipping and sipping, and is suddenly taken drunk ('*Josephine may not attend a wedding*,' observes the narrator sagely) and has to be asked to leave. Alone at last, the Bride (who has put on a little tutu) and Groom dance a brief *pas de deux*, which is followed – when the Bride has left the stage – by a Tango in which the Groom partners a group of his former mistresses. The Bride returns, faints – we hope with delight – and as night falls, the guests leave ('*Thank you. Thank you*'), and the happy couple exit, leaving the disconsolate Julia alone on stage save for the comforting presence of Pepé.

A Wedding Bouquet is a unique ballet which has always aroused the most passionate admiration among its devotees. The combination of neat and funny dances, the inconsequential relevance of the words, the splendid characterizations (Helpmann unforgettably brilliant as the original Groom) and the delicacy and lightness with which Ashton has put together this bouffe makes it a connoisseur's piece, particularly since it is far too infrequently performed.

Symphonic Variations

A ballet in one act. Choreography: Ashton. Music: César Franck (Variations Symphoniques for piano and orchestra). Décor: Sophie Fedorovich. First performed Sadler's Wells Ballet, Covent Garden, 24th April, 1946.

Symphonic Variations presents an essence of Ashton's classic genius; it is perfectly attuned to the music – he is totally responsive to a score – and it is, throughout, warmed by a 'drama of the emotions' that flavours the dancing with a strong character that never bursts through the classical surface though it is readily perceptible: it reflects with uncanny skill the dramatic shifts and emphasis of the score itself.

In February 1946, the Royal Ballet took up residence at the Royal Opera House, and in a world sated with six years of war's tragedies, still constrained by shortages and rationing, the opulent revival of *The Sleeping Beauty* re-affirmed the traditional order and splendour of the classic dance. Three months later the first performance of Ashton's *Symphonic Variations* was as significant an event for ballet in this country as *Beauty*'s triumph. On his return from military service Ashton found that 'there seemed to be a clutter of ballets with heavy stories, and I felt that the whole idiom needed purifying. So I made *Symphonic Variations*, and it was a kind of testament.' A testament, as we now see, not only for Ashton, but for the Royal Ballet and its audiences about the supremacy of classicism as the most fruitful means of future development

The ballet had originally been intended – and how rightly – as the first creation by the company at Covent Garden, but an injury to Michael Somes, who was to dance the central male role, necessitated a month's postponement, and Helpmann's *Adam Zero* had the honour of baptizing the stage, on April 10th. A fortnight later, on April 24th, 1946, *Symphonic Variations* had its première, with Margot Fonteyn, Pamela May, Moira Shearer, Michael Somes, Henry Danton and Brian Shaw as its cast, and with designs by Sophie Fedorovich who, twenty years before, had decorated Ashton's very first ballet, *A Tragedy of Fashion.*

The ballet was recognized as a masterpiece from the start; Ashton's 'testament' was a declaration of faith and intention whose importance has been enhanced with each succeeding year. It was, significantly, his first major 'plotless' ballet, but in a conversation with Richard Buckle, recorded in the magazine *Ballet* in November 1947, Ashton commented on the various themes that had occupied his thoughts in the period immediately prior to the ballet's creation. It is important to stress that *Symphonic Variations* is a plotless ballet, free of any direct literary or dramatic incident, but the strength of its formal structure (which follows the scheme: a, b, a, b,) is best explained by reference to the themes that sparked off Ashton's creativity. The work owes something to Ashton's seeing a reflection of the Seasons in human relationships; in brief, the opening *poco allegro* was 'the woman, winter, the period of waiting', the *allegretto* saw 'the arrival of the men, the sun's rays, the summer . . . Life, Love'; the *molto piu lento* was 'the search, the wound of love, and rapture caused by the spark of love; the dance of union; fertility'; while the final *allegro non troppo* became 'the festival, the summer, the marriage, the heart's joy in union'. But Ashton insisted: 'All these things were only "put in" the ballet, if they *were* "put in", to be eventually refined and eliminated. I did not want to load the work with literary ideas; and I was quite willing for people to read whatever they liked into it.'

Scènes de Ballet

A ballet in one act. Choreography: Ashton. Music: Stravinsky. Décor: André Beaurepaire. First performed Sadler's Wells Ballet, Covent Garden, 11th February, 1948.

Ashton's *Scènes de Ballet* is a classic ballet about classic ballet. Stravinsky had originally written the score for a revue staged by the American impresario Billy Rose, in which it was choreographed by Anton Dolin; he intended it as a recreation of the forms of the classic dance in which, to use his own words, 'the parts follow each other as in a sonata or in a symphony in contrasts or similarities'.

Ashton has made the ballet what Stravinsky intended: a study in the formulae of the classic dance. In a broadcast he stated: 'When I was doing this ballet I immersed myself in geometry and Euclid . . . and the fact that you could make the front anywhere, not necessarily, as it were, where the public sit and see. So that *Scènes de Ballet*, if you were to sit in the wings, would still have the same effect as it has from being viewed from the auditorium. You would get a different, but logical, pattern, and this was a fascinating problem for me. I used to place the dancers in theorems and then make them move along geometric lines and then at the end I would say: "Well, Q.E.D." when it worked out. Sometimes we got into the most terrible muddles, but it was a very interesting problem for me to unravel them.'

Ashton wrote the work for a ballerina and her cavalier, four male soloists and a *corps de ballet* of twelve girls. With these forces he has made a ballet which offers, in an amazingly succint way, a fascinating and revealing study of the emotional and technical attitudes of the classic dance of Petipa. Here are variations, ensembles, *pas de deux* – even an apotheosis; the ballerina seems at times the heroine of any great Maryinski spectacle; the male soloists and the *corps de ballet* of girls evoke memories of the most brilliant passages in the classic repertory; and yet Ashton's language – though entirely classical – has a freshness and a novelty of outline that are constantly exciting. It is a work whose ingenuities, and it is most deft and allusive in structure, never weigh down the actual quality of the invention, which shows Ashton at his most masterly.

Cinderella

A ballet in three acts. Choreography: Ashton. Music: Prokofiev. Décor: Jean Denis Malclès. First performed Sadler's Wells Ballet, Covent Garden, 23rd December, 1948. Moira Shearer as Cinderella, Michael Somes as the Prince, Frederick Ashton and Robert Helpmann as the Ugly Sisters, Pamela May as the Fairy Godmother. (Re-designed by Henry Bardon [sets] and David Walker [costumes], 23rd December, 1965.)

ACT I: A room in the house of Cinderella's father.

At curtain rise Cinderella sits quietly by the fire while her two Ugly Step-sisters are busily sewing a scarf, in anticipation of the ball to which they are going that evening. They bicker – do they ever do anything else? – about the scarf, which is finally torn in half, and they exit to start their preparations, leaving Cinderella alone. She too dreams of going to the party; she dances with her broom, but suddenly becomes sad, and going to the fireplace she lights a candle before the picture of her dead mother. Her father, brow-beaten within an inch of his life, enters and is seized with remorse at this sight, but the two termagants return, nagging him for indulging the girl and chiding Cinderella for not working. A shimmering, magical

tune announces the arrival of an old beggar woman; the Sisters
jeer at her, but Cinderella offers her a crust of bread, and just
as the old woman leaves she strikes the bossier of the two sisters
dumb for one agonizing and glorious moment. Now the
cohorts of attendants needed to prepare the two Sisters for the
ball arrive, bringing clothes, wigs, hats, jewels, maquillage, plus
a handsome dancing-master over whose charms the two old girls
squabble as they squabble about everything. In a final flurry of
powder and malevolence they leave for the ball, with their step-
father in depressed attendance, leaving Cinderella alone. She
dances again with the broom, but suddenly the old beggar-
woman returns to reveal herself as Cinderella's Fairy Godmother. The walls of the room melt away to show the four
Fairies of the seasons who each in turn dance a variation, with
a culminating dance for a group of stars during which time the
pumpkin is transformed into a coach which bears the now
gorgeously dressed Cinderella away to the ball – but not before
the Fairy Godmother has issued the traditional warning that at
midnight everything will be turned back to rags.

Act II: The Ballroom.

The guests are already moving through the formal patterns
of a court dance, while a Jester leaps and curvettes among them.
The Ugly Sisters make a devastating entrance, followed by an
even more devastating dance from each one as they are introduced to their partners. The Prince's four friends herald the
arrival of the Prince himself, which is followed soon by the
magic appearance of Cinderella, revealed as the loveliest of young
women. The Prince, of course, falls in love with her, and their
pas de deux and variations make the glowing romantic heart of
the act. The Prince presents Cinderella with an orange, and
then also makes a gift of an orange each to the two Ugly Sisters
(which occasions yet another display of temper), and the ball
progresses, with Cinderella lost in delight, until suddenly the
ominous ticking of a clock is heard. Desperately she tries to
flee, but she is hindered by the guests and by the Prince. As
she rushes away, midnight sounds and her clothes are turned
again into the rags she wore in the kitchen – save for a shoe

left on the stair. The Prince picks it up, and swears that he will find and marry the owner.

Act III: The Kitchen.

A front cloth scene shows the Ugly Sisters returning homeward with the other guests; soon they are back in the kitchen. Cinderella is asleep; as she wakes she asks herself if she has been dreaming of the ball and the Prince, but suddenly she discovers a dazzlingly beautiful shoe in the pocket of her apron: her delight is interrupted by the return of the Ugly Sisters, reliving with customary bickering the splendours of the ball. A fanfare announces the arrival of the Prince who has come in search of the girl who owns the slipper. The Ugly Sisters eagerly protest that it is their shoe; but despite their agonized attempts they cannot fit the slipper on their bunioned feet. Cinderella moves forward, and as she does so, the other slipper falls from her apron. The Prince realizes that she is the girl he had met and loved; the sisters are aghast when the Prince declares that he will marry Cinderella, but they realize that she is the rightful bride and hobble away to their beds.

The scene is transformed into a magic garden where the Fairies and stars dance once again; Cinderella and the Prince enter, grandly attired, and they leave for a life of ideal happiness as the curtain falls.

In *Cinderella*, Ashton took up the challenge of the full-length ballets of the Maryinski repertory which had featured so significantly in the development of the Royal Ballet. It was the first important long classic ballet created in England. In a sense Ashton had been preparing himself for this task for years – his mastery of the classical vocabulary was complete, and by choosing a tale that had been hallowed in the British theatre through years of pantomime, he was making a very apt and clever choice of subject. He further strengthened the link with a native tradition by having the roles of the Ugly Sisters played by men, first – and subsequently – performed with superlative comedy and finesse by Helpmann and Ashton himself. Helpmann, looking like a roguish horse, was the bossy one; Ashton, paddling about the stage like the ugliest of duck-

lings was the sadly put-upon nervous Sister. The two interpretations complement each other perfectly: Helpmann
rampages shamelessly with eyes in a permanent ogle; Ashton
gets into frightful neurotic muddles, and can suddenly be seen
overcome with a dreadful attack of the Sylphides – and contrives to be so endearing that one often longs for the shoe to fit.

The writing for Cinderella (a role intended for Fonteyn,
though first danced by Moira Shearer because of Fonteyn's
illness) is effortlessly lovely, from the skittish and charming
dance with the broom in Act I, to the ecstatic walk down the
ballroom which Fonteyn does with a superb sense for the
dreaming enchantment the girl feels, and the wonderful *pas de
deux* and variations with the Prince. The soloist roles for the
Fairy Godmother and the Season Fairies are equally fine –
there have been slight changes over the years, none of which
detract from the delight of the ballet. The only complaint which
can be levelled at the work is that structurally it is weak; the
first act is something too long; the second act is ideal in size and
shape, but the third act tails away to nothing, lacking even a
final grand *pas de deux* for the happy pair. The fault here lies in
the score: Prokofiev provided a lengthy travel *divertissement* in
which the Prince journeyed round the world in search of
Cinderella, but the music is hardly of the quality of the rest of
the piece, and Ashton suppressed it in his version. In Soviet
versions, this *divertissement* is used, as also is the character of
the stepmother, but both of these are rejected in the Ashton
staging.

Daphnis and Chloe

*Ballet in three scenes. Choreography: Ashton. Music: Maurice
Ravel. Décor: John Craxton. First performed Sadler's Wells
Ballet, Covent Garden, 5th April, 1951. Margot Fonteyn as
Chloe, Michael Somes as Daphnis, Violetta Elvin as Lykanion,
John Field as Dorkon, Alexander Grant as Bryaxis.*

Scene I: A sacred Grove before the Cave of Pan.
A group of young shepherds and shepherdesses are bringing

gifts to the god Pan, and dancing in his honour; among them are Daphnis and the girl he loves, Chloe. Another shepherd, Dorkon has also fallen in love with Chloe, and after he has paid rough and lusty attentions, which she rejects, there is a dance contest arranged between the two men in which Dorkon's coarse dancing is easily outshone by the grace of Daphnis. After Chloe has given Daphnis a kiss as the victor, she leaves with her friends, and Daphnis remains alone dreaming of his beloved. Lykanion, a beautiful girl, appears and makes determined advances to him; he is excited by her, but quickly dismisses her. Suddenly the scene is invaded by pirates who pursue the village girls and capture Chloe; Daphnis, held by Dorkon, cannot rescue her, and he sinks despairingly to the ground. The nymphs of Pan appear, waken Daphnis, reveal the god Pan to him, and Daphnis prays that the god will help him recover Chloe.

Scene II: The Pirate Camp.

The pirates are celebrating their raid with dances. Chloe is brought in with hands bound, by the pirate chief Bryaxis, who is determined to keep her for himself. She pleads with him, but Bryaxis is adamant. Just as he is about to attack her, the god Pan appears; Chloe's bonds mysteriously fall off, the pirates cower in terror, and the god leads Chloe away.

Scene III: By the Sea Shore.

Daphnis is lying in despair as dawn breaks. His friends come to console him, and he learns that Chloe has been restored to him. She appears, and they are reunited amid general rejoicing.

In 1911 Maurice Ravel was commissioned by Diaghilev to write the score for *Daphnis and Chloe*, with choreography by Fokine. The ballet was first given the following year with Karsavina and Nijinski as the two lovers, and with a beautiful classic setting by Léon Bakst. In his version Ashton rejects the idea of an 'antique' appearance, and his choice of a designer for

the work fell on John Craxton, a painter who knew and loved
Greece; the result was a staging that happily caught the timeless quality of Longus' great love story despite modern dress; it
is remarkable how the trousers of the shepherds, the girls'
dresses and the intervention of Pan are made to work har-
moniously together.

The choreography contains some of Ashton's loveliest writing; he has avoided any 'archaisms' in the general dances of the
first act which recapture the feeling of ritual and homage to the
god (as he does also in *Persephone*) in beautifully simple and
convincing terms; they catch, without aping, the innocence of
folk-dances.

The contrasted dances for Daphnis and Dorkon, the fierce
passion of Lykanion, are all dramatically exciting, and the
pirates' dances of the second scene are excellently crafted. But
it is in the final scene (in which Ashton has rejected the interpolated mimeplay about Pan and Syrinx called for in the
original libretto: it is his only real departure from it) that the
ecstasy of the two reunited lovers and the joyous gaiety of their
friends are so wonderfully expressed.

The ballet was misunderstood by the majority of the critics
after its première, but continued acquaintance soon revealed
that it is one of Ashton's most moving and rewarding short
ballets.

Ondine

*A ballet in three acts. Choreography: Ashton. Music: Hans
Werner Henze. Décor: Lila de Nobili. First performed Royal
Ballet, Covent Garden, 27th October, 1958. Margot Fonteyn as
Ondine, Michael Somes as Palemon, Julia Farron as Berta,
Alexander Grant as Tirrenio.*

Act I, *Scene I:* Outside Berta's Castle.

Berta has returned from hunting, and Palemon courts her
by offering her an amulet, which she rejects. He is left alone in
the courtyard, when a mysterious creature, Ondine, appears
from a waterfall in the garden. From a hiding place Palemon

watches Ondine as she dances in the moonlight, frolicking delightedly with her shadow. Attracted to her, he shows her the amulet which she takes from him. Suddenly she feels his heart beating; she flees into the forest, and Palemon, by now in love with her, rushes after her. Berta's friends witness this, and organize a hunt to pursue Palemon.

Scene II: The Forest.

Tirrenio, Lord of the Mediterranean, and his water sprites lie in wait for the lovers. Tirrenio tries to separate them, but when this fails he warns Palemon that if he should be unfaithful to Ondine he will die. Ondine defies Tirrenio, and together with Palemon finds a hermit who marries them. As they leave, Berta and the hunt enter, only to be driven in terror from the forest by Tirrenio and his creatures.

Act II: On Board a Ship.

Palemon and Ondine decide to take passage in a ship; Berta, who has followed them but does not know of Palemon's marriage, also comes on board unobserved. When they have set sail, she is made jealous by seeing Palemon offer the amulet again to Ondine, who accepts it. Berta now accuses Palemon of faithlessness; Ondine promptly gives her the jewel, but Tirrenio, rising from the sea, snatches it from Berta. Ondine seeks to compensate Berta for this loss by pulling a magical necklace from the sea, but Berta rejects this witchcraft and tosses it back at her. The sailors are by now thoroughly alarmed at the presence of Ondine on board, and threaten her. Tirrenio arises in fury from the sea again, creates a great storm in which the ship is endangered. He carries Ondine away to the bottom of the sea, and Palemon and Berta escape ship-wreck by climbing on to a rock.

Act III: Palemon's Castle.

Palemon and Berta, saved from the storm, have just been married, and Berta shows Palemon her wedding gift to him, a portrait of herself. She leaves him alone while she goes to welcome their guests, and Palemon has a vision of Ondine mourn-

ing him below the waves. His reverie is interrupted by the arrival
of the guests who join in a series of brilliant dances, suddenly
disturbed by the appearance of Tirrenio with a host of sea-
sprites. They drive the guests away, Berta is led out, and
Tirrenio causes Ondine to appear. Palemon realizes that he
loves her still, and though Ondine tells him that if he kisses her
it will mean his death, he cannot resist her beauty and his love
for her; they kiss, and he falls dead in her arms. A final scene
shows Ondine back at the sea-bed, cradling her dead lover in
her arms.

Friedrich de la Motte Fouqué's tale of *Ondine* appeared first
in 1811, and was soon to prove a happy hunting ground for
Romantic choreographers: Paul Taglioni, Jules Perrot (in the
celebrated ballet for Cerrito which contained the *pas de l'ombre*)
and a second version by Paul Taglioni, all used the tale within
thirty years of its publication. In making his version, Ashton
has in some part been influenced by this Romantic tradition –
even to the extent of providing a *pas de l'ombre* for his Ondine,
too. The interest in this, his fourth full-length ballet, though,
lies in the fact that Ashton was completely in control of all its
elements; he devised his own libretto, and worked for the first
time with a commissioned score, rather than with one already
written. The result is a ballet imbued with a splendid mystery.
Throughout its length one is conscious of the sea; the movement is largely inspired by it, the mysterious forest of the
second scene is plainly near water, the second act takes place at
sea, and the castle of the last act looks out on to the sea, and
indeed is invaded by the waters with magical effect. It is also
a ballet which depends, more than any other of Ashton's large
works, on one great central role, that of Ondine, which Ashton
made as a superlative statement about Fonteyn's gifts. It is
part of the ballet's quality that so much of the background
seems misty and strange; the characters other than Ondine are
given little detail, they exist as subordinate figures to the
central portrait of the water-sprite. In it, too, Ashton has rejected the formal devices that he adapted from Petipa for his
other big ballets: the work's structure is freer. Like water

itself, it flows along, with none of the set-pieces that one might expect, its central act, in fact, being almost entirely devoted to the scenic possibilities of the presentation of a ship in full sail and its wrecking. In this there is a return to the older traditions of the Romantic ballet (as *Le Corsaire*, for example, contains a celebrated wreck), but we must under no circumstances suggest that Ashton has been niggardly with the dancing. The ballet is filled with superb movement, much of it, of course, given to Ondine, but there is also a magnificent, though over-long, *divertissement* in the last act, which was first intended to be given by Tirrenio's creatures in disguise. At its close they were to throw off their costumes and drive the guests into the sea. Alas, this thrilling idea did not prove possible. What is most remarkable about the ballet, though, is its atmospheric quality; partly due to a marvellous design by Lila de Nobili, more particularly because Ashton has devised a style that manages to evoke the mysterious quality of a doomed and impossible love set against the constant surge of water.

La Fille Mal Gardée

A ballet in two acts. Choreography: Ashton. Music: Hérold (arranged Lanchbery). Décor: Osbert Lancaster. First performed Royal Ballet, Covent Garden, 28th January, 1960. Nadia Nerina as Lise, David Blair as Colas, Stanley Holden as Widow Simone, Alexander Grant as Alain and Leslie Edwards as Thomas.

Act I, *Scene I:* The Farmyard.

Lise, the only daughter of Widow Simone, a prosperous farmer, is in love with Colas, a young farmer. Unfortunately her mother plans a far more advantageous marriage for her. At dawn the farm labourers go off to work, and a cockerel and hens wake up to the new day. Lise starts her work but her thoughts are on Colas: she leaves a ribbon as a token of her love and when Colas enters he finds it. The lovers' meeting is interrupted by Simone who chases Colas away, and sets her daughter churning butter. The lovers contrive to meet and express their devotion, but soon the farm girls come in and Lise dances with them. Simone dispatches her workers off to the field, and Lise tries to escape with them. Just as her mother is chastising her, Thomas, prosperous owner of a vineyard, enters with his simpleton son, Alain, who is destined to be Lise's husband. Lise is far from impressed by Alain's antics, but she and her mother accompany Thomas and Alain to the harvest field.

Scene II: The Cornfield.

The harvesters have finished their labours and Colas leads them in a joyful dance. When Lise arrives with Alain and their parents, she manages to escape with Colas, while the harvesters make fun of Alain. Lise and Colas express their love in a *pas de deux.* When Simone discovers this she is angry, but is persuaded to show off her prowess in a clog dance. However, a storm interrupts the merrymakers, and they scatter to shelter.

Act II: Inside Simone's Farmhouse.

Mother and daughter return, soaked to the skin. They sit down to work, but Simone nods off to sleep, and Lise contrives to talk with Colas across the locked door of the kitchen. The farm-workers bring sheaves from the field, after which Simone leaves to give the harvesters their celebration drink. Left alone, Lise talks to herself about the delights of marriage and motherhood. Suddenly Colas springs from his hiding place under the piled-up sheaves. They declare their love yet again, until Simone suddenly returns. In desperation, Lise sends Colas to hide in her bedroom. Simone bustles in, suddenly suspicious: she is sure that Lise has been meeting Colas, but cannot prove anything. She hustles Lise up to her bedroom, locks her in, telling her to get ready for the signing of the marriage contract with Alain. Thomas and Alain now arrive, with the village notary and the marriage contract is signed. Alain, given the key to Lise's bedroom, is told to go and claim his prize. As he unlocks the door, Lise and Colas are revealed in each other's arms. Thomas is furious, but the young couple plead with Simone. Thomas storms out, tearing up the contract, and dragging his hapless son with him; Simone relents, blesses the happy pair, and the ballet ends in a dance of general rejoicing.

Ashton's *La Fille Mal Gardée* is an entirely new version of one of the most famous and most significant ballets of the eighteenth century. In 1789, in Bordeaux, Dauberval staged the original, which made a complete break with the formal classical/heroic ballets of his time; in *Fille* (whose staging in the very year of the French Revolution is symbolic) Dauberval was following the precepts of his great master Noverre, in providing truthful observation, a *ballet d'action* rather than the stultified display pieces so prevalent at this time. Here were real peasants, as opposed to the artifices of the French court playing at shepherds and shepherdesses. Here was observation based in life, and a true and urgent dramatic intrigue that went back to the good sense of Molière's greatest comedies. The ballet went through a variety of stagings, including the acquisition of an entirely new score; and in 1885, Virginia Zucchi, the dramatic ballerina, scored an immense success in the work in St Petersburg. As a touching link with this great past, the mime scene for Lise in Act II was revived by Tamara Karsavina for the Ashton staging.

From the moment that the curtain went up on the first night Ashton's *Fille* was a triumph. The wonderful eccentric dance for the cockerel and hens caught the audience, and when Nerina spun prettily through her first variation; when Blair bounded through his, and Stanley Holden poked Simone's outrageous old face out of the window and started hurling artichokes and almost (but not quite) a flower pot at Colas, the success was absolute. The ballet seemed to convey everything that was happy, sun-lit and pastorally delightful; its construction was masterly – dances and mime flowed one into another; its action was purposeful, and told with a gorgeous sense of fun – and at moments, of seriousness; its dances seemed to pile delight on delight. Ashton was writing the ballet for two fine virtuoso dancers, and he responded to all the needs to show off their prowess in dazzling inventions. Nerina's superbly easeful technique – with a lovely jump and *à terre* clarity; Blair's dashing skill, and his dramatic strength; Holden's comic talent, and the immense eccentric resource of Alexander Grant, inspired Ashton to make a masterpiece of comedy without peer. The dancing bubbles along, seeming to gain in momentum and brilliance throughout each act, and yet the dramatic development is never lost. We feel for Lise and Colas – as we feel for the lovers in a Molière comedy – and we rejoice in their tricking of authority so that their love may win in the end. For all the artificiality of its means, *Fille* is still a work of truth; its dancing is inspired by real characters, real and touching situations, all shown with a radiant sense of joy and a feeling for the countryside that is a particular quality of Ashton's poetic genius. Above all, the ballet celebrates the quality and achievement of the new English School.

The Two Pigeons

Allegory in two acts. Choreography: Ashton. Music: Messager. Décor: Jacques Dupont. First performed Royal Ballet Touring Section, Covent Garden, 14th February, 1961. Lynn Seymour as the Girl, Christopher Gable as the Painter, Elizabeth Anderton as the Gipsy Girl, Richard Farley as Her Lover.

ACT I: A Studio in Paris:

A young painter is trying to make a portrait of his girl friend, but her inability to keep still infuriates him. The painter, too, is restless; he feels bored, not only with his life, but even with the charms of his lady-love. His mother enters with a group of young girls, friends of his model, but they cannot distract him from his disconsolate mood, and the young girl is upset that all her charms and her sense of fun cannot affect the painter's feelings. The sound of a troupe of gipsies is heard in the street below; quickly they are invited up, and the arrival of these dashing creatures – and particularly a beautiful girl, mistress of the chief of the gipsies – brings the painter to life in no uncertain manner. Despite the wiles and entreaties of his beloved, he manifests the greatest interest in the gipsy girl. When the gipsies leave, he follows them, abandoning his lady-love.

Act II, *Scene I:* The Gipsy Camp.

The gipsies are dancing, and mingling with the passers-by who have come to see bohemian life (and lose their valuables). The painter enters in pursuit of the gipsy girl, who at first greets him with pleasure; gradually the gipsy leader manifests his anger at this interloper, they essay a trial of strength and the young man is set upon, bound and mocked by the gipsies, including the lovely girl whom he has followed. He staggers from their camp, and makes his way sadly home.

Scene II: The Painter's Studio.

The girl lies sorrowing and alone in the studio, faithfully awaiting her lover's return. As he comes down the staircase, she greets him with unbelieving joy, and their *pas de deux* expresses all the happiness of true love found again.

To say that a ballet has charm nowadays is often to dismiss it as unworthy of further comment; yet *The Two Pigeons* is a work of the greatest and most engaging charm, as it is also a masterpiece of poetic choreography. Together with its companion piece, *La Fille Mal Gardée*, which was created a year previously, *The Two Pigeons* shows Ashton's complete mastery of the two-act ballet. His previous full-length works, *Cinderella*, *Sylvia*, *Romeo and Juliet*, and *Ondine*, had demonstrated how he could develop the traditions of the Maryinski grand ballets and suit them to the needs of the twentieth century theatre. In the most clearly individual of them, *Ondine*, he made a strong personal statement on the form of the big ballet as he understood it, giving it an emotional force that it had rarely known before, but even so there remained problems of spacing the dramatic action significantly throughout the length of an evening. With a two-act ballet these problems are solved, without *divertissements* and interpolated dances to break into the flow of the drama, and in *La Fille Mal Gardée* Ashton showed a complete control of form, telling the story in dances that developed the action through buoyant, sparkling inventions. This is not to decry the achievements of his larger ballets, but in *Fille*, and *The Two Pigeons*, we are presented with long, lyric works as concentrated in their poetic imagination as his finest short creations. The sun-lit extrovert *Fille* is a study in young love at its happiest; Lise and Colas are positive, yea-saying in their view of life; *Pigeons* is the reverse of the coin – softer, gentler, and more searching in its emotional appeal. Ashton called it an 'allegory', and it probes and explores our experience in precisely the way that allegories should. The young painter's wanderlust, his search for sensation and the illusory delights of a 'different' passion, and his eventual realization of the truth of his first love are all aspects of human behaviour that must awake a response in an audience. By casting them in terms of young people seemingly just on the brink of life Ashton has also expressed a great deal about the dreams and aspirations of youth and their adjustment to life itself; the greater marvel is that we are shown all this in choreography of such beauty and freshness.

The Two Pigeons was first staged for the Royal Ballet's touring section, and, like every Ashton ballet, sums up a particular stage in the development of his company. Just as *Fille* is a comment on the virtuoso dancers who first created it, so *Pigeons* presents the lyric gifts of the second company's young stars in 1961. It had its origins in the discovery at Covent Garden of Messager's score, first performed at the Paris Opéra in 1886 – which he had staged in 1906 when he was musical director at the Opera House. Its enchanting melodies and tremendous 'dancing' qualities were inspiration enough for Ashton, but the scenario as originally written – set in eighteenth-century Thessaly and devised to give its first ballerina a double, Odette-Odile role as both innocent girl and gipsy seductress – was plainly unworkable. In transposing the action to a *vie de bohème* Paris, and separating the two female roles, Ashton gave the piece a far greater poetic sensitivity.

And how sensitive the dances are. By presenting the

dramatics in deliberately free terms, with little specification as to the day-to-day reality of the characters, Ashton conveys – as allegorical style requires – the truth of certain emotions in a 'universal' form. The supporting dance action of the gipsies and the young girl's friends is treated as abstract *ballabili* against which, as in a plotless ballet, the principal characters are seen. This in itself is a brilliantly effective innovation for a dramatic work; we do not worry about the whys and where-fores of the drama, we accept the varied – and very exciting – dances for the *corps de ballet* as an accompaniment to Ashton's analysis of his main characters. The ballet can even be seen to be following, in this respect, concerto form, with the principals as the solo instrument set against the orchestration provided by the *corps de ballet*.

Ashton's dramatic works have always been distinguished by the clarity with which emotional states are captured and moods evoked. Ballets as diverse as *Nocturne* and *A Wedding Bouquet* are two examples that spring to mind. In *The Two Pigeons* he shows us sentiment without sentimentality, the tender feelings of youth without mawkishness, emotion communicated with a rare truth and understanding. This alone would make the ballet a fine achievement; but to have done so through dancing of such freshness, lyricism and wit has made *The Two Pigeons* a very special joy to watch.

The Dream

Ballet in one act, adapted from 'A Midsummer Night's Dream' by Shakespeare. Choreography: Ashton. Music: Mendelssohn (arranged Lanchbery). Décor: Henry Bardon. Costumes: David Walker. First performed Royal Ballet, Covent Garden, 2nd April, 1964. First performed Royal Ballet Touring Section, décor and costumes: Peter Farmer, 3rd May, 1967.

Oberon and Titania are quarrelling over the changeling Indian Boy, so Oberon sends his sprite, Puck, to fetch a strange flower, whose juice, when dropped in the eyes during sleep, causes the sleeper to fall in love with the first living being

seen on waking. He intends in this way to spite Titania by causing her to fall in love with some unsuitable creature. Enter two
happy lovers, Lysander and Hermia, and two unhappy lovers,
Helena and Demetrius. Oberon tells Puck to drop some of the
magic essence into Demetrius' eyes so that the unhappy pair
may be reconciled. Oberon meantime, squeezes the magic
flower over Titania's eyes, and causes her to be awakened by
the coarse rustic, Bottom (on whom Puck fixes an ass's head –
which scares Bottom's companions, who flee into the forest).
Titania wakes and falls in love with Bottom, but Puck has
charmed the wrong human lover and Oberon, by endeavouring
to redress this mistake, brings it about that both Lysander and
Demetrius are in love with poor Helena, while Hermia is
now unloved. To right this tangle, Oberon causes a mist to
rise; the correctly paired lovers are guided to sleep, Oberon
arranging that Lysander on waking shall first see Hermia and
fall back in love with her. Titania is shown the ass-headed
Bottom, is reconciled with Oberon and gives him the Indian
Boy; the lovers wake to happiness, and Bottom, with his
human head restored, is left to puzzle out what seems to him a
dream. 'I will get Peter Quince to write a ballet of this dream.
It shall be called Bottom's Dream.'

For nearly two hundred years Shakespeare's plays have
attracted choreographers who have hoped, usually in vain, to
transpose both the action and the poetry into dance. With the
play treated simply as a scenario, success has been possible –
though what merit there lies in setting this dramatic skeleton
dancing when the original offers poetic flesh as well is highly
arguable. But to translate Shakespeare's poetry into dances, to
devise movement able to capture or mirror its verbal splendour,
demands a genius denied all but the greatest choreographers.
The three Shakespeare works that the Royal Ballet offered as
its contribution to the quatercentenary celebrations in 1964
were notable for the originality with which the adaptation to
the lyric stage was achieved. Robert Helpmann's *Hamlet*
showed the action in the fevered, Freudian imaginings of the
dying Hamlet; Kenneth MacMillan's *Images of Love* presented

studies in human passion developed and extended from a series of quotations; Ashton proved that the magical element in *A Midsummer Night's Dream* could with advantage be displayed within the conventions implied by Mendelssohn's ethereal, incidental music. With characteristic sensitivity he captured the essence of this double inspiration and produced a piece that was true both to Shakespeare and to Mendelssohn. The sheer mastery of his craft (not the least important element in Ashton's genius) can be clearly judged in his treatment of the *scherzo*, where the imponderable scoring is perfectly matched in the layout of Oberon and Puck's choreography with its flashing entries and the brief intervention of Titania's attendants. Spinning, soaring, barely touching the ground, the dancers seem buoyed up on the feather-light music which in its turn has captured the essence of their dramatic and poetic qualities. Throughout the ballet this same sureness of touch fixes the essential midsummer magic of the play – even the antics of the mechanicals are touched with some special enchantment; the work does more than justice to Shakespeare – and Mendelssohn – and most importantly, boasts a clear lyricism of its own that shows, once again, that Ashton is a great English poet.

Monotones

MONOTONES I. *Ballet in one act. Choreography: Ashton. Music: Satie, 'Trois Gnossiennes' (orchestration, Lanchbery). First performed Royal Ballet, Covent Garden, 25th April, 1966. Antoinette Sibley, Georgina Parkinson, Brian Shaw.*

MONOTONES II. *Ballet in one act. Choreography: Ashton. Music: Satie, 'Trois Gymnopédies (orchestration, Debussy and Roland Manuel). Lighting: William Bundy. First performed Royal Ballet, Covent Garden, 24th March, 1965. Vyvyan Lorrayne, Anthony Dowell, Robert Mead.*

Monotones II was first given as a *pièce d'occasion* at the Royal Ballet Benevolent Fund Gala in March 1965. Despite the competition offered by the Royal Ballet's staging of the *Polovtsian Dances from Prince Igor*, and such Gala fare as a *pas de six* from *Laurencia* with a stellar cast, *Monotones*, with three dancers in white leotards, no décor other than sensitive lighting, and just ten minutes of choreography, made the greatest and most lasting impression. Since Ashton is intensely musical, the key to the work lay in the pure, uncluttered lines of Satie's music – music stripped down to its essentials, marvellously calm, beautifully ordered. The dancers seemed like three athletes involved in some celestial game, Henry Vaughan's 'angels in some brighter dream', moving calmly, deliberately, unemotionally through their rites, borne along on the clean, spacious sonorities of the music, sharing its qualities of peace and measured beauty. The trio cluster together, separate into solos and duets, rejoin again, always with an unhurried grace, forming sculptural poses of great plastic beauty. Ashton concentrated on exploiting his dancers' qualities of line, with movement followed through to its conclusion with superb logic, as if stating and proving some choreographic theorem with tranquil assurance.

Monotones I, which followed a year later, reversed the casting of No. II by offering two women and one man, and the stronger pulse of the *Gnossiennes* inspired Ashton to create movement that seems more sharply accented than in the earlier trio. There is the same insistence on beauty of line and control of extension, and the same essentially classic nobility, but the dancers are treated as separate entities in a pattern rather than as links in a chain of dynamics. There is a fascinating counterpoint of dancing, with shapes echoed and repeated, lines of movement interweaving and answering each other; the effect, as in the earlier trio, is of timeless beauty.

Enigma Variations
Ballet in one act. Choreography: Ashton. Music: Elgar. Décor: Julia Trevelyan Oman. First performed Royal Ballet, Covent Garden, 25th October, 1968.

In *Enigma Variations* Ashton created one of his most original and moving ballets. Superficially it may seem that he has

provided a skilful realization of 'the friends pictured within' of
Elgar's Variations. Curtain rise shows Elgar's house and the
surrounding garden and countryside; the Variations have been
written, Elgar holds the score and there are the friends whose
inspiration he has acknowledged in the music. Mrs Elgar stands
watchful on the stairs as Dorabella, an enchanting girl, dashes
in and hugs the composer, and slowly the *tableau vivant* of
the opening pose comes to life. First Stewart Powell enters on
his bicycle, dances briefly, knocks out his pipe on his heel and,
suddenly conscious that it is getting late, rushes off. Then
Baxter Townshend arrives on his tricycle, surrounded by a
group of children – readers of his 'Tenderfoot' books, who
dance with him as he struggles with his ear-trumpet. Then
Meath Baker bounds down the stairs, brandishing a list of
arrangements for the day, in a boisterous character solo, which
ends with a bang as he rushes back into the house. Now Isobel
Fitton rises from the hammock where she has been lying, with
Richard Arnold in attendance, and in two linked variations they
express a lyrical affection, before returning to the hammock.
Next Troyte Griffith bursts on in a dazzling classical variation
and dashes off, and it is the turn of Winifred Norbury to rise
from the table where she has been sitting with A. J. Jaeger,
Elgar's close friend and publisher, to dance a graceful variation. Then Jaeger rises, and in the most celebrated section of
the work (Nimrod) he walks slowly across the stage, and is
joined by Elgar in a danced conversation referring to the close-
ness of their friendship, in which they are joined by Mrs Elgar.
(This trio emotionally, though not technically, brings memories
of the *Monotones* trios to mind.) As they leave, Dorabella
enters in a *scherzo* (which includes swift hesitant steps recalling
the fact that she had a slight speech impediment), ending her
variation by dancing with her adored friend Elgar. As they
exit, G. R. Sinclair comes on with a troupe of children; the
musical variation really refers to Sinclair's dog, Dan, who
dashed with much barking into the River Wye, and Ashton
shows Sinclair making pawing gestures during his solo. Now
Basil Nevinson pulls forward a stool and sits playing the cello
while Elgar and his wife dance a *pas de deux* expressing all her

desire to comfort and sustain him, and his reliance upon her support in his whole life. The mysterious opening of Lady Mary Lygon's variation brings a vision of that lady (who was absent on a voyage at the time Elgar was writing) surrounded by curls of mist, as she drifts across the stage like some unattainable ideal. The martial strains of the final variations find all the friends returning to the stage; a telegraph boy brings on the telegram from Richter announcing he will conduct the first performance of the Variations, Elgar is summoned and receives the news with almost uncomprehending joy, as does his wife, and in a final pose the entire group of friends join together while Stewart Powell photographs them.

This is the surface of Ashton's ballet, the first layer of his creativity, and very fine it is, with its well-made variations, its contrasts, its humour, its unerring sense of style and effortless realization of the music. But the true concern of the ballet is with something more serious and more enduring; the artist's life, his loneliness, and those inner doubts of the creator that not even the love and affection of friends or wife can ultimately touch. This theme runs through the ballet, supporting and giving it shape, just as Elgar's theme does to the score. At the opening, when the musical theme is stated, and leads into Caroline Elgar's variation, we see how Dorabella's youth and joyful affection could delight the composer, and how his wife's 'romantic and delicate inspiration' could sustain him. Then Ashton's theme runs underground until Variation IX for Nimrod. Here it bursts out into the most deeply emotional section of the work, in which we sense the intense relationship of love and affection between Elgar, his wife and Jaeger, which helped the creative artist at his most self-doubting moments. With Dorabella's variations the theme runs underground again, but it reappears in the *pas de deux* for Elgar and his wife in Nevinson's cello passage, and it takes a different form in Lady Mary Lygon's solo, in which that lady becomes a vision of some imagined ideal. The resolution of this 'interior' action comes in the finale, where the recognition of an artist's creativity is seen as the true climax of the work.

ANTONY TUDOR (b. 1909)

Considering his small output of ballets, Tudor has made an extraordinary impact on both sides of the Atlantic. Although never well known in Britain before he went to America in 1939, his ballets continue to maintain their influence here over dancers, critics and choreographers. This impact is due in part to the strong personal style of his choreography, the result of a constant search for original classical movement. But it derives mostly from the contemporary problems which compose his themes and which have helped to bring the art of choreography into closer touch with everyday life. Therein lies his principal contribution to the art.

Tudor is one of those many people whose lives were changed by Pavlova's missionary travels. Having seen her dance, then visited the Diaghilev company, Tudor was no longer satisfied at the age of 19 to pursue the prospect of a business career; he decided to become a dancer. His late start, though it drove him forward in passionate study to make up lost ground, inevitably affected his acquisition of the classical vocabulary, and his application of it on stage. It explains to some extent his leaning towards dance drama and avoidance of any kind of technical display.

Launched as a choreographer by Marie Rambert in 1931, much influenced by Fokine and the expressionist work of Kurt Jooss, Tudor developed Fokine's ideas in terms of mood, psychology and character. He examined the emotional stress in human lives always presenting living characters, as opposed to types. Their emotional relationships one with another provide the substance of his ballets.

Jardin aux Lilas

Ballet in one act. Libretto and choreography: Tudor. Music: Chausson. Scenery and Costumes: Hugh Stevenson. First performed Ballet Rambert, Mercury Theatre, London, 26th January, 1936. Revived for American Ballet Theatre, Centre Theatre, New York, 15th January, 1940. For the Royal Ballet, Royal Opera House, Covent Garden, 12th November, 1968.

Characters:

Caroline, the Bride-to-be	The Man she must marry
Her Lover	The Woman in his Past

Scene: The lilac garden of Caroline's house.

Tudor's way of naming his characters explains exactly the motivation of the ballet. The period is Edwardian, when marriage is 'sacrosanct'. Caroline's marriage is one of convenience, therefore she and her lover seek desperately for a moment together in the garden to take a last farewell. The husband equally insists that the woman in his past must end their former relationship. At the end Caroline must leave on the arm of her fiancé without having had an opportunity to take the last farewell of her lover, which was her principal reason for giving the party. It is a ballet of meetings soon disturbed, hurried partings and imploring glances.

Very varied in theme and origin, Tudor's ballets are presented through a choreography which is more cerebral than Ashton's. Each work is the result of a search for some style of movement particularly applicable to the subject and the music. In this ballet he uses classical technique to indicate the aristocracy of his characters, modifying it with the gestures and images necessary to indicate their tension and frustration underlying perfect manners. Hence *Jardin aux Lilas* shows very well Tudor's development of the mood *genre* from the point where Fokine left it. The characters are carried along on an endless belt of movement which arises from their conflict, one with another. It is the application of the mood *genre* to psychology.

The ballet's creation is interesting, also, for the insight it gives into Tudor's way of working. He tends to choose one or two dancers – often in Rambert days one or other of the principals in this ballet, Maude Lloyd (Caroline), Peggy van Praagh (The Woman in his Past) or Hugh Laing (Her Lover) – to find a dance style before transferring it to the rest of the cast. Often his whole ballet will be worked out first in this way. He has always depended very much on sympathetic collaboration, not only with his dancers, but his designer. Hugh Stevenson, for example, was the author of *The Planets*, Tudor's first lasting success for Rambert in 1934, and played an equally significant part in the birth of *Jardin aux Lilas*, ultimately suggesting its title.

Dark Elegies

Ballet in two scenes. Libretto and choreography: Tudor. Music: Gustav Mahler (Kindertotenlieder). Scenery and costumes: Nadia Benois. First performed Ballet Rambert, Duchess Theatre, London, 19th February, 1937.

The ballet is an intensely human portrayal of grief and bereavement in which young parents mourn the loss of their children after a disaster has struck their village. Nadia Benois' sombre backcloths and severe costumes give the tragedy a maritime setting. The first scene of bereavement is conveyed through five songs – first a solo for one woman; second a *pas de deux*; third, male solo and ensemble; fourth, female solo; fifth, ensemble. The second scene of resignation is for the ensemble.

Like Nijinski's *Le Sacre du Printemps* and Nijinska's *Les Noces*, *Dark Elegies* represents a whole community, not just an individual. Such ballets distil the essence of a community, rising to epic heights as if impelled by communal emotion. No other ballet in the English repertory has succeeded so well in the epic *genre*. Its principal stylistic influence is expressionist, reflecting the tensions of the thirties, although the choreography derives also from folk movement and classical technique. Classical turn-out and *pointes* are discarded for the *corps*, but retained for the three principal characters, providing a contrast which helps to emphasize choreographically the sense of grief and personal loss. Tudor's choice of music illustrates an aspect of his creative method. He prefers to use existing music, which he can study, rather than music specially composed. Generally, he is attracted to the high emotional content of the late romantics and moderns (Chausson, Strauss,

Mahler, Schönberg, Koechlin), finding in such music the response to the social and psychological themes which move him.

Pillar of Fire

Ballet in one act. Libretto and choreography: Tudor. Music: Arnold Schönberg ('Verklärte Nacht'). Scenery and costumes: Jo Mielziner. First performed American Ballet Theatre, Metropolitan Opera House, New York, 8th April, 1942.

The time is the turn of the century; the place, an open space across which two houses face each other. A young woman, Hagar, fears that she will lose the man she loves ('The Friend' in Tudor's cast list) to her flirtatious youngest sister. Maliciously her older sister encourages the youngest in her efforts to attract the Friend. Terrified of being left an old maid like the elder sister, Hagar gives herself to a man she does not love. The episode brings her nothing but shame and misery until, in her despair, The Friend returns with sympathy and understanding. The ballet ends with the lovers walking away into the forest, their shoulders touching.

Tudor left Britain for America in 1939, to work with the newly-established Ballet Theatre. There he received opportunities which consolidated his position as one of the outstanding choreographers of the day. In the long run, perhaps, the move was less beneficial than it seemed at first for his creative development. He was separated from the sources which had stimulated him until then, and the working conditions of the American theatre, especially the crippling restrictions of rehearsal time, were not congenial to his creative method. At first, in *Pillar of Fire*, however, America provided his masterpiece. It was an extension of the method first used in *Jardin aux Lilas* to express through movement the strain and stress of emotional upheaval. In such ballets Tudor probed beneath the surface of actions and behaviour to show the 'why' as well as the 'how'. In so doing he enlarged the frontiers of ballet in directions where few other choreographers have followed.

Pillar of Fire illustrates once again Tudor's dependence on people for creative stimulus, especially Hugh Laing who went with him to America and created the 'other man' in *Pillar of Fire*. Out of the abilities of his dancers he creates his characters. Hagar was superbly interpreted by Nora Kaye, so that the ballet established her as a dramatic ballerina as firmly as it established Tudor in America. After this Tudor's extension of the mood ballet into psychological drama, his particular development of expressive dance gesture and preference for contemporary stories and types of people, became part of the tradition of American choreography. The best ballets he had created for Rambert in Britain, as well as others newly created, like *Pillar of Fire*, became classics in America, if not American classics. They gave artistic stability to the erratic, proudly American, self-consciously national venture which was Ballet Theatre in its early days.

Shadowplay

Ballet in one act. Libretto and choreography: Tudor. Music: Charles Koechlin ('Les Bandar-Log' and 'La Course de Printemps'). Scenery and costumes: Michael Annals. First performed Royal Ballet, Royal Opera House, Covent Garden, 25th January, 1967 with Anthony Dowell as the Boy with Matted Hair.

The scene is a forest; a great tree with hanging rope structures for the monkey folk (Arboreals) and, below it, the hero, the boy with matted hair, alone. To the boy come inhabitants of 'the penumbra', people who communicate experience, the world, its social attitudes. Among them the Arboreals, silly and annoying; then Aerials, seeming like Cambodian dancers, communicating perhaps more worthwhile values; then Terrestrial, a male dancer representing passion and experience; finally, the Celestials offering the boy choice and combat. At the end, after great struggle, he returns to his place below the tree, sitting as we found him.

This obscure but magnificent work appeared at a time when

many people thought they had seen their last new Tudor ballet.
Two more essays in the same *genre* had followed *Pillar of Fire*
in 1942, *Dim Lustre* was staged in 1943; *Undertow* in 1945.
Nothing of the same quality had appeared since. Tudor left
Ballet Theatre in 1950, worked briefly with New York City
Ballet, and was associated for many years with the Metro-
politan Opera as well as teaching for the Dance Department of
the Juilliard School of Music. It seemed that creativity had
passed. Then in 1963 he produced *Echoes of Trumpets* for the
Royal Swedish Ballet, a major work which contained all his old
dramatic strength, psychological perception and theatre sense.
A second phase of choreographic creation had begun in which
Shadowplay takes its place as an extension of the psychological
drama in which he is a master. Using symbols suggested by
Kipling's *The Jungle Book* which had inspired Koechlin's
music, *Le Livre de la Jungle*, he burrows deep beneath the surface of society to show the forces which mould individuals, and
the individual struggling for self-assertion against these forces.
The point of departure is Koechlin's music. The composer
sees the monkeys as symbols of anarchy and vulgarity in
opposition to the order and mystery 'of things and beings',
represented by the jungle and its 'noble' creatures, and of
course, Mowgli himself. In Tudor's treatment Anthony Dowell
danced the boy; Derek Rencher the Terrestrial and Merle
Park the Celestial.

Knight Errant

*Ballet in one act. Libretto and choreography: Tudor. Music:
Richard Strauss (from 'Le Bourgeois Gentilhomme' and the
Overture to 'Ariadne auf Naxos'). Scenery and costumes: Stefanos
Lazaridis. First performed Royal Ballet, Opera House,
Manchester, 25th November, 1968.*

Characters:

A Gentleman of Parts   Ladies of Quality
A Woman of Consequence   Ladies of Position
Gentlemen of Standing   Gentlemen of Means
                    Postillions

The plot is suggested by an incident in Choderlos de Laclos' novel, *Les Liaisons Dangereuses*, where reference is to an incidental character, Prévan, who seduces 'three inseparables'. The action presents three ladies, lately married, whom the Chevalier, a gentleman of parts, contrives to seduce during one hectic night and then betrays to their respective husbands. In turn, the Chevalier is betrayed by the Woman of Consequence who tosses his clothes from the bedroom window during *her* bout with him. He is then confronted by his three earlier conquests who leave him – more in sorrow than in anger – while he shrugs his shoulders philosophically as the curtain falls.

Few ballets illustrate more clearly Tudor's habit, and need, to create ballets around one artist, or at most a very few, for whose talent he has a special sympathy. In this case the artist is David Wall, applying in his performance principles of acting *à Stanislavski* which Tudor has sought to adapt to ballet throughout his career. The result is a witty, mocking commentary on love and the preposterous nature of amorous intrigue given with a good deal of psychological insight, which becomes at the same time an outsize compliment to exceptional artists.

ANDREE HOWARD (1910–1968)

Andrée Howard, trained in the forming ground of Rambert's Ballet Club, made her first attempt at choreography in 1933. *Our Lady's Juggler* showed at once an ability to sustain mood and create atmosphere with a remarkable economy of movement, which remained her strength.

In her early days she was influenced by the two senior choreographers of the Ballet Club, Ashton and Tudor, inclining towards Ashton. Her qualities as an artist resemble his in flow of movement, taste, sensitivity and a restraint which is very English in its understatement but which in her case, has led to her worth being much undervalued. For Ballet Rambert in 1947 she created in *The Sailor's Return* the first British two-act ballet; her *Death and the Maiden* remained a classic of the Rambert repertory for over twenty years after its first performance in 1937; while the enormous popularity of *La Fête Etrange*, which contained so many of her best qualities, indicates better than anything else the appeal of her work.

La Fête Etrange

Ballet in two scenes. Libretto: Ronald Crichton, based on an episode in 'Le Grand Meaulnes'. Choreography: Andrée Howard. Music: Gabriel Fauré. Scenery and costumes: Sophie Fedorovitch. First performed London Ballet (with Ballet Rambert), Arts Theatre, London, 23rd May, 1940.

On the terrace of a young bride's castle, young guests in carnival costume celebrate by dancing and playing in the wintry sunlight. A country boy, wandering in the woods, stumbles upon this world he has never experienced before. The guests welcome him and his happiness mounts to ecstasy when the bride allows him to dance with her. The gaiety is stilled and the mood changes when the bridegroom arrives. He misunderstands his bride's kindness to the boy, and leaves her, in spite of the pleading of all the guests. The unhappy boy tries to console the bride, but she turns from him and goes into the castle. As evening falls the boy who so unwittingly caused the tragedy, retraces his steps alone through the woods.

The London Ballet was one of the first small companies to raise the flag of ballet in the early days of the war after the theatre shutdown of 1939. Andrée Howard's tender choreography became a memorial of that event. It showed her preference for literary subjects – *Lady into Fox* and *The Sailor's Return* were likewise based on stories – as well as her mastery of the mood form. The choreography of *La Fête Etrange* evoked the adolescent wonder of *Le Grand Meaulnes* with a quite extraordinary intensity, aided by Fedorovitch's wintry, pale backcloth and the sweet melancholy of Fauré's songs and piano music. Bride, bridegroom and country boy are linked in tragic conflict never directly expressed by any of them, but ending in solitary grief for all three, having been visible as a whole only to the audience.

WALTER GORE (b. 1910)

One of the first male dancers to make a reputation at Marie Rambert's Ballet Club and one of the best British character dancers of his day (he created the Rake in de Valois' *The Rake's Progress*) Gore received an early training at the Italia Conti School plus some encouragement from Massine, but owes most of his training as dancer and as choreographer to Rambert. His ballets fall into three main categories: strongly dramatic works like *The Night and Silence*; light comedy ballets like *Street Games*; and ballets of mood. Although the development of his style has suffered from working for too many groups for too short a time, he remains one of the most original and prolific of choreographers.

Street Games

Ballet in one act. Libretto and choreography: Gore. Music: Jacques Ibert. Scenery and costumes: Ronald Wilson. First performed New Ballet Company, Wimbledon Theatre, London, 11th November, 1952.

Scene: A wharfside stretch of ground near Blackfriars Bridge, London. To the left a stylized house with a window; to the right a dark wall. The dancers, as children, prepare to play games. First comes Hopscotch for the girls followed by Rugger for the boys, Skipping for the girls and *pas de deux* for screen-struck lovers who have just left a cinema. The boys search for a lost ball, which a girl hides. And so the games continue with Statues, Dressing-up and Mock Battles linked by the progress of the lovers.

Although *Street Games* is at least one game too long it illustrates very well the twists of humour and wry observation which Gore habitually introduces to his comedy ballets, so that humour is sometimes never far from tears. He is above all an inventor of situations and a commentator on the human state. This ballet entered the repertory of Western Theatre Ballet, with designs by André François, soon after that company was formed and owes its place in the English repertory largely to their loving performances.

The Night and Silence

Ballet in one scene. Libretto and choreography: Gore. Music: Bach, arranged Mackerras. Décor and costumes: Ronald Wilson. First performed Edinburgh International Ballet, Empire Theatre, Edinburgh, 25th August, 1958.

Jealousy of a man for a woman finally destroys them both.

In 1958 the Edinburgh Festival presented a series of 'Ballet Premiers' with guest artists and guest choreographers. This ballet, danced by Paula Hinton and David Poole, was one of the most memorable contributions and a singularly powerful study of its theme. In his early work as a choreographer for Rambert at the end of the thirties Gore seemed influenced by Tudor in a style marked by strong musicality, sense of rhythm and an original approach to movement. *The Night and Silence* shows these qualities in maturity. A ballet of mood, it is also a strongly dramatic work in Gore's eccentric and individual manner, such as he has repeated since, with variations, for the Gulbenkian company in Lisbon where he has spent the last few years. Both roles in *The Night and Silence* were remarkable performances by their two creators, each outstanding as a dramatic artist.

JACK CARTER (b. 1923)

Jack Carter's experience as dancer and choreographer has been gained outside Britain as much as with British companies. He danced with the Ballet Guild in 1946, then with Original Ballet Russe, Ballet Rambert (creating a number of excellent works for Ballet Workshop), and Festival Ballet, where he is now resident choreographer. Much of his experience was gained in Holland where he worked from 1954–57 with the Ballet der Lage Landen, and also in Sweden. His ballets like *Past Recalled* (originally named *Ouverture*, to a theme by Proust), *Agrionia*, *The Witch Boy* and *Cage of God* are strong in atmosphere and tell their stories through well-drawn characters which indicate a marked narrative ability in their creator. As resident choreographer to London's Festival Ballet during the last few years, he has also had to handle the largest ensemble in Britain outside the Royal Ballet. For this company, his productions of large classical ballets like *Swan Lake* and *Coppélia* (both with his own choreography) show also an ability to handle large numbers of dancers on stage and organize the dramatic and other climaxes of full-length works.

The Witch Boy

Ballet in one act and three scenes. Libretto and choreography: Jack Carter. Music: Leonard Salzedo. Scenery and costumes: Norman McDowell. First performed Ballet der Lage Landen, Amsterdam, 24th May, 1956. First performed London's Festival Ballet, Opera House, Manchester, 27th November, 1957.

A ballet on the American ballad of Barbara Allen.

Scene I: The General Store.
Barbara Allen, repelled by the unwelcome advances of the Preacher, flees to the mountains.

Scene II: On the mountain side.
Barbara Allen meets the Witch Boy, child of the Conjurman. They fall in love.

Scene III: Saturday night at the General Store.
Barbara Allen brings the Witch Boy back to the village where they join in the dancing. The Preacher turns the people against the Witch Boy. Accused of witchcraft he is beaten up,

then lynched. As his body hangs from the rope the Conjurman appears, and the Witch Boy is reborn.

It is hard to judge Carter properly beside his English contemporaries because so much of his work is scattered through theatres in Europe and South America. This ballet illustrates his sense of theatre and place in the tradition of English dramatic choreography.

Cage of God

Ballet in one act. Libretto and choreography: Jack Carter. Music: Alan Rawsthorne ('Concerto for ten instruments' and 'Theme and variations for two violins'). Scenery and costumes: Patrick Procktor. First performed Western Theatre Ballet, Sadler's Wells Theatre, 20th June, 1967.

It is said that in Eden God created Adam . . . Eve too. And that, through the Serpent, he holds them and their kind encaged forever. This is an allegory of the Fall, of jealousy, and Cain and Abel in terms of dancers and their conflicts. When Cain finally is slain his dead body clings to the murderer who is joined in turn to all the other characters in an endless chain of guilt.

Probably Carter's best and most original ballet in the dramatic narrative *genre* for few characters – which seems most suited to his talent. It is perhaps significant that he should have created it for Western Theatre Ballet, a company trained in ballets by Peter Darrell whose dramatic and choreographic requirements are close to Carter's own.

JOHN CRANKO (b. 1927)

Born in Rustenburg, South Africa, John Cranko created his first ballet (an individual interpretation of Stravinsky's *Soldier's Tale*) for the Cape Town Ballet Club at the age of

sixteen. By the time he came to England in 1946 and joined
Sadler's Wells Theatre Ballet as a dancer he had already
mounted several more works. He soon showed Ninette de
Valois two short *divertissements* which she accepted for the
company's repertory in 1947. One of these, *Tritsch-Tratsch*,
has remained ever since a popular item for concert programmes. Further creations for the company followed, and for the
1950–51 season Cranko was designated Resident Choreographer. *Pineapple Poll*, created that year, won great popularity; other notable works from this period were an imaginatively
romantic duet, *Beauty and the Beast*, and the poetic *Harlequin in
April*.

Cranko's first ballet at Covent Garden was *The Witch*,
created during New York City Ballet's season there in 1950 as
part of an exchange arrangement. From 1952, Cranko created
ballets alternately for the resident companies at Covent
Garden and Sadler's Wells, including in 1957 the first full-
evening ballet entirely by British artists, *The Prince of the
Pagodas*, for which Benjamin Britten wrote the music, his only
commissioned score for ballet. Cranko's opportunities with
these two companies, however, amounted on average to not
more than one new work a season, though he used his remaining time adventurously. Naturally he accepted commissions
from other companies, creating two works for Ballet Rambert,
La Belle Helène for the Paris Opéra, and the Prokofiev *Romeo
and Juliet* for La Scala, Milan. He organized a special season
of ballets, most of them new, jointly with the painter John
Piper in a small theatre near Piper's home at Henley. He also
experimented in other branches of the theatre, most successfully with an unusual intellectual revue, *Cranks*, which he
wrote and directed, and which was reproduced subsequently in
many countries.

In 1960 Cranko went to Stuttgart to revive *The Prince of the
Pagodas* and was asked by the general director whether he
would accept the post of ballet director. Feeling by this time
impatient for greater responsibility, he accepted. The Stuttgart
Opera was already among Germany's leading companies;
the ballet company was sound, but undistinguished. Cranko

took up his new post in 1961, and by 1963 the company was strong enough to appear at the Edinburgh International Festival. Since then it has established itself as unquestionably Germany's leading company, with an international reputation built during several tours, including an exceptionally successful season in 1969 at the Metropolitan Opera House, New York.

Part of Cranko's success in Stuttgart has been in creating a strong company. He insisted on the foundation of a ballet school attached to the theatre; he secured able assistants and gave them responsibility. Some outstanding dancers were imported, but Cranko's real secret lay in developing an exceptional team spirit and in his own rare ability to recognize, cherish and nurture the talents of his dancers. In particular, he helped his leading ballerina, Marcia Haydée, to grow into one of the best dancers in any company anywhere today, and built an unusually strong group of male dancers.

Cranko also created a series of ballets which not only showed off his dancers to good advantage but also had a direct and immediate appeal to audiences. He has a sense of theatre and a genuine wish to entertain people, coupled with a keen sense of humour. As a storyteller he is probably unrivalled among choreographers today. Frequently his ballets are based on literary sources, but always these are translated (and often drastically adapted) into a form that can be expressed in dancing. The situation and characters remain recognizable but the incidents are often new. By this process Cranko ensures a rare depth and liveliness of characterization for his works and an unusual degree of narrative interest.

Simultaneously with works of this nature, Cranko has always shown an inclination to experiment: both in the form of his ballets and in their content, which was often influenced by philosophical or artistic ideas. Some people found even *Harlequin in April* difficult to follow, although to a generation brought up on T. S. Eliot's poetry it was straightforward. In *Reflection* and *The Angels* for the Royal Ballet, and *Variations on a Theme* for Rambert, he created enigmatic narratives illuminated by flashes of poetic or psychological understanding.

This strain continued at Stuttgart with such ballets as

Opus 1 (a reworking of themes from some of these early ballets in abstract terms with a free choreographic style), *The Interrogation*, with its Kafkaesque drama inspired by paintings by Francis Bacon, and *Oiseaux Exotiques* to Messaien's music. Such ballets, although their appeal was inevitably less wide than that of his more conventional ballets, kept Cranko and his dancers full of new ideas which enriched all his work.

In his early days, Cranko (like most young artists) was influenced by the work of other choreographers and experimented in their various styles to the extent that successive ballets by him might almost have been by different creators – the works of Balanchine, Massine and others were at different times Cranko's models. Gradually he welded these eclectic influences into his own recognizable, distinctive and flexible style. Even so, although he has created several plotless ballets, it is not as a creator of pure dance that Cranko is outstanding. His distinction lies in using dance to express the richness of the human spirit, whether in serious mood or with the robust and irreverent sense of humour that is one of his most endearing features.

Recently Cranko assumed additional responsibilities as principal choreographer to the resident ballet company at Munich, about two hours' drive from Stuttgart. His aim, if it proves practicable, is eventually to combine the two companies into one large South German Ballet. His ambition remains as large and his resourcefulness as ingenious as ever.

Pineapple Poll

Ballet in three scenes. Plot freely adapted by John Cranko from 'The Bumboat Woman's Story' by W. S. Gilbert. Music from the operas of Arthur Sullivan, chosen and arranged by Charles Mackerras. Scenery and costumes by Osbert Lancaster. First performed by the Sadler's Wells Theatre Ballet at Sadler's Wells Theatre, 13th March, 1951.

Scene I: Portsmouth.
Sailors gather with their sweethearts and wives outside a

quayside inn. Poll, a 'bumboat woman' who lives by selling
trinkets, enters and her wares are in great demand. Jasper, a
potboy, loves her but she scorns him. Captain Belaye, commander of HMS 'Hot Cross Bun', arrives; he is so handsome
that all the women fall in love with him. He has come, however, to meet his fiancée Blanche, who is chaperoned by her
constantly chattering aunt, Mrs Dimple. In spite of this, his
crew are rebellious to see the effect he has on their womenfolk,
and stalk off followed by the harassed Belaye.

Scene II: The quayside.

Poll arrives, gazing lovestruck at Belaye's ship. She decides
to disguise herself as a sailor and go to sea with him. Other
members of the crew arrive, their faces hidden beneath their
large sailor's hats, their stride curiously careful. Jasper comes
looking for Poll. Finding her abandoned clothes, he decides she
must have drowned and leaves sorrowfully.

Scene III: Aboard the 'Hot Cross Bun'.

Belaye is surprised at some of the mannerisms of his crew,
and even more so when one of them (Poll) faints because a
cannon is fired. He goes ashore and the crew wait impatiently.
His return with Blanche in her wedding dress, accompanied by
Mrs Dimple, causes great commotion. Poll tears off her
disguise and declares her love for Belaye, whereupon the rest of
the crew reveal themselves also as girls in disguise for the same
reason. At this point the real crew are heard angrily approaching, led by Jasper. Mutiny is averted only by Blanche and Mrs
Dimple who persuade the sailors to forgive their women.
There is nearly a relapse when Belaye reappears more splendid
than ever, having been suddenly promoted to the rank of
Admiral, but this is averted. Jasper is appointed Captain in
Belaye's place and Poll decides she will marry him after all. A
celebratory dance concludes with the transformation of Mrs
Dimple, with the addition of a flag and a trident, into the figure
of Britannia.

Pineapple Poll was the first example of Cranko's gift for

14. Vaslav Nijinski's *L'Après-Midi d'un Faune*, Paris, 1912, with Nijinski as the faun in the costume designed by Léon Bakst

15. Leonide Massine's *La Boutique Fantasque*, London, 1919.
Shown here, Massine in a costume designed by Derain

16. *La Boutique Fantasque*. Lydia Lopokova as one of the Can-can dancers, in a costume designed by Derain

17. Bronislava Nijinska's *Les Biches*, Monte Carlo, 1924, with designs by Marie Laurençin. Georgina Parkinson as the page-boy in Nijinska's revival of the work for the Royal Ballet, 1964

18. Ninette de Valois' *The Rake's Progress*, London, 1935, based on the Hogarth paintings. The orgy scene in the original Vic-Wells production with Walter Gore (*extreme right*) as The Rake

19. Dancers of The Royal Ballet in Frederick Ashton's *La Fille Mal Gardée*, London, 1960. Act I, scene 2, showing the Fanny Elssler *pas de deux*: Nadia Nerina as Lise, David Blair as Colas

20. The original cast of Frederick Ashton's *Symphonic Variations*, London, 1946. *Left to right:* Henry Danton, Moira Shearer, Michael Somes, Margot Fonteyn, Pamela May and Brian Shaw

21. Dancers of the Royal Ballet in Antony Tudor's *Shadow-play*, London, 1967, designed by Michael Annals with Anthony Dowell as Boy with Matted Hair, and Frank Freeman as an Arboreal

22. Dancers of the Wurtemberg State Ballet in John Cranko's *The Taming of the Shrew*, Stuttgart, 1969, designed by Elisabeth Dalton with Richard Cragun as Petrucchio and Marcia Haydée (in white) as Kate

23. Kenneth MacMillan's *Romeo and Juliet*, London, 1965, designed by Nicholas Georgiadis. Lynn Seymour as Juliet

24. Jerome Robbins' *Afternoon of a Faun*, New York, 1953. Danced here by Wilma Curley and John Jones

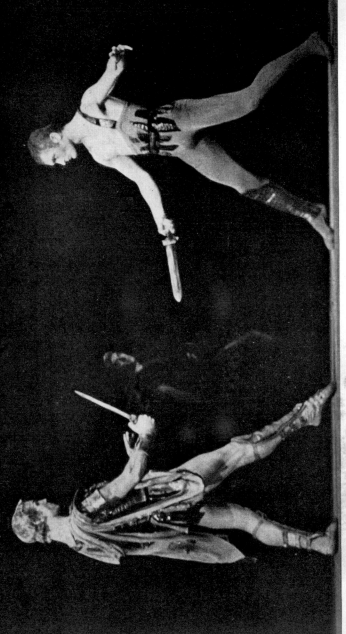

Yuri Grigorovich's *Spartacus*, Moscow, 1968, designed by Suliko Virsaladze, with *left to right*: Maris Liepa as Crassus and Mikhail Lavrovsky as Spartacus

taking a popular tradition (in this case, that of the Gilbert and Sullivan operas) and transforming it into different but equally popular terms as the basis of a ballet. The whole work was treated, by Cranko and his collaborators, with a particularly light-hearted zest. The characters are not intended to be at all realistic, but they are well contrasted and sketched with lively humour. Also, they are revealed almost entirely in dancing, not mime. The roles were excellently designed to bring out the individual qualities of the original cast, especially the dashing manner of the young David Blair as Belaye, dancing a hornpipe with splendid bravado and accepting the adulation of all the girls with superbly confident aplomb. Subsequently the work proved capable of bearing a number of different interpretations, and the many dancers who took the leading roles almost always managed to preserve the vigorous humour which is the main cause of the ballet's lasting success.

The Lady and the Fool

Ballet in one act. Libretto by John Cranko. Music from the operas of Verdi, selected and arranged by Charles Mackerras. Scenery and costumes by Richard Beer. First performed by Sadler's Wells Theatre Ballet at the New Theatre, Oxford, 25th February, 1954. Moondog: Kenneth MacMillan. Bootface: Johaar Mosaval. La Capricciosa: Patricia Miller.

PROLOGUE: A Street.

Guests are arriving for a ball. One of them, La Capricciosa, a famous beauty, is pleased by a little dance performed by two shabby clowns, Moondog and Bootface, and she invites them to accompany her.

Scene: A Ball.

The clowns entertain the guests with an outwardly comic but fundamentally romantic dance with a rose: after this they are hurried out of sight. La Capricciosa, who hides her beauty behind a mask, is courted by three admirers who represent wealth (Signor Midas), gallantry (Capitano Adoncino) and rank (The Prince of Arragonza). Each in turn removes her mask only to find another beneath. Spurned, they depart into an adjoining room to which the other guests have already gone. Left alone, La Capricciosa takes off her remaining mask and reveals herself as a lonely and unhappy woman in spite of the grandeur that surrounds her. Moondog has meanwhile crept back into the ballroom; he falls in love with her and she with him. The other guests return and are shocked: they turn on La Capricciosa and reject her. She departs with Moondog. His friend Bootface, now alone, huddles shivering in a corner, but almost at once the couple return for him, and the trio go off together.

EPILOGUE: The Street.

Poor but happy, the three friends are seen sharing a bench which must be their bed for the night.

In its original version, *The Lady and the Fool* proved rather muddled and achieved only a partial success. The next year, Cranko revived the ballet at Covent Garden with some drastic revisions, and it is this version which has survived, and has also been mounted in Stuttgart and in Australia. The main changes were the elimination of a sub-plot involving a flirtatious society hostess, Signora Scintillarda; the omission of the epilogue; and the transformation of the roles for La Capricciosa's suitors from purely acting and partnering into more vividly characterized parts with a solo apiece.

The simple moral of *The Lady and the Fool* – that love is more important than riches, fame or power – is attractive but hardly enough to explain the ballet's success. More to the point are the effectiveness of many of the dances, combined with the grandeur and drama of Verdi's music. The big adagio for La Capricciosa and her suitors especially has a bold sweep and powerful climaxes. Again, the various roles are virtually caricatures, but drawn with wit and style. The romantic passages, too, although at times they come dangerously close to sentimentality, are saved by their simple sincerity and also by the sharp humour which serves as a contrasting sauce to prevent the ballet from cloying.

Antigone

Ballet in one act. Libretto freely adapted by John Cranko from various versions of the Greek legend, especially Racine's play. Music by Mikis Theodorakis. Scenery and costumes by Rufino Tamayo. First performed by the Royal Ballet at the Royal Opera House, Covent Garden, 19th October, 1959.

The chorus mourn. Old King Oedipus dies and his sons, Polynices and Etiocles, wrangle for the crown. Creon, brother of the dead king, sides with Etiocles. Polynices is expelled but returns to stir up his followers. Jocasta, mother of the warring brothers, pleads with them to live in peace. When her words have no effect she kills herself on their two swords in an attempt to shame them into reconciliation. Her action has no effect: they remain bitterly opposed. To counterbalance Creon's support for Etiocles, Antigone sends her lover, Haemon, (Creon's son) to aid Polynices. While the men prepare for war, the women lament; Antigone bids Haemon farewell. When the men return from battle, they bear the corpses of Haemon and the two brothers. Creon crowns himself king. Etiocles and Haemon are buried with honour, but when Antigone goes to perform the same service for Polynices, Creon forbids it and orders the body to be flung aside without ceremony, on pain of death. Antigone defies him, straightens her dead brother's limbs and spreads her own cloak over the body. Creon orders his guards to kill her, but as they close in she stops them with a gesture, chooses one of them, feels his sword to make sure it is sharp, and beckons him alone to follow her. A moment later he returns, lays his bloodstained weapon at Creon's feet and backs away in horror. All the people turn from Creon, who is left alone with his crown and the bloody sword.

Cranko's main purpose when he started producing *Antigone* was to create a dramatic role for Svetlana Beriosova, who had previously been cast only in classical, lyrical or occasionally comic parts. In this he succeeded, but he achieved much more besides, partly inspired by the depth and variety of effect in the ballets of Jerome Robbins, whose company was appearing in

London during Cranko's rehearsal period. One minor result was that Antigone, originally intended to dance on point, became a simpler, more natural and expressive figure in soft shoes. Less obvious but more important influences caused Cranko to depict in the ballet's action a subtle study of the politics of power, with clear implications for our own day. Aided by his collaborators, the Greek composer Mikis Theodorakis and the Mexican painter Rufino Tamayo, Cranko produced a ballet that was raw, harsh but powerful. It contained, besides the leading role (later danced with success by Anya Linden in London and Marcia Haydée in Stuttgart), two strong roles for the fratricidal brothers and a shiftily dominating part for Creon. This was the work in which Cranko, previously thought of (rather unfairly) as an amusing but light-weight choreographer, proved himself capable of seriousness, passion and even tragedy.

Jeu de Cartes

Ballet in 'three deals' (one act). Choreography by Cranko. Libretto adapted by Cranko from the original synopsis by Igor Stravinsky and M. Malaieff. Music by Stravinsky. Scenery and costumes by Dorothea Zippel. First performed by the Württemberg State Ballet, Stuttgart, 22nd January, 1965.

First deal: The scene is a card table.

Huge playing cards are moved from side to side, as if being shuffled. The first hand is dealt, and the cards themselves disappear to reveal the dancers playing the roles: two sevens, two tens and a queen. They are agitated about their prospects. From beneath the player's hand (painted on the backcloth) there appears the Joker who can represent any card he wishes. Imperiously banishing the Queen of Hearts, he supplants her and converts the two pairs into a winning full house.

Second deal:

The next hand to be dealt is a straight flush: the Two, Three, Four, Five and Six of Hearts. They dance a lively march and a solo each. The Joker tries to gatecrash but cannot improve their strength and he is strenuously rejected.

Third deal:

The Ace, King, Jack and Ten of Spades are indignant at the poor little Two of Diamonds who is spoiling their prospects of winning. The Joker arrives, converts himself into the Queen of Spades (complete with tutu and crown) and by taking the place of the Two of Diamonds produces a royal flush. Triumphantly, the Joker leads all the other cards in a wild chase back and forwards across the stage. As the curtain falls, he is peering slyly round the back of another card, waiting for his next chance.

Although *Jeu de Cartes* can be described in terms of a game of poker, Cranko actually simplified the original plot a great deal (only one hand, for instance, is shown in each deal) and declared in a radio interview that 'it is in fact a kind of abstract ballet' but that people did not notice this because the characters were given names and the action was funny. Certainly it was the dancing that was the real point of the ballet. This involved, for the Joker, a virtuoso role, with ingenious solos also for the five men in the second deal and a strenuous finale for the whole cast. Even the straight dancing was almost always comic, too, with unexpected timing and impudent details, and in addition the ballet was full of satirical touches. Some of these were fairly obvious, such as a parody of the Rose Adagio from *The Sleeping Beauty* danced by the Joker in his Queen of Spades disguise. Others were simply deft, cunning asides: a momentary burlesque of many other ballets including several of Balanchine's. The uninformed spectator could take it as knockabout comedy: the other allusions were a bonus for the connoisseur. Besides remaining continuously in the Stuttgart repertory, this ballet has been revived for several other companies, including a particularly successful production by the Royal Danish Ballet with Niels Kehlet as the Joker. It was given (under the title *Card Game*) by the Royal Ballet at Covent Garden in 1966, together with a new plotless ballet to

Bach's Brandenburg concertos numbers 2 and 4. Christopher Gable and Anthony Dowell both danced the Joker, and there were notably witty performances by Annette Page as the Queen of Hearts and Lynn Seymour as the Two of Diamonds.

Onegin

Ballet in three acts. Choreography by John Cranko. Libretto by Cranko after Alexander Pushkin. Music by Tchaikovsky, chosen and arranged by Kurt-Heinz Stolze. Scenery and costumes by Jürgen Rose. First performed Württemberg State Ballet, Stuttgart, 13th April, 1965. Onegin: Ray Barra. Tatiana: Marcia Haydée. Olga: Ana Cardus. Lensky: Egon Madsen.

ACT I, *Scene I*: Madame Larina's garden.

Her daughters Tatiana and Olga dance with their friends. Olga's fiancé, Lensky, arrives and introduces his dandified friend Onegin, with whom Tatiana immediately falls in love, in spite of his amused and condescending manner towards her.

Scene II: Tatiana's bedroom.

She is trying to write a letter to tell Onegin of her love. As she gazes longingly in her mirror, he appears to her confused imagination and dances a romantic duet in which he returns her affection.

ACT II, *Scene I.* A party at Madame Larina's house.

Tatiana looks anxiously for Onegin while the guests dance. When he arrives he gives her back the torn fragments of her letter, indicating that it was unwise of her to send it. She tries to plead with him and, to put her off, he flirts conspicuously with Olga, precipitating a quarrel with Lensky which ends with a challenge to a duel.

Scene II: A deserted park.

Tatiana and Olga beg Lensky to forgive Onegin, the latter is ready for a reconciliation, but Lensky insists on the duel. The girls watch as the men, a little way off, raise their pistols. Both fire; Lensky falls dead.

ACT III, *Scene I:* A ball at Prince Gremin's palace.

Onegin, after years of remorse and attempts to find forgetfulness in wandering, returns to Russia and visits an old friend, Prince Gremin, who introduces his wife. She proves to be Tatiana. Onegin determines to visit her.

Scene II: Tatiana's boudoir.

She is reading a letter, obviously overcome. Onegin arrives, begs forgiveness and declares that he loves her. She tears his letter into pieces and returns them to him. In spite of his pleas she proudly insists that he must leave for ever. He stumbles away in despair; as soon as she is alone she too collapses.

Cranko's first idea was to produce a ballet to the music of Tchaikovsky's opera on this subject. When this proved impracticable he had a score prepared from mainly lesser-known pieces of Tchaikovsky's music. His handling of the action is surprisingly domestic; even at points like Madame Larina's party he concentrates on the individuals rather than seizing the opportunities for large-scale dances. Inspired by the talents of Marcia Haydée, who had already danced with great success in his own distinctive (and widely copied) productions of *Romeo and Juliet* and *Swan Lake*, Cranko made of Tatiana a truly tragic character of impassioned depth and understanding. Although the other roles were always also well played, the title part proved more difficult to cast ideally. Both Ray Barra and (as guest artist) Donald MacLeary gave interesting interpretations, but the ballet really came into its own in a slightly revised new production in October 1967 when Heinz Clauss proved a worthy match for Haydée's constantly maturing and expanding qualities.

Présence

Ballet in one act. Choreography: Cranko. Music: Bernd Alois

Zimmermann. Scenery and costumes: Jürgen Schmidt-Oehm. First performed Württemberg State Ballet, Stuttgart, 16th May, 1968. Molly: Marcia Haydée. Don: Heinz Clauss. Roy: Richard Cragun.

Don lights a cigarette and watches a screen where formal patterns are shown, and then huge, alluring female portraits which blend into a photograph of Marcia Haydée. She appears in silhouette; in a shadowplay she performs a striptease; then coaxes amorously a man with a bull's head. This proves too much for Don who plunges through the screen to join them.

There follow disjointed individual scenes in which the three principals play out the roles of three archetypal characters from fiction. Don, a helmeted knight, is Don Quixote; Molly is James Joyce's slovenly heroine, Molly Bloom; and the fat brutal Roy is Ubu Roi from Alfred Jarry's play. In the course of scenes involving mass murder, an operation, and Molly's languorous disappearance into a living sofa, they suggest three aspects of human nature concerned with idealism, sex and power. The mime scenes, in a broad, effective and often comic style, are interspersed with dance passages in which, stripped to tights and leotards with just a single identifying initial on their breasts, the characters continue their action in more abstract terms.

Présence, which Cranko regards as one of his best ballets, is an example of the experimental mode he has always continued alongside his big narrative works. The music, written in 1961 by the avant-garde composer Bernd Alois Zimmermann, was intended as a ballet, but the composer wanted it treated very differently from the classical tradition where the music 'carries' the dance; rather as part of a complex 'space-time structure' in which individual elements would be juxtaposed. Each character is associated, however, with a single instrument: violin (Don), piano (Roy) and cello (Molly). The danced passages are set to Zimmermann's trio; the pantomimes which precede or separate them are performed to a mixture of taped sounds, speech, noises or music. Some people found the result puzzling; others discovered in it a marvellous series of insights and a step towards a new kind of dance-theatre.

The Taming of the Shrew

Ballet in two acts, after Shakespeare. Libretto and choreography: Cranko. Music: Kurt-Heinz Stolze, after Scarlatti. Scenery and costumes: Elisabeth Dalton. First performed Württemberg State Ballet, Stuttgart, 16th March, 1969.

ACT I, *Scene I:* Outside Baptista's house.

Three suitors (the cockscomb Hortensio, the silly student Lucentio and the old roué Gremio) arrive to serenade Baptista's pretty young daughter, Bianca. Her older sister Kate interrupts the idyllic scene. Baptista declares that Bianca shall not marry until Kate is wed. The noise attracts a large crowd of neighbours whom Kate soon sends packing.

Scene II: A tavern.

Hortensio, Lucentio and Gremio are nursing their battle scars received at this affray. Petrucchio arrives rather tipsy and is robbed by two whores of all his money. Unable to pay his bill, he is told by the others that they can introduce him to an heiress. To their delight, he accepts the offer.

Scene III: Baptista's courtyard.

Petrucchio arrives and asks for Kate's hand; after a stormy courtship she agrees. Meanwhile, the three rivals in disguise pretend to give Bianca a music lesson as an opportunity to press their claims on her.

Scene IV: Kate's wedding.

Petrucchio behaves outrageously at the wedding and immediately afterwards compels Kate to accompany him to the country.

ACT II, *Scene I:* The journey to Petrucchio's house.

The newly-weds travel through a storm on a worn-out old horse.

Scene II: Petrucchio's kitchen.

Kate arrives hungry and soaked through. Petrucchio prevents her from eating under the pretext the food is not good enough. She refuses to go to bed with him and spends a miserable night on the kitchen floor.

Scene III: A carnival.

Lucentio, bribing the two whores to wear cloaks and masks like Bianca's, tricks his rivals into marrying them, leaving himself free to marry Bianca unopposed.

Scene IV: Petrucchio's house.

After a chilly night, and still starving, Kate is further provoked by Petrucchio finding fault with her new clothes and sending them away too. Eventually she capitulates and recognizes him as her master. After this they both admit they love each other.

Scene V: The journey to Bianca's wedding.

Now happy, Kate travels through sunshine with Petrucchio to her sister's wedding, proving her loyalty by accepting his whims even when he pretends a water pump is a peasant and a bystander is the pump.

Scene VI: Bianca's wedding.

Bianca, like the wives of Gremio and Hortensio, acts disdainfully towards her husband. Kate, with a return to her old shrewishness, cows them into submission and shows them how a wife should behave. Left alone, she and Petrucchio dance lovingly together.

While preserving the essentials of Shakespeare's plot, Cranko's ballet departs from it in most of its details, although his inventions (the weddings of Gremio and Hortensio, for instance) often have a decidedly Shakespearean flavour. Apart from its lively humour (rare in a full-evening ballet), the work is notable for its many spirited characterizations and above all for the two leading roles, created by Marcia Haydée and

Richard Cragun. These are both virtuoso parts, with many leaps, high lifts in the *adagios* and such rare steps for the man as triple *tours en l'air* performed with nonchalant perfection. Even more important is the fact that they seem credible characters, whose genuine love for each other (visible even beneath the sparring of their early scenes together) gives richness and humanity to the ballet.

KENNETH MACMILLAN (b. 1930)

Born in Dunfermline, Kenneth MacMillan was trained at the Royal Ballet School, and graduated from there to the Sadler's Wells Theatre Ballet on its formation. For this company he danced many leading roles, and then moved to the Covent Garden company in 1948. He returned to the Wells company in 1952, and made his apprentice ballets – *Laiderette* and *Somnambulism*–for the Wells Choreographic Group. Three years later he staged his first professional ballet, *Danses Concertantes*, whose dazzling, spikily witty inventions revealed that an extraordinary new choreographic talent had been found. That same year he made his first dramatic work – *House of Birds* – a version of a Grimm fairy-tale, following this in the next year with his first work for the Covent Garden company: *Noctambules*. This was a dramatic work, concerned with a magician in a back-street theatre who hypnotizes his audience so that they reveal their innermost feelings and desires: a Faded Beauty recaptures her youthful loveliness, a Soldier revels in slaughter, an innocent girl is loved by a rich young man, and at the end the Magician is trapped in his own bizarre fancies. All three ballets indicated an original talent, blessed with fluency of invention, and a refreshingly different – though entirely classical – choreographic manner. All three ballets were also marked by an excellence of their design by Nicholas Georgiadis, introducing a collaboration which still continues. In these works MacMillan was concerned to consolidate his knowledge of his craft (he described *Noctambules* as a dramatized version of the last act of *The Sleeping Beauty*). He returned to working for the Sadler's Wells Theatre Ballet with two more ballets – the dramatic *The Burrow* (1958) which portrayed a group of people hiding from oppressors and the light-hearted *Solitaire* (1956) 'a kind of a game for one'. There followed another work for the Royal Ballet at Covent Garden, a version of Stravinsky's *Agon* (1958) which extended his earliest faceted dance style in a study of a house of pleasure; it was a mysterious and beautiful piece, but it failed to find much favour with the public at the time. He also made two ballets for American Ballet Theatre in this year: *Winter's Eve*, a story of a blind girl, and *Journey*, which treated the theme of death with considerable success. A major change in his style was announced with *Le Baiser de la Fée*, for Covent Garden in 1960. Here, working with three lyrical dancers – Lynn Seymour (who was to become the Muse for many of his greatest ballets thereafter), Svetlana Beriosova and Donald MacLeary, his choreographic manner became softer and more expansive. The ballet was notable for the skill with which MacMillan overcame the problems of staging what has always been considered a difficult work to realize, and also for the acutely sensitive way in which the choreography echoed Stravinsky's homage to Tchaikovsky by offering a parallel homage to Petipa – particularly in the Mill Scene for Seymour and MacLeary. The ballet was further distinguished by Kenneth Rowell's décor, which arguably ranks as the most beautiful and poetic ballet designs seen at Covent Garden since the war.

Baiser was followed in the December of 1960 by Mac-Millan's most assured and compelling dramatic work, *The Invitation* (*q.v.*), and in the following September he made a piece of pure dancing: *Diversions*. With *Rite of Spring* in May 1962 (*q.v.*) he showed a new mastery in manoeuvring large masses of dancers, and his next ballet, staged for the Stuttgart ballet, was *Las Hermanas* (*q.v.*). Another plotless work – and one of his finest – came in 1963, when *Symphony* (to Shostakovich's first symphony) was staged at Covent Garden. It was a beautiful piece, one of his most personal statements on what he felt about dancing, having a profusion of choreographic invention. He returned to working with the Royal Ballet's

Touring section in January 1964, making a pop-art version of Milhaud's *La Création du Monde*, and for the Shakespeare quatercentenary celebration in June of that year he produced *Images of Love*, a series of dance incidents, each inspired by a quotation from Shakespeare. The work was uneven, but in two sections for Lynn Seymour (with Gable and Nureyev) he indicated a new plasticity of manner that was extremely impressive, and the ballet also provides an interesting hint of his reaction to a written text, which was to be extended in his *Romeo and Juliet* (*q.v.*) the following year. In June 1965 he created a work that he had long been contemplating, a ballet that has been recognized as one of his finest, *The Song of the Earth* (*q.v.*) It was first staged in Stuttgart, and was enhanced there – as it was at its later staging for the Royal Ballet – by the presence of Marcia Haydée as the woman.

In 1966 MacMillan was released for three years by the Royal Ballet to take up the post of Director of the Ballet of the Deutsche Oper, West Berlin – where he was joined by Lynn Seymour as ballerina, and there he staged a variety of works, many designed to help shape and train his company: works like *Valses Nobles* and *Concerto* (1966), and *Olympiade* (1968) were all basically exercises in setting a somewhat raw company dancing with clarity and precision. While in Berlin he also created two fine dramatic ballets: *Anastasia* in 1967 for Lynn Seymour, and *Cain and Abel* (1968). He also mounted two classic stagings: a tremendously opulent *The Sleeping Beauty* (which preserved all the Petipa choreography but aimed at a more sensitive and logical production) in 1968, and a *Swan Lake* in 1969, his last gift to the company before returning to London, preparatory to taking up the joint directorship of the Royal Ballet in 1970.

Of all his contemporaries, MacMillan is the only one in our experience with genius, and it is the peculiar gift of genius to have entirely personal laws. MacMillan's whole creative approach concerns movement; to him, the action of bodies is the food for his gift. He stated, early in his career, how the sight of dancers sitting at rest excited his imagination (consider *Danses Concertantes* and *Agon*) and we know that visits to football games sparked off some of the imagery in *Symphony:* the long, dashing lines of dancers; Lynn Seymour, hands outstretched in front of her as if she had just thrown a ball into a line-out.

With MacMillan, like Degas, it is the movement of things that excites the creative instinct, but there are also the psychological springs of action and behaviour which offer a comparable stimulus to his creativity. MacMillan is a Freudian choreographer, showing us the sexuality that underlies so much of the behaviour of his characters, as in *The Invitation, Romeo and Juliet* and *Las Hermanas.*

He is the poet of passion, of dark, unhappy desires and frustrations and self-deceits. He can show us the gnawing appetites and needs, the loneliness, that polite society masks behind its superficial behaviour, but which MacMillan exposes in burningly clear movement. His *Romeo and Juliet* is as much a ballet about passion as *The Invitation*; *Images of Love,* flawed though it was by its score, was a potent exercise in the range of human sexual need: *Rite of Spring* showed primitive man obsessed and haunted by the sexual urgency of a tribe which must placate its divinities and guarantee the harvests by the virgin's first orgasm, which is her death and the earth's life. But one over-riding fact must never be forgotten: MacMillan's only means of expression is movement; his classical training has mercifully provided him with a built-in formal equipment that shapes, canalizes and guides his dance imagination. All his ballets are classical in that they are clear developments (no matter how far ranging, in *Rite* or *Cain and Abel*) of the academic dance.

Danses Concertantes

Ballet in one act. Choreography: MacMillan. Music: Stravinsky. Décor: Nicholas Georgiadis. First performed Sadler's Wells Theatre Ballet, Sadler's Wells Theatre, 18th January, 1955, with Maryon Lane, Donald Britton and David Poole.

When the curtain fell after the first performance of *Danses Concertantes*, the excitement of the occasion must have been obvious to the whole audience. This first professional work by a young Royal Ballet dancer was an amazing piece, glittering with inventiveness, intensely personal in its expression. It seemed a kaleidoscope in which all the old, accepted dance ideas had been thoroughly shaken up by this new talent, to form fresh and intriguing patterns. Not many first ballets can retain their place in a repertory year after year, but whenever it has been revived, *Danses Concertantes'* interest seems to increase, for here are many of the qualities that have been so richly extended in MacMillan's later work. This cool view of a hot-house was full of unexpected allusions: dancers are as interesting sitting down on chairs as they are when working in class; fingers can make mysterious masks; dancers are like horsemen and gymnasts and movie sirens. It was an explosion of bright dance ideas that never lost sight of those fundamental truths of the classic tradition that had produced and educated Mac-Millan, and nothing he has created since has departed from this basic belief in the academic dance. This ballet lives because it perennially suits young dancers in a young company.

The Invitation

Ballet in one act. Choreography: MacMillan. Music: Matyas Sciber. Décor: Nicholas Georgiadis, First performed Royal Ballet Touring Section, New Theatre, Oxford, 10th November, 1960.

In a wealthy household in some warm climate at the turn of the century a houseparty has been arranged by a wealthy widow with three daughters. The two eldest girls are of marriageable age, and are carefully guarded from the world by their mother. The youngest girl plays with her boy cousin and their friends, who, with their parents, are guests at the house. She is revolted by the sly, sexual innuendoes of the other children, and is unable to understand the gentle, budding sexuality of her cousin's affection for her. At the afternoon reception we see the guests arrive, among them an unhappy husband and wife; when the guests go to watch the children at their dancing lesson, the husband manifests an interest in the girl which flatters her, though it angers the girl's mother.

That night, the guests are watching a group of acrobats who have come to entertain the house-party; as the guests disperse through the gardens, the husband and wife quarrel yet again, and the husband angrily leaves. The young boy, disturbed by his own feeling of urgently awakening sexuality, comes into the garden, and the wife, sensing his needs, seduces him. The girl, innocently intrigued by the husband, steals out of the house and seeks him out in the garden. He misinterprets her presence, and unable to resist her virginal beauty, savagely rapes her. Aghast at what he has done, he goes back to the house, where his wife, realizing what has happened, still finds strength and understanding to support him. The girl, shattered by her experience, returns distraught to the house, and her cousin endeavours to console her. She believes that his tender passion is exactly the same as the husband's brutality, and with fierce energy drives him from her; as the curtain falls she walks with frozen gaze and rigid gait away from all chance of future happiness.

The Invitation is a ballet about sex; from the moment the curtain rises and we see the young boy gazing at the naked female statue, the theme is plain. In setting his ballet in some unspecified warm climate at the turn of the century, MacMillan was able to use certain recognized social attitudes and conventions to underpin his dramatic structure. The ballet was inspired indirectly by two novels: Beatriz Guido's *The House of the Angel*, and Colette's *Le Blé en Herbe* – these provide, respectively, germs of the girl's and the boy's characters. But the extension of the incidents is entirely MacMillan's. He is concerned with the sexual needs of adolescence, the sexual greed of the husband, and the sexual frustration of the wife – whose seduction of the boy is her only answer to her husband's neglect. It is the particular quality of *The Invitation* that the characters seem to have a life that extends far beyond the stage action; we can sense both their past (notably the reason for the disintegration of the marriage between husband and wife) and their future, in which the boy will be unaffected by the night's events, while the girl will freeze into a spinsterhood as embittered as that of her governess. The hectic sexual air of the ballet becomes more and more intense as the action progresses: the acrobats impersonate two cocks in rivalry for a hen; the flashing trajectories of the guests in the night scene show men and women bent upon gratification – one of the men, rejected by a girl, makes a brief pass at a male acrobat. But lest this seem lurid and overemphatic, it should be stated that Mac-Millan's expressive choreography is remarkably sensitive and beautiful. In the dancing lesson, the man's increasing interest in the girl is suggested by the gradually wider arcs in which he lifts her; when he attacks her the physical act of rape is portrayed with such subtle symbolism that it is beautiful but never offensive. *The Invitation* is supremely a ballet in which glances and slight gestures play a vital role. At the afternoon reception we can see the moment when the husband is first aware of the girl and sizes up her youthful beauty; a moment later when the wife greets the young cousin the husband's jealousy is sharply stated as he interposes his body between them. At the dancing lesson the husband eyes the girl, and she, aware of his gaze, darts sudden, shy glances at him; when they start to ·dance the wife's embarrassment and her nervous excuses are tellingly shown. The young cousin's characteristic action at the start of the ballet when he tries to lay his head on the girl's breast, is a *leit-motiv* that returns when he essays the same gesture with the wife. *The Invitation* is compact with such small, revelatory detail: it is they which give such truth and intensity to the principal characters.

The original cast – Lynn Seymour as the Girl, Christopher Gable as her Cousin, Anne Heaton and Desmond Doyle as the Husband and Wife – were superb; in particular the ballet announced Lynn Seymour as one of the most beautifully expressive dramatic dancers of our time.

The Rite of Spring
A ballet in one act. Choreography: MacMillan. Music:

Stravinsky. Décor: Sydney Nolan. First performed Royal Ballet,
Covent Garden, 3rd May, 1962.

The action of MacMillan's version is, in outline, very simple.
The first tableau, *The Adoration of the Earth*, presents a tribe
in a rocky setting; groups of adolescents, men and women,
dance in a frenzy preparatory to the choosing of the maiden
who is to be the central figure of their fertility rite.

For the second tableau, *The Sacrifice*, a back-cloth featuring
an enormous gold phallus shape is revealed, and the tribe are
first seen sitting in a semi-circle round the edge of the stage.
Six maidens move into the centre and one is chosen as the
sacrificial figure. She is ritually daubed on the face by the
Elders, and then she dances with the tribe, sometimes held
aloft, sometimes moving among their prostrate bodies.
Gradually her dance becomes more ecstatic and frenzied until
she collapses dying on the ground; the tribe cluster round and
her lifeless body is tossed high in the air as the curtain falls.

The first performance of the *Rite of Spring* by the Diaghilev
Ballet in Paris on 29th May, 1913, has passed into the annals of
theatrical history as one of the most celebrated brawls in a
theatre. The shock administered by Stravinsky's score to the
decorous ear-drums of *le tout Paris* and the originality of
Nijinski's choreographic conception, all produced howls of
outrage that still echo down the years. The score is now
recognized as one of the most influential masterpieces of this
century's music – in it Stravinsky was inspired by 'the violent
Russian spring' when the whole earth seems to crack open
into life. He noted that he 'saw in imagination a solemn pagan
ritual; wise elders, seated in a circle, watching a young girl
dance herself to death. They were sacrificing her to propitiate
the god of spring'. Diaghilev produced a second version, with
choreography by Massine in 1920, and other choreographers –
including Maurice Béjart – have also been attracted by the
score, notable among them being Kenneth MacMillan, whose
staging was made for the Royal Ballet.

MacMillan has noted, 'In *Rite* I wanted the movement to be
primitive, but with a "primitiveness" of my own invention

rather than an attempt at an imagined pre-history. It does not deal with any specific race, and I believe that the actions and feeling that are shown may still be observed in people today.'

In thus de-localizing the score MacMillan's choreography manages to dominate Stravinsky's massive creation so that the Russian flavour of the music does not obtrude through being un-realized. In the first section he presents an image of the tribe as a single entity through his use of blocks of dancers who move almost in unison; these people have no individuality, only a corporate existence at this crucial moment of their year. Their movement is frenzied; their desperate couplings, their arms thrust forward or up, the blind urgency, the almost animal intensity with which they move – faces and bodies hideously daubed – is extraordinarily communicative of primitive society. At the pause in the music that precedes the final crescendo which ends part one, the three Elders, lion-masked, move forward to lie flat on the ground at the very edge of the stage, preparatory to the choosing of the Virgin.

The second section finds the tribe sitting in a semi-circle awaiting the appearance of the six maidens from among whom the sacrificial victim will come. The Elders wait at the back as six girls, seemingly impelled by the music, move into the centre of this arena, and then one of them is singled out and collapses to the ground. From that moment she ceases to be a girl and becomes a tribal symbol. She is passed, prostrate, over a long column of males, she forms the central, hierarchic figure held high above the outstretched hands of the tribe, like an Egyptian goddess; she dances a solo among the prostrate figures of her people, and her movements become more and more excited. The tribe joins in agitated and eagerly anticipatory dances, and suddenly she collapses again in an orgasm that is her death and the renewed life of the earth for the tribe. They gather round the body and toss it exultantly up to the sky as the curtain falls. The ballet is compact of fierce imagery in which MacMillan has admirably suggested the urgency of the ritual and the girl's terror, submerged in a resolute acceptance of her fate. The choreographic manner was the freest and least classical that MacMillan had made to date, and yet it was possible to see in the shaping of the work and in much of the dance outlines a strong classically trained intelligence at work. But what distinguishes this version from any other is the intellectual approach of the choreographer to his score. The central role of the Virgin was first interpreted by Monica Mason, whose ability to invest her dancing with a superhuman grandeur and an outstanding muscular weight was wonderfully revealed in the role. Her performance has never been equalled for sheer power. Eyes gleaming with terror, driven seemingly by forces outside herself, she gave an unforgettably moving interpretation.

Las Hermanas

Ballet in one act. Choreography: MacMillan. Music: Frank Martin (Concerto for harpsichord and small orchestra). Décor: Nicholas Georgiadis. Based on Lorca's play, 'The House of Bernarda Alba'. First performed Stuttgart Ballet, 13th July, 1963, with Marcia Haydée as the Eldest Sister, Ray Barra as the Man. First performed Western Theatre Ballet, New Theatre, Cardiff, 22nd June, 1966.

The curtain rises in silence to reveal a claustrophobic white and grey interior of a house; the mother limps down the staircase, her walking stick thumping out each step. Her five daughters sit in rocking chairs, aimless, despondent; they move towards the mother and sit each of them in a line springing from the old woman's belly. Gradually the characters of three are revealed; the eldest is an agonized spinster; the middle sister (hunch-backed in Lorca's play) is envious and embittered; the youngest, still a girl, first comes to our attention when she tries on the bridal veil from a wedding dress draped over a dummy in the corner of the room. The eldest sister, for whom it is intended, next puts it on and the three other sisters dance with it; all the while we are made conscious through the taut and almost desperate dancing of the eldest sister that she is declining unhappily into spinsterhood. Now the mother brings on the prospective husband for the eldest –

marriage must go by seniority – and we meet a man who reveals, under the stiff best suit, a brutal sensuality. The eldest sister goes out with him, leaving the others rocking and fanning themselves in their chairs as the light fades. The second scene takes place by night. The man returns, freed of his constricting coat, to an assignation with the eldest sister. He tosses gravel to her window, she comes down and they commence a *pas de deux* which is to reveal much of their characters: the man is coarsely sensual, the sister, at first frigid, is yet eager for love though she has to conquer years of repression. Her clenched fists and tense arms indicate how great are her fears; just as it seems that she is warming to her lover, she realizes that the middle sister has been watching them from a balcony. Swiftly she kisses the man, shakes his hand formally and goes indoors. Almost at once the youngest sister rushes out to meet the man and they embark on a frankly sensual duet culminating in a sexual embrace. The middle sister again has been watching and she at once arouses the household, showing the eldest sister with relish just what her future husband is like. The eldest sister eddies over the stage in agony of mind while the mother raises her stick and tries to strike the man, but the youngest girl snatches the stick from her. The mother flings the girl to the ground, and drives the man from the house, while the eldest sister expresses her suffering in a solo. The youngest girl rushes upstairs, the mother gathers her family of women about her, and the eldest sister takes one terrifying look out of the window at her lost freedom and happiness. The mother locks the door with a ferocious finality, and climbs the stairs in search of her youngest child. She pulls back the curtain at the stair head and reveals the swinging body of the youngest girl who has committed suicide. The curtain falls.

As with each of his dramatic ballets – from *The Burrow* up to the latest *Cain and Abel* (Berlin, 1968) – MacMillan is concerned with the interaction of personalities, and the resolution (often the explosion) of tensions that bring about a final tragedy. His habit is to take a dramatic theme, and sometimes by changing and compressing it extensively, to extract what he feels is its emotional essence. In the brief, concentrated

Hermanas he presents a claustrophobic house of women where passions, desires and longings are firmly controlled by clearly defined social and sexual conventions. There are feline jealousies among the girls, and a terrible sense of frustration in the personalities of the eldest sister and the embittered middle sister. Dominating and controlling is the watchful presence of the mother, a wardress/matriarch presented in rigid, menacing dance images. Each of the principals is sharply characterized: the eldest sister cuts tense, frustrated arcs of movement with her arms, and when the man comes to court her she undergoes a curious blossoming. With the destruction of her hopes we witness the turning inward of her emotions – one last despairing run towards the window, and then isolation and total despair freezes her body. The man is depicted in equally powerful manner: the ape-like stance, the pungent sexuality, are brilliantly shown – MacMillan always contrives imagery that is entirely apposite and revealing: nothing could be more succinct than the chain of sisters, each sitting on the other's lap, springing from the old mother's body; nothing could better suggest the sense of frustrated waiting than the row of girls rocking in their chairs as the ballet begins. *Hermanas* is tight in structure – MacMillan compresses the very detailed action with entire success into the brief space of the Martin Harpsichord Concerto – and the result is an excellently shaped work whose tensions never slacken.

Romeo and Juliet

Ballet in three acts after Shakespeare. Choreography: Mac-Millan. Music: Prokofiev. Décor: Georgiadis. First performed Royal Ballet, Covent Garden, 9th February, 1965.

ACT I, *Scene I:* The Market Place.

It is early morning; Romeo enters with Mercutio and Benvolio, and declares his love for Rosaline who is walking through the square. Gradually the town awakes, and among the market activity are three whores who dance playfully with the three young men. Tybalt, Capulet's nephew enters and provokes a quarrel with the Montague faction which develops into a street fight; Capulet and Montague enter with their wives and followers and a pitched fight ensues, with many slain, but the arrival of the Prince of Verona with his guards ends the slaughter. He orders the two families to live peaceably, and commands them to lay their swords in front of the pile of the slain.

Scene II: Juliet's Ante-room.

Juliet runs in and plays with a doll while her nurse watches fondly. Her parents enter with Paris, who is destined to be Juliet's husband. He pays his respects to her, but as he leaves Juliet tries once more to play childishly with her doll, until her nurse shows her that her childhood is over and that she is a woman. A final pose shows Juliet standing with her hands on her breasts.

Scene III: In front of the gates of the Capulet Palace.

Romeo and his two friends are amusing themselves as masked guests arrive for a ball at the Capulet's house. Romeo flirts with Rosaline, though the watchful Tybalt tries to drive him away. As the guests enter, Romeo and his friends, masked and carrying lutes, decide to run the danger of attending the ball, too, so that Romeo may see Rosaline yet again.

Scene IV: The Ballroom.

The guests are moving in a stately dance as Romeo and his companions arrive. Juliet enters, a shy child at her first ball, and dances with Paris. Suddenly, for an eternal second, Romeo and Juliet see each other. Juliet sits and plays a mandoline as six of her friends dance, but Romeo bursts among them and dances for Juliet. She dances again with Paris, but Romeo manages to dance with her too; Tybalt intervenes, and as the guests leave Juliet pleads an indisposition so that she is alone in the ballroom when Romeo appears. He takes off his mask and reveals who he is, and they dance ecstatically together. Tybalt observes this and provokes a quarrel with Romeo but Capulet enters and makes Romeo welcome to the party.

Scene V: Outside the Capulet House.

The guests depart, and Tybalt follows Romeo, and would pursue him were he not restrained by Capulet.

Scene VI: The Capulet Garden.

Juliet appears on her balcony. A sudden noise in the garden tells her that Romeo is there, and she runs swiftly to him. They express their passion and love in a *pas de deux*.

Act II, *Scene I:* The Market Place.

The market is bustling with activity; through it passes a wedding procession, but Romeo is caught up with thoughts of his new love. The Nurse enters, bringing a letter from Juliet, proposing a secret marriage; Romeo, delirious with joy, rushes out.

Scene II: Friar Laurence's Church.

Friar Laurence enters and prays and then Romeo arrives; a moment later Juliet and her nurse enter, and the Friar unites the two while the nurse sobs.

Scene III: The Market Place.

The celebrations and bustle of the market are continuing as Romeo returns from his marriage. Tybalt endeavours to pick a quarrel with him, but Romeo, determined that the ancient strife between the two families shall cease with his marriage to Juliet, refuses to fight. Aghast at what he thinks is cowardice, Mercutio joins battle with Tybalt. Romeo begs him to stop, and Tybalt stabs Mercutio in the back: in his death agonies Mercutio still makes a gallant figure but as he collapses he curses both houses. Romeo, unable to restrain his anger, seizes his sword, fights Tybalt and kills him. Lady Capulet enters, frantic with grief at Tybalt's death; Romeo holds pleadingly to her skirt, but she rejects him and rocks the dead body of Tybalt in her arms.

Act III, *Scene I:* Juliet's Bedroom.

As dawn breaks, the lovers are in bed; Romeo tries to steal away, but Juliet rushes to him and seeks to delay his departure

in a passionate embrace. But he must leave as sounds indicate
that someone is stirring. The nurse enters, followed quickly by
Juliet's parents and Paris. Their marriage must now take place;
Juliet frantically rejects Paris, and her father driven to anger,
orders her to marry the husband he has chosen and stalks out.
Juliet sits for an agonized moment on her bed, then seizes a
cloak and rushes to consult Friar Laurence.

Scene II: Friar Laurence's Chapel.

Juliet begs for help from the Friar and he gives her a phial
containing a drug that will produce a cataleptic trance when
she swallows it; her parents will think her dead, and she can
then be rescued from her tomb by Romeo. Friar Laurence says
that he will ensure that Romeo is told of the plan.

Scene III: Juliet's Bedroom.

Juliet hides the phial under her pillow; when her parents
enter she pleads once more not to be married to Paris, but then
yields to their insistence. She dances with Paris moving
like a ghost in his arms, and content that she will comply with
their wishes, her parents leave with Paris. Juliet knows that she
now must take the potion; she delays for a second, then
swallows it; as the drug courses through her body she creeps to
her bed and lies there. Her friends enter, ready to prepare her
for her wedding; as they dance they are puzzled that Juliet
should still sleep, and when they go to touch her they find her
cold and apparently lifeless. The old nurse, bringing the
wedding dress, is distraught with grief, and Juliet's parents,
entering soon after, are heart-broken at the tragedy.

Scene IV: The Capulet Family Crypt.

Juliet lies on a central bier while monks and the Capulet
family pass in front of her, black-cloaked in mourning. Paris
remains behind to bid farewell to her. Romeo, unaware of
Juliet's stratagem, reveals himself, throwing off the black
cloak he has worn so that he may see Juliet for the last time.
He kills Paris, then lifts Juliet's body from the bier in an agony
of grief. He dances briefly with it, then placing it back on the

cold stone, he takes out a phial of poison, swallows it, and dies at her side. Now Juliet awakes from her sleep, and as she surveys the crypt she sees Paris's body, and then comes upon Romeo's corpse. She snatches up the dagger with which he has killed Paris, and stabs herself, stretching her arms out in a final embrace to Romeo.

MacMillan's Juliet *is* Lynn Seymour, in the same way that Fonteyn *is* Ondine and Chloe and every other role that Ashton has written for her. This identification with a character is one of the most fascinating aspects of the marriage between a choreographer and his chosen ballerina, in which the dancer's gifts are a challenge to the creator and are in turn challenged by his creation. For twenty-five years Ashton and Fonteyn worked in such a partnership; since 1958 (when he made *The Burrow*) MacMillan has been similarly exploring the qualities of Seymour as a glorious and highly dramatic dance instrument.

This production reflects her dramatic gifts, for Juliet is the machine that drives the ballet along; wilful, reacting with extraordinary passion against her world, she has the temperament to try to change her destiny. MacMillan sees the character as a 'positive' girl whose tragedy lies in her defiance of all the conventions of the society she lives in, and his concern is with the psychology of this central characterization. In each of his major dramatic ballets – *The Invitation, Las Hermanas, Anastasia* come to mind – MacMillan has sought to explore the springs of behaviour, to catch those images of love and lust that are all-revealing of personality. (How right that the ballet in which he brought this Freudian approach first to Shakespeare should have been called *Images of Love*.) It is almost as if MacMillan becomes an analyst to his characters, forcing them to delve into their psyches and bring out their fantasies into the light of day – this was, in fact, the whole action of his early *Noctambules*, where the cast relived their dreams under the Hypnotist's spell. In MacMillan's version, *Romeo and Juliet* becomes as much a ballet about sex as *The Invitation*, and there are even parallels to be observed between Juliet and the Young Girl in that earlier work. Both are first seen on the brink of sexual awareness, rejecting their logical partner (Paris in *Romeo*, and young cousin in *The Invitation*) and succumbing to another and ultimately destructive lover – the Husband and Romeo. Juliet is shown first as a child; the crucial moment at the end of the second scene when she stands, hands on breasts, suddenly aware that she is now a woman, is the clue to the sudden expansion of her personality from that of a girl playing with her doll to that of a women overwhelmed by her first great passion.

Juliet is self-willed; it is she who suggests and engineers the marriage; she is a personality at odds with her surroundings, in rebellion against her parents and the conventions they represent. Romeo takes his colour from her – his arrival in the garden can best be interpreted as another example of that youthful dalliance that finds him serenading Rosaline at the start of the ballet. The ballet exists as an increasingly close observation of the two lovers; MacMillan's choreography bears down on them like a lens, revealing more and more of their passion. As always with MacMillan there is an under-pinning of psychological understanding that inspires the intense revelations of the choreography; Juliet when she is taking the sleeping draught curls in fœtal position on the bed; awakening in the tomb her hand moves across the bier as if searching for Romeo's body in bed. The relationship between Tybalt and Lady Capulet is seen as having a strong emotional basis: Tybalt's actions throughout show him as if trying to supplant Capulet's authority, and Lady Capulet's frenzy at his death is to be explained by the strong, though unexpressed passion she feels for him. The role of Romeo, of necessity, comes second in this production; the character is something of a roaring Veronese boy, caught up in a love far greater than he could have imagined; if the dramatic opportunities are less exciting than Juliet's the technical demands of the role are great, and have been admirably met by most of the Royal Ballet's interpreters, especially Christopher Gable on whom it was created. Of the subsidiary roles, two are particularly satisfactory: Mercutio, debonair, dashing and wonderfully interpreted by David Blair, and Tybalt, icily fierce, a role taken with total rightness by Desmond Doyle.

The Song of the Earth

Ballet in one act. Choreography: MacMillan, Music: Mahler (Das Lied von der Erde). First performed Stuttgart Ballet, 7th November, 1965. First performed Royal Ballet, Covent Garden, 19th May, 1966. Both with Marcia Haydée as the Woman.

Das Lied von der Erde is strictly speaking Mahler's Ninth Symphony, but superstitiously (because ninth symphonies had been final symphonies for Beethoven and Schubert) he refused to give it the title. This symphony for tenor and alto voices and orchestra was composed in 1907–8, using recently published translations of Chinese poems as text, and to the final poem, *The Farewell*, Mahler added the following lines:

'The dear Earth blossoms in the Spring and buds anew
Everywhere and forever the luminous blue of distant space!
Forever . . . forever . . . forever . . . forever . . .'

These are the clue to the work, which is Mahler's farewell to the joy and beauty of the world, which are all transitory, but which are always renewed. MacMillan's realization of Mahler's work is in no sense a literal translation of words into dance; as in *Images of Love* (where he took phrases from Shakespeare's sonnets as a springboard for his imagination) and in *Romeo and Juliet*, where he seized on the sense of a speech or a scene, he has sought out an imagery that catches the essence of the poems. The ballet is ultimately about Death, not as a menacing and dreadful figure, but as the inevitable companion and participant in all human activity: the masked figure who is one of the trio of central characters in the work was called in Germany *der Ewige* – the eternal one – though in England he is named *The Messenger of Death*. The ballet's subject is that of a man and a woman: Death takes the man and then they both return to the woman, and in the last song, *The Farewell*, there is a promise of renewal.

The first song, *The Drinking Song of Earthly Sorrow*, shows the Man running on with five other boys, leaping and soaring, celebrating the brief joys of the world. At the end the Messenger of Death claims the Man. The slow movement, *The Lonely One in Autumn*, is written for the Woman with three other girls; at first they are partnered by four men, but these leave and there follows a *pas de deux* for the Woman and the Death figure, which ends with the woman solitary and sorrowing ('O sun of Love, never again wilt thou shine, gently to dry my bitter tears ?')

Then come three *scherzi:* the first, *Of Youth*, shows a group of young people enjoying themselves in games and chatter around a green and white porcelain pavilion (there are no sets in the ballet: costumes are simple leotards and tunics, with the Messenger of Death wearing a half-mask; but so vivid is MacMillan's imagery here – and throughout the work – that we seem to see the settings and locations). When the poem speaks of everything mirrored in the smooth surface of the quiet pool that surrounds the pavilion, MacMillan shows his soloist momentarily inverted. It is a fresh, youthful scene filled with innocent joy – and at the end the Messenger enters to carry off the principal girl soloist.

The second *scherzo, Of Beauty*, shows a group of girls picking lotus flowers by the river's edge; on dash young men on horseback. 'The loveliest of the maidens sends the rider glances of yearning' – and MacMillan shows us just this; passion and happiness are perfectly expressed.

The following *Drunkard in Spring* finds the Man carousing with two cronies, but there is a fourth member to their party, the Death figure, and at the end – as spring comes with the chatter of birds – he claims the Man.

The final section, the heart of the work, is a long sequence (lasting nearly thirty minutes) which brings together the Man, the Woman and the Messenger of Death. It is a marvellous sequence of dancing that captures everything of the intensity and beauty of the theme. Death brings back the Man to the Woman; they dance, and at the end the promise of renewal is miraculously suggested when the three figures move slowly forward as the curtain falls.

Song of the Earth is a very great ballet – arguably Mac-Millan's finest. In it his inspiration catches and matches all the elegiac beauty of Mahler's symphony; the dance language (which owes something to the manner of *Symphony*, of *Images of Love* and of *Diversions*) is freely shaped, though entirely classical, and utterly and magnificently revelatory and moving. It also enshrines a superlative role for a ballerina: in this case for Marcia Haydée, the Stuttgart ballerina, one of the most poetic and thrilling of dancers. Her interpretation has the complete rightness of genius; in a ballet where any attempt to 'act' is fatal, she makes the Woman a figure of the utmost beauty and grace.

Concerto

Ballet in one act. Choreography: MacMillan. Music: Shostakovich (piano concerto No. 2). Décor: Jürgen Rose. First performance: November, 1966, Deutsche Oper Ballet, Berlin, with Lynn Seymour and Rudolf Holtz. First performed Royal Ballet Touring Section, Covent Garden, 26th May, 1967.

Musicality is a clumsy word, but inescapable when talking about ballet. It implies that quality of harmonious accord between dance and music, a feeling for what the score is about, that is – somehow unexpectedly – one of the prime gifts of English dancers. Naturally enough it is also highly characteristic of our best choreographers. Kenneth MacMillan has intense 'musicality' – he had it as a dancer, too; attracted predominantly to the music of this century (he has not yet created a ballet to music dating before 1900) he is sensitive to both mood and structure of his scores. His chief concern is always to realize as much as he can of these factors in movement, and 'the finer the score, the finer the ballet' is a not imprecise yardstick with which to judge his works.

Like Balanchine and Ashton he seems able – in Martha Graham's phrase – to refract music into dancing, as naturally as a prism breaks up light into the spectrum. This is clear in *Concerto*, which is set to the joyous youthful second piano concerto which Shostakovich wrote for his son and the Moscow Youth Orchestra. The ballet has a fresh, open style that matches the airy textures of the score with neat assurance. The opening movement is set for a principal couple with attendant soloists and corps; movement is bright, dashing, with the principals often identified with the piano while the corps impersonate the orchestral *tutti*; at the end of the movement, as the cheery opening theme sounds for the last time, the dancers march off in formation, and then the two leading dancers march back on stage for the final chord in a merry, inconsequential fashion.

The lighting dims for the second movement, a sun blooms on the mottled pearl grey of the back-drop and as the piano starts its long, elegiac theme the ballerina and her partner walk on from opposite sides. The *pas de deux* – for this *adagio* is an extended and radiant duet – starts with the ballerina bending and unfurling her arms in slow *ports de bras* (the *pas de deux* has its inspiration in the sight of Lynn Seymour warming up in class, and it evokes her presence in marvellous fashion). The duet is lyrical, flowing effortlessly and beautifully, with occasional reflections of its movement in three couples of dancers who appear at the back of the stage, echoing and underlining certain movements of the principal couple (rather as MacMillan did in *Diversions*). At its close, the sun fades, the lights come up and we are whisked into the jollity of the last movement. One leading girl opens this rondo with a sprightly solo, and gradually the other principals, the soloists and the corps are also involved; the dancing is laid out in blocks of movement for wheeling and turning squads of dancers, and at the close the whole cast are involved in a joyous finale.

Kenneth MacMillan staged this happy, light-weight work for his Berlin dancers when he took up his post as Director of the Deutsche Opera Ballet: its form and style are very much dictated by the need he felt to guide and train these dancers in clean, academic choreography, and give his troupe a cohesive and classical style.

PETER DARRELL (b. 1932)

Darrell was trained at the Royal Ballet School, danced with Sadler's Wells Theatre Ballet for three years, and then joined Festival Ballet, working later with several continental companies before taking up choreography. His first creations were seen in Ballet Workshop at the Mercury Theatre, and he also worked extensively in television, but his career is chiefly linked with that of Western Theatre Ballet, of which he was joint Artistic Director with its founder Elizabeth West. For the company he made several ballets which did much to crystallize its early style – pieces as diverse as *The Prisoners, Non-Stop* and *Chiaroscuro*. The ideals of the company were implicit in its title: *theatre* was to be as important as *ballet*. The company, originally Bristol based, surmounted extraordinary difficulties in its early days, and gradually gained a reputation for a lively and firmly contemporary view of what ballet should do. Darrell's gifts for dramatic ballets were seen also in *A Wedding Present*, and his comic range extended to works like *Salade* and *Mods and Rockers*. In 1962, the tragic death of Elizabeth West meant that Darrell became sole Artistic Director: but he continued to choreograph, creating *Home, Sun into Darkness* in 1967, *Francesca* and *Ephemeron* in 1968. In 1969 Western Theatre Ballet, who four years earlier had been invited to take over responsibility for the Sadler's Wells Opera Ballet and share seasons at the Sadler's Wells Theatre, took another and even more important step in their progress, by moving to Glasgow and assuming a new identity – though retaining all their former prestige – as Scottish Theatre Ballet.

In his years as Artistic Director of Western Theatre Ballet, Darrell has done much to enlarge the repertory's range, inviting Kenneth MacMillan, Jack Carter, Peter Wright, Flemming Flindt and Walter Gore, among others, to stage ballets and also acquiring two important classic revivals: Fokine's *Le Carnaval*, and Bournonville's *La Ventana*. Thus Darrell's choreographic career is indissolubly bound up with the growth and success of Western Theatre Ballet; from its inception the company was dedicated to the idea of original ballets in which the particular qualities of the dancers could shine, and Darrell was called upon to provide a considerable number of new works. His understanding of dramatic construction, his fluent choreographic style, even his ability to produce agreeable and workmanlike *pièces d'occasion* when the *occasion* arose, all showed him to be a sound balletic craftsman. At his best in dramatic pieces – *The Prisoners*, *A Wedding Present*, *Home*, *Jeux* – he combines dance and drama with sure skill. In lighter pieces – *Mods and Rockers*, *Non-Stop* (a lovely joke about a *jeune fille fatale* and a juke box) and *Salade* – he shows a sharp eye for quirks of character and the observation of social attitudes which are characteristic of all his ballets.

The Prisoners

Ballet in one act. Choreography: Darrell. Music: Bartok's 'Music for Strings, Percussion and Celeste'. Décor: Barry Kay. First performed Western Theatre Ballet, Dartington Hall, 24th June, 1957. Barry Salt as Baudin, Erling Sunde as Christophe, Suzanne Musitz as Madeleine.

We first see two prisoners, Baudin and Christophe pacing in agony in their cell. Christophe so engineers events that they are able to snatch the keys from the warder who brings them food, and they escape, and make for Christophe's home. There his wife Madeleine shelters them, but she falls in love with Baudin and persuades him to kill Christophe. Tormented now by guilt and by his fears of society, Baudin allows Madeleine to keep him confined in her house: he has exchanged one prison for another.

The Prisoners was one of the earliest and most successful of Peter Darrell's dramatic ballets; taut, well constructed, it offers excellently conceived roles for its three principals in which the conflict of their personalities is sharply externalized in movement. The unrelenting pace of the work, the momentum of its action, are excellently judged, and it has ever received fine performances. It is one of the ballets that first helped establish Western Theatre Ballet as a company of strong dance actors, and its best qualities – of urgent dramatic power – are well reflected to this day in the dancers of the Company.

A Wedding Present

Ballet in one act. Choreography: Darrell. Music: Bartok, 'Piano Concerto No. 3'. Décor: Judith Wood. First performed Western Theatre Ballet, Empire Theatre, Sunderland, 19th April, 1962. Laverne Meyer as the Groom, Brenda Last as the Bride.

At Mrs Bellamy's boarding house preparations are under way for her son's wedding breakfast, but beneath the hectic jollity we sense the undercurrents of emotion that are to destroy the new marriage. Among the guests is a young man who has been the Bridegroom's lover, and through some neurotic compulsion he slips an indiscreetly inscribed book into the Groom's suitcase. The Bride discovers this on the first morning of the honeymoon, and her questionings force the Groom to confess his earlier liaison. Despite her ultimate understanding of his plight, he feels that the marriage has been destroyed; on their return to the boarding house his failure to accept her forgiveness drives her into making public issue of the affair, and the final moments show the Groom's isolation surrounded by a whirling – and to him, mocking – group of guests.

This is the dramatic basis for a cleverly conceived study in human relationships, which Darrell dresses with lively, convincing characters. Mrs Bellamy is a garish, coarsely knowing creature surrounded by lodgers whose personalities are lightly but tellingly sketched in – notably a Friend of the Family, whose friendliness is distinctly ambiguous. The son and his Bride are caught, helplessly it must seem, in an emotional trap, and their ecstatically sensual duet on the honeymoon soon gives way to a terrible lack of mutual understanding. The ballet works in those sharply theatrical terms which have ever marked Peter Darrell's dramatic pieces; his choreography catches all the shifting changes in the young couple's relationship with a blend of naturalistic movement, passages of lyrical invention, and clear-cut observation of human behaviour.

Jeux

Ballet in one act. Choreography: Darrell. Music: Debussy. Décor: Harry Waistnage. First performed Western Theatre Ballet, Citizen's Theatre, Glasgow, 7th March, 1963. Clover Roope, Sylvia Wellman, Simon Mottram.

'A Black Comedy: Three people have been playing tennis but the game continues after the match is over.' So says the programme note for this intriguing ballet which conceals menace and mayhem beneath the sunniest of exteriors. At curtain rise we see the stage bare save for a table and four chairs. We then meet the three characters – whose relationship is never made clear – a man and two women (is one his wife and the other his mistress ? We shall never know). The man and one of the women have been playing tennis, and they are joined by the second woman who brings on a tray of drinks. The man goes into the house (we must imagine it lies just off-stage) to change; in his absence there is a certain feeling of tension between the two women; the man returns, and his partner exits also to change, leaving him alone with the other woman, who proceeds to flirt mildly with him. The first woman returns, and there follow a series of polite but plainly insincere exchanges between the trio. The second woman slips something into the other woman's glass; and she, in her turn, feeling in the man's jacket for a cigarette case, brings out a revolver, which she promptly hides in her hand-bag. All three go off and there is a pistol shot – but a moment later they all return unharmed, though slightly jittery in manner. The man hands drinks to each of the women and picks up his glass: they toast each other, and we realize suddenly that one of the glasses has poison in it. But which one ? The curtain falls . . . we shall never know.

This is a consummate tease-piece; nothing happens, yet

everything happens – there are undercurrents of hatred, love and frustration that are stated with a subtlety and an atmospheric delicacy that seems entirely in accord with the shimmering sensuous quality of the score. The very mystery that surrounds the identity and relationships of the three is part of the ballet's strength: we return to see it time and again, determined that *this* time we shall solve the enigma – though we never do. The dancing is nicely-shaped and entirely suited to the music – more than compensation for our failing to elucidate the basic puzzle of this very mixed treble.

Mods and Rockers

Ballet in one act. Choreography: Darrell. Music: The Beatles. Décor: Desmonde Downing. First performed Prince Charles Theatre, London, 18th December, 1963.

The theme of *Mods and Rockers* is an archetypal love story that probably wasn't young when Romeo and Juliet first met. Into a coffee-bar come two contrasted and rival groups; a gang of leather-clad Rockers with their leather-clad girls (fresh from doing a 'ton' on some motorway) and a natty collection of Mods in their ultra-fashionable suits with their equally fashionable dollies. The tensions between the two simmer with minimal violence, but the chief Rocker finds a Mod girl rather more to his taste than his own bird, and as the Beatle banalities clatter out from the record-player these two contrive to slip away. The last we hear is the roar of the motorcycle on which this sheik of the sixties is bearing away his beloved.

This is one of those slight ballets which sum up a particular time so pertinently that they endure when more serious works have slipped into oblivion. *Mods and Rockers* is now a piece of social history; Western Theatre Ballet's dancers up-date their clothes, but the Beatle tunes endure, as does the basic dramatic idea, and the work has built-in charm – plus some very soundly made choreography – which should ensure it a continuing career in the theatre.

Home

Ballet in one act. Choreography: Darrell. Libretto: John Mortimer. Music: Bartok's 'String Quartet No. 5'. Décor: Peter Cazalet. First performed Western Theatre Ballet, Empire Theatre, Sunderland, 3rd February, 1965. Nadia Nerina as the Girl.

The story of *Home* reduces itself in essence to that truism: Home is where the heart is. We are presented with a greyly awful family of Husband, Wife, Son and Daughter, who are unable to cope with the nervous, maladjusted girl who is the other daughter. Inept in everything she does, pathetically eager to please, a compulsive eater of sweets, she infuriates and exasperates her parents, who take her to a mental hospital for treatment. There, amid the bizarre occupants of a psychiatric ward, she finds the acceptance—and eventually – the love that she has never known before. When her family return to bring her home she refuses to leave, preferring the new 'home' that she has found among these kindred spirits.

Home was initially created as a vehicle for Nadia Nerina, on leave from the Royal Ballet; the ballet provided her with the sort of strong dramatic meat that any classical ballerina must sometimes require as a rest from incessant Swan Queens and Auroras. Written with considerable sensitivity as a portrait of a sad ugly-duckling of a girl, the role offered excellent opportunities for dramatic playing. The frantic eagerness to please her family, the clumsy failure of every attempt at normalcy, the desolation that only once gives way to a frantic outburst when she first realizes she is trapped in the mental institution, were all excellently done by Nerina – and by later interpreters from among Western Theatre Ballet's own artists. The work has undergone some re-writing of its choreography, because it was hampered at first by lack of shape in its scenario and the inherent difficulties of using the Bartok 5th quartet. Its sincerity and the skilful choreography of its central character now make it a moving experience in the theatre.

Sun into Darkness

Ballet in three acts. Choreography: Darrell. Music: Malcolm Williamson. Décor: Harry Waistnage. Libretto: David Rudkin. Producer: Colin Graham. First performed Western Theatre Ballet at Sadler's Wells Theatre, 13th April, 1966. David Jones as Ridd, Elaine McDonald as Mrs Ridd, Laverne Meyer as their Son, Donna Day Washington as their Daughter, Gary Sherwood as the Stranger.

ACT I: The scene is a Cornish village.

Mr Ridd is the garage owner and mayor, Mrs Ridd a house-wife. Their daughter is at school and their son – a 'sensitive' youth – helps out at the garage. At curtain rise we see the garage workers, meet the Ridd family, and witness the arrival of two comic carrier's men who indulge in a knock-about routine with a ladder, and then bring on a draped throne which they place on a platform. Already we sense that things are not quite what they seem; Ridd is a frozen, severe character, ill at ease with his wife; their daughter is a simple, charming girl, excited with a new dress she has bought for the carnival that evening; the son, timorous and nervous, is made the butt of rather coarse jokes by Ridd's garage hands, who tie an apron on him. Plainly, he is a disappointment to his parents.

The villagers arrive to prepare for the evening's festivities, and there enters a young stranger wheeling his motorcycle which has broken down. The Ridd's daughter is at once attracted to him, and the son also manifests a deep interest in both the motorcycle and its owner. Mrs Ridd invites the Stranger to spend the night with them, and when he enters the Ridd House, the two Carriers come on bearing a large wooden chest. With them comes the local Cleric, who opens the chest and produces the vestments used to dress the carnival's Lord of Misrule. The problem now remains of choosing the Lord: the Cleric offers the clothes to several men who refuse them, though the young Ridd shows a frantic eagerness to put them on. Then the Stranger returns with Mr and Mrs Ridd, and we realize Mrs Ridd's role in the forthcoming drama as the Priestess of the festivities; she indicates that the Stranger is to be the Lord of Misrule, and the curtain falls as the Cleric and the two Carriers, now masked, present the robes to the Stranger.

ACT II: It is night.

The villagers are arrayed in their best clothes, but there is an air of constraint which is broken only when the two Carriers appear dressed as monkeys and gradually excite the assembled villagers. There follows a *divertissement* for two whores and the Carriers which involves a strip-tease and a mock flagellation sequence. The Ridds' son, thoroughly frightened by the Carriers, is carried and pressed face to face with the Stranger during a general dance. The villagers leave and the Stranger and the Ridds' daughter dance a *pas de deux*. At its end the villagers return with the Cleric; the Ridds mount the platform, tear off the draperies that hide the throne and are revealed as High Priest and High Priestess for the forthcoming ritual. The Cleric produces the vestments for the carnival's Ruler; the Ridds' son tries once again to snatch them, and then they are offered to the Stranger. He refuses them, but is seized, carried to the throne, and forced to don the costumes, while wine is poured down his throat. Now the ritual can begin. The dancing of the crowd becomes more brazen and orgiastic; each member of the community mounts the throne to kiss the Stranger. He is borne to the ground and the entire village line up in turn to straddle his prostrate body. The villagers exit and Mrs Ridd returns to seduce the drunken and completely bewildered young man; her husband and some of the villagers return and witness this . . . as the curtain falls we realize fully something that has been hinted at throughout the earlier scenes: Ridd is impotent.

ACT III: Just before dawn.

The carnival continues. Mrs Ridd taunts her husband by dancing with several of the village youths, and suddenly it is time for the second part of the ritual to commence: the Trial. The Cleric produces masks from the chest which the village men don, and Mr Ridd is revealed as the judge. The villagers

first dismantle the Stranger's motorcycle – when he enters he is
horrified at this act – and force him to kneel at the foot of the
throne which now serves Ridd as judgement seat. The evidence
of his rape of Mrs Ridd is presented (in the form of her petti-
coat), and he is mauled, beaten-up and castrated. Next his
mangled body is dressed in a goat-skin and the Ridds' son is
terrified by the sight of this weird creature. The villagers force
the boy to couple with the mutilated figure; the Stranger appeals
for help to the boy and to the Ridd girl, but the boy is so
terrified that he attacks and strangles the unrecognizable
Stranger. The ritual has been fulfilled: the villagers creep away
as dawn breaks; Mrs Ridd leads her son indoors. The daughter
casts one backward glance at the body of the Stranger and
shuts the house door, as the curtain falls.

Sun into Darkness was a brave attempt at a brave ideal: a
full-length ballet on a contemporary theme, with specially
composed score, and the participation of some of the brightest
talents in the British theatre. The work's failings were those of
a theme too lurid in manner, lending itself to excessive coarse-
ness of choreographic expression. Structurally, the first act
took too long to set the scene and the second act *divertissement*
for the whores and Carriers was hardly justifiable. Despite these
flaws, the piece packed great theatrical punch, and has
occasioned some splendidly – and characteristically – well-
thought-out performances from Western Theatre Ballet's
artists.

NORMAN MORRICE (b. 1931)
Born in Mexico, educated in Scotland, Norman Morrice
studied at the Rambert School and joined the Company in 1953.
Marie Rambert, with her eye for choreographic talent,
nurtured Morrice's creative abilities and he made a very
successful first work in 1958: *Two Brothers*. From then on
each Rambert summer season in London saw a new Morrice
ballet; *Hazaña* in 1959; *Wise Monkeys* in 1960; *A Place in the*

Desert in 1961; *Conflicts* – which was the fruit of a study period with Balanchine and Martha Graham in New York – in 1962; *The Travellers* in 1963; *Cul de Sac* in 1964, in which year he also made the highly successful *The Tribute* for the Royal Ballet Touring section. In 1965 came *Realms of Choice*, but in the following year the complete reorganization of the Ballet Rambert required all Morrice's energies when he was appointed Associate Director of the new company. Its re-shaping was to enable this oldest of British ballet companies to return to the lively creative policies obscured by the harsh necessities of touring and the constantly nagging financial problems of ballet in Britain in the '50s and '60s.

His first ballet for two years, *Hazard*, was a triumphant vindication for the 'new' Rambert, and his next works for the Company were seen in the early summer of 1968: *Them and Us* and *One, Two, Three*, and in March 1969 another new work: *Pastorale Variée*. He has also mounted *Side Show* and *Rehearsal* for the Batsheva Dance Company of Israel for whom he originally made *One, Two, Three*.

Norman Morrice's early ballets were notable for their strong dramatic themes; the dancing in them was neat but seemed less interesting than the psychological motivation he gave to his characters and the theatrical structure of the pieces.

Then in works like *Conflicts, Cul de Sac, The Travellers* and, notably, *The Tribute*, Morrice showed a greater maturity and more adventurous choreographic style, coupled with a strong sense of dramatic situation. The list of locales of his ballets – a Mexican church, a desert, Oxford Circus underground (for *Cul de Sac*), an Iron Curtain airport (for *The Travellers*) – all indicated this, and he forged a commendably revealing style to present his themes. His choreography did not seem, though, as it does now, to linger in the memory: it was the dramatic imagery rather than the *enchainements* that caught and held the imagination. Thus the cross, the ramp and the sweating labourer straining towards the church formed a series of dramatic rather than dynamic images in *Hazaña*. Morrice could pin-point emotional states most tellingly: the wife dipping her hands in water and cooling her husband's brow in *Hazaña;*

the Cain-brother curled in fœtal position in *Two Brothers*; the
unhappy girl resting her forehead against the man's back in
Conflicts.

This last was one of Morrice's most satisfying early ballets, a
cunningly constructed exercise in reality, with situations
nestling inside one another like those Russian dolls that always
contain other dolls. It was a ballet concerned with three
problems: the first was the nature of the choreographer's task
when faced with a group of dancers awaiting the life that his
inspiration was to give them as stage characters; then there
were the facts of their personal relationships as human beings
and interacting with this their relationships as personages in
the choreographer's work. The conflicts that were implied in
this were sufficient explanation of the ballet's title. There were
emotional tensions arising from the unrequited love of a girl
understudy for a leading dancer, and a further drama in the
relationship of the understudy with the ballerina she was
covering, since the latter was loved by the leading dancer, and
this particular theme was explored by Morrice with fine
sensitivity.

Of the works that he created before the very considerable
re-shaping of Ballet Rambert's identity in 1966, *Realms of
Choice* afforded a very interesting pointer to the future. It was
a ballet which started from a décor which was designed, as it
were, *in vacuo*; this was shown to the composer who created a
score inspired by it, and it was only then that Morrice devised
the steps. What could have turned into an empty study in
aleatory techniques, became in fact an exciting and rewarding
ballet thanks to Morrice's inventive choreography. The idea of
chance, implicit in this ballet, was given a more dramatic expression in *Hazard* which came two years later in 1967 and
represents Morrice's finest achievement to date.

As a pendant to it, Morrice made *One, Two, Three* in the
following year, premiering this with *Them and Us*, a densely
written and allusive piece. In the spring of 1969 he made the
light-hearted *Pastorale Variée*, which aimed to do no more than
charm its audience with neatly made dances, as well as balance
a company repertory overloaded with dramatic works.

Hazaña

Ballet in one act. Choreography: Morrice. Music: Carlos Surinach. Décor: Ralph Koltai. First performed Ballet Rambert, Sadler's Wells Theatre, 25th May, 1959, with John Chesworth as the Man, Gillian Martlew as his Wife, June Sandbrook as the Child, Norman Morrice as the Priest.

The action takes place in a South American village on the eve of a local religious festival. The new church for the village stands nearly completed at the back of the stage, and the labourers are resting in the sunshine. The huge stone cross that is to surmount the church lies on one side, but when the local priest urges the men to place it in position, they find it too heavy. One man is determined that it shall be erected, and despite the mockery of his workmates and his wife's attempts to dissuade him, he tries to lift it. The priest and the man's young daughter encourage him, and gradually he strains and levers the cross up the scaffolding and sets it on the roof.

Morrice's first ballet, *Two Brothers*, had been a moving study of a backstreet boy jealous of his older brother's happiness in love; goaded by what Freudians would term sibling rivalry and by his sense of isolation and loss when his brother becomes engaged, the boy kills him. For his second work, *Hazaña* – which means 'achievement' – Morrice demonstrated a remarkable sureness in his handling of what is an unlikely and not especially balletic theme. The whole course of the ballet charts the man's fierce determination to achieve something, despite the mocking rejection of his workmates and the more insidious wiles of the wife to distract and dissuade him. Inspired also by his daughter's innocent faith in him, and the encouragement of the priest, he succeeds. Morrice extracted the maximum excitement from the agonized and laboured progress of the man, the cross roped across his body, as he struggled with it up a wooden ramp. Atmosphere, a directly stated theme that also served to reveal much of the attitudes of the surrounding characters, and a notable unity of style, made this a rewarding ballet to watch. As in *Two Brothers*, the characters were real, unromanticized, pinpointed in movement with all the freshness of acutely observed personalities.

Hazard

Ballet in one act. Choreography: Morrice. Music: Leonard Salzedo. Décor: Nadine Baylis. First performed Ballet Rambert, Theatre Royal, Bath, 12th June, 1967, with Christopher Bruce as leading male, Jonathan Taylor and Sandra Craig.

Morrice's subject is man's birth from chaos, his acquisition of identity, the arrival of woman in his life, and the structure of love, passion, jealousy, anger and sorrow which man himself has created. Equally important is the fact that mere hazard in natural selection and choice is a seed from which man's nature and his tragedy can grow. The setting is a golden glow of metallic plaques (the initial chaos being suggested by vast black screens that soon disappear), in the middle of which rises a tree structure from which the central male character descends in Darwinian fashion. Then a second male appears, soon to be joined by three other men, and they disport themselves in innocently muscular games. The entrance of four women, moving with sensuous grace, excites the men, and three couples pair happily off, leaving the central female with the two principal males. Here is the primeval problem, and Morrice states the central fact of his ballet: the crucial factor of chance, the hazard in the choice of a mate from which the rest of the ballet's action – and mankind's development – must depend. After a trio in which both men court the woman, her choice falls upon the second man, and they retire behind a golden screen, leaving the first man to mourn his outcast fate, while the other couples dance in celebration. The fortunate male is revealed exultant in his union with the woman, but when he leaves, the first man dances with this now unattainable mate.

The second man's return precipitates a fight for her, in which the outcast male strangles his rival. There follows a superbly organized sequence in which the woman's grief is elaborated by the mourning of the other couples. She curses the murderer, and the other men now turn on him. He flees from them by climbing up the tree, but they move the structure away, leaving him turning aimlessly and tragically from the great curve of a metal crescent that has dominated the set throughout the ballet.

Morrice's theme is a tremendous one, and his exposition, which is lucid, beautiful in manner, profoundly touching in expression, is among the finest things he has done. The story is told in a seamless sequence of ten numbers, which he fills with intricately wrought references and symbolism which nevertheless do not seem over-elaborate. The central figure is Adam, but also Cain; the woman mourns her mate's death in a pose that recalls a pietà; ; womankind is not always shown in sympathetic terms; courtship is presented in animalistic dances that suggest male display and female enticement; conformity is the rigorous norm for the group, which rejects the unattached outcast.

The work's structure is tight, cogent, without an ounce of fat or excessive decoration, and the dance language is free, certainly influenced by Martha Graham, but clearly springing from Morrice's earlier ballets – owing something to *Conflicts* and even going back as far as *Two Brothers* in its picture of masculine rivalry for a female. It is also that rarest of choreographic birds, a philosophical ballet, taking a clear stand on the nature of man and his plight.

One, Two, Three

Ballet in one act. Choreography: Morrice. Music: Ben-Zion Orgad (designer not named). First performed Batsheva Dance Company, Israel, 11th January, 1968. First performed Ballet Rambert, Jeannetta Cochrane Theatre, 29th May, 1968, with Christopher Bruce, Peter Curtis, Mary Willis.

One, Two, Three treats of a problem which has occupied Morrice in two previous ballets. Hinted at in his first work, *Two Brothers*, and largely explored in *Hazard*, it is the disruption of a relationship between two men by the arrival of a woman. In *Hazard* the drama was shown on a large scale; in *One, Two, Three* it is reduced to its basic components of two men and one woman. When the curtain rises we hear the sounds of heart beating and laboured breathing, and see the fœtus born from under a vast waving sheet of polythene. The image is telling, the gradual arrival of the male child into its world is admirably detailed as it moves and clambers over the wide plastic sheeting, swimming towards life, gaining in awareness. It learns to use legs and arms, discovers its faculties of speech, and then winding the polythene round itself like a cocoon, eventually emerges as a man. He moves and surveys his world; then from another cocoon a second man is born, whom the first proceeds to educate in movement. They sport and play together in harmony. A female enters their world; at first she joins in their games, innocently happy as they, but as she leaves, one of the men makes as if to follow her, though he is prevented from doing so by the other man. Rivalry has been born, and it reaches a greater intensity when the woman returns, marvellously draped in white; each of the men dances with her, and their mutual jealousy eventually brings about a fight which the woman stops by throwing her draperies over both of them. They are embroiled in them and at the ballet's end they stand, separated, gazing at her.

The theme is simple enough; where Morrice reveals his qualities is in the sculptural and sensual imagery he has invented for his cast. The men are shown in beautiful, statuesque groupings, their dances have a fine muscular thrust and rhythm; the woman – particularly when she returns trailing yards of white drapery – is portrayed in wonderfully fluid movement. Throughout the ballet Morrice's use of his props – polythene sheet and the woman's trailing gauzes (which he manipulates with the skill that Graham brings to her use of costume) – is constantly inventive and exciting.

Chapter Seven

The Americans

The United States is the only nation which has had a flourishing tradition compounded of two independent and equal forms of serious theatrical dancing. Both ballet and modern dance exist side by side, but, historically, America had a vital modern dance movement before ballet was firmly established. So that while there are choreographers who work almost purely in the ballet tradition, such as George Balanchine and John Taras, there are numerous others who have consciously set out to create a form of dance expression that partakes of elements of both. These choreographers are mainly in their twenties and early thirties, and represent a type of choreographic evolution which is unique in the world of dancing. Three of the most interesting are John Clifford of the New York City Ballet, Gerald Arpino of City Center Joffrey Ballet, and Eliot Feld of The American Ballet. As a reflection of how deeply the movement has taken hold of the American Dance scene, it has only to be remembered that the last strictly classical ballet company formed in the United States was New York City Ballet and that the half-dozen other companies established since then have been created in the mixed classical/modern mould.

Basically, ballet choreographers have been attracted by the creative vigour of the modern dance movement and, in an effort to extend the expressive range of ballet, they have borrowed heavily from it. American dancers tend to work closer to the floor as a result of the creative use that modern dancers have made of that surface and the freedom of the modern dance torso has found many reflections in ballet.

The yeast-like proliferation of modern dance companies has not been a pattern which one can observe in the ballet world, although Eliot Feld, almost alone among young ballet dancers, has felt impelled to create a company around himself. As well as being one of the leading dancers, he proposes to create its basic repertory by himself. His first ballet, *Harbinger*, showed an original talent, oriented to those urban jazzy rhythms which are so much a part of American life, but was funnelled into the mould of classical ballet. The *fit* was not quite perfect, so Feld bent the mould a bit to suit the shape of his conception and further introduced some modern dance gestures and phrasing that showed his debt to that tradition. His second ballet, *At Midnight*, pursued the modern dance and ballet amalgam even further, using Mahler's song cycle, *Kindertoten-lieder*.

Gerald Arpino, who has created about half of the City Center Joffrey repertory, must be considered its chief chore-ographer. His eclectic taste in dance has found expression in subjects as widely diverse as black magic (*Incubus*), and inter-national athletics (*Olympics*). Arpino has choreographed works for dancers in traditional ballet shoes and the rarely seen (in ballet) unshod foot. *Sea Shadow*, performed by a ballerina in toe shoes and a man with bare feet, was an especially felicitous combination of the two styles of dancing. The boy and girl who encountered one another on the strand at the edge of the sea were characterized as partaking of the earthy as well as the lighter airborne sensibility, suggested by the large amount of point work included for the girl. The piece also required balancing skills of a high order such as might be expected of a gymnast. The resultant mixture created an exceptionally effective *pas de deux*. Throughout his work Arpino has displayed an agile talent exceptionally apt at creative adaptation.

Similar to Arpino is John Clifford of the New York City Ballet. As one who has danced the Balanchine repertory extensively, it is not surprising to see Balanchine influences in his work such as *Stravinsky Symphony*. Clifford uses the Balanchine vocabulary of movement as naturally as any child would use the alphabet in forming new words. Often, with Clifford, Balanchinian fluency becomes a heated frenzy as he attempts to choreograph every jot and tittle of a particular musical score instead of interpreting its inner life. His most successful piece, *Fantasies*, was a ballet for four people, two of whom were dressed in recognizably civilian clothes and the other two in blue dream costumes. Though the piece was athletically demanding it showed Clifford in a relaxed state of rapport with his music. In addition to works for the New York City Ballet, he also prepares showpiece trifles for the company school which show an inventive imagination as well as experimental daring.

Classical ballet has always made itself sympathetic to the national characteristics of the countries into which it has been introduced. It has been able to incorporate elements and personality traits of each of its host countries so that one can speak of English, Russian, American or French ballet and know that while they share a common vocabulary of steps each nation has bent the form to the shape most suitable to them temperamentally. It is one of the wonders of ballet, this supremely adaptable nature which can partake of local coloration and yet retain the core of a shared common heritage. The blend of classic and modern dance elements which is emerging in the United States is, unquestionably, another phase in the perpetual dialogue between classic dance and indigenous dance forms.

GEORGE BALANCHINE (b. 1904)

Judged only on the prodigious volume of his output throughout forty years as an active choreographer, George Balanchine is assuredly a major dance figure. Against the range and imaginative variety of his ballets he must be considered in that rare company of major innovative talents and ranked with the seminal figures of the dance world along with Noverre and Petipa. He has, throughout the course of his creative work, striven toward the classical ideal of presenting his dancers in the purest light unmarred by idiosyncratic movement.

Early in his career Balanchine decided that he wanted to

'move people to music,' and has subsequently been attracted to and claimed for the ballet stage some of the most distinguished scores of the past and present. His musical taste has found sympathetic dance scores in Mozart ('Divertimento No. 15'), Bach ('Concerto Barocco'), as well as the twentieth century master Igor Stravinsky (*Apollo, Orpheus, Baiser de la Fée, Agon, Movements for piano and Orchestra, Variations*). That which distinguishes Balanchine's handling of these diverse musical talents is his incisive recognition of the inner pulse of the score and his creation of a suitable musical parallel for it. By his own testimony, Balanchine considers music as the *floor* for the dance and found his own development as a choreographer changed after understanding the construction of Stravinsky's *Apollo*. He perceived that his creative energy would be best served by creating families of gestures and restricting his inventiveness to those related movements which would culminate in a structured whole. In his subsequent work he has not deviated from this decision.

Balanchine's ballets have, since *Apollo*, been characterized by a distilled clarity of movement and scrupulous elimination of gesture which would not be wholly consistent with the character portrayed. Primarily, his ballets have not had narrative continuity but have been pure dance works of a plotless nature, yet they have a continuous flow which elaborates on the essential thrust of the dance idea being portrayed, and move forward with an apparently effortless fluency. The Balanchine dancer moves with dignity which stems from the organically linked pattern of movement which comprises any role in his ballets. This is easily noticeable in the appropriateness of the gestures which the dancers are given in order to elaborate a role. They are never asked to transgress that logically evolving line which delineates a characteristic mode of behaviour in order to perform a movement inconsistent with the character's sensibility. The ballets are thus the combination of unfailing inventiveness and a subtle distillation of experience. As a result, Balanchine's ballets lend themselves to continual reviewing with the reward of fresh insights.

Balanchine began his career as a student in the Imperial

Ballet School in St Petersburg. His studies were interrupted by the Russian Revolution of 1917 and his graduation from the school delayed until 1923. He left Russia with a small group of dancers for a tour of Western Europe and was engaged by the impresario Serge Diaghilev in 1924. He was the last of the great choreographers who worked for Diaghilev and produced ten ballets for him. Two of these are still in current repertory – *Apollo* and *The Prodigal Son*. With the dissolution of the company in 1929 after Diaghilev's death, Balanchine worked with various companies including the Royal Danish Ballet and finally formed his own troupe, *Les Ballets 1933*. The company lasted for only one season, but Balanchine was encouraged by Lincoln Kirstein to go to the United States and form a school and company there. He accepted and within two years was invited to become the resident ballet master of the Metropolitan Opera. It was an unhappy period in Balanchine's life, for the directors of the Metropolitan regarded ballet lightly, if at all. The company left the Metropolitan after a particularly virulent argument between management and the choreographer and Balanchine then supported himself by means of Broadway and film assignments for the next fifteen years.

In 1948, a newly formed ballet company (which was presented under the title of Ballet Society) became the resident company of the New York City Center and then changed its name to New York City Ballet. Within the secure home of the City Center and, subsequently, the New York State Theater, Balanchine has proceeded to create a major performing ensemble and a body of work which has fused the raw energy of his adopted American society and the classicism of his Imperial training into a neo-classical repertory of ballets that stems directly from the mainstream of classical dancing.

Apollo (Apollon Musagète)

Ballet in one act, two scenes. Choreography: Balanchine. Music and book: Igor Stravinsky. Décor: André Bauchant. First performed Ballets Russes, Théâtre Sarah Bernhardt, Paris, 12th

June, 1928, *with Serge Lifar* (*Apollo*), *Alice Nikitina* (*alternating with A. Danilova*) *as Terpsichore, Lubov Tchernicheva* (*Polyhymnia*), *Felia Dubrovska* (*Calliope*). *Has also been mounted for Ballet Theater, Paris Opéra Ballet, Royal Danish Ballet, and Royal Ballet.*

Apollo opens with the birth of the young god, Apollo, who emerges in swaddling sheets and is released by his attendants. He spins about strongly and then sinks into a coltish slump.

In the second scene, Apollo is depicted in his young manhood as the one who will be the teacher of the Muses. Three girls, representing Calliope, Muse of Poetry, Polyhymnia, Muse of Mime, and Terpsichore, Muse of Dancing and Song advance from the corners of the stage to appear before him. He takes their hands and draws them toward him. They dance together. They follow him, echoing his movements. He circles the stage in a series of rapid leaps and returns to join hands and lead them.

After this initial introductory dance, which establishes the relationship of the graceful Muses and the awkward but growing young god, he presents each of them with a symbol representing their art. Calliope receives a writing tablet, Polyhymnia the mask of mime and Terpsichore the musical lyre. Each of the Muses dances her variation. Calliope during hers makes broad declamatory gestures leading outward from her body. Polyhymnia has a spritely variation full of youthful enthusiasm. Terpsichore has a classical restraint. Apollo finds the first two slightly flawed in their presentation, but finds no fault in Terpsichore's dance. Apollo in his own variation teaches the Muses the full power of expressiveness that they must possess and shows his own mastery after his initial tentativeness. He chooses Terpsichore, his favourite, for a *pas de deux* that culminates in a 'swimming lesson' with her stretched in a beautiful proud curve on his back as they move their arms in swimming motions. The other Muses join in a fast *coda* in which the three, seated on the stage, humbly lift one foot up to touch the palm of Apollo in unison. They rise and he leads them like a team of horses. At the end, he ascends a steep staircase leading to a heavenly locale and the Muses form a line behind him.

Apollo was, for Balanchine, a turning point in his creative life. It was the first time that he had worked with a Stravinsky score and it indicated the course of his future career. From the time of *Apollo* Balanchine developed the line of neo-classic choreography which has been his particular contribution to twentieth-century ballet. In later works he was to push the dance element of his ballets even further to the fore while dispensing almost entirely with naturalistic incident. However, in this ballet, the narrative line is still retained although it is a much attenuated one compared with those works which had preceded it.

One of the special distinctions of this ballet is the way in which it is fragmented. The young god, Apollo, is shown in his early awkwardness by clear breaks in the choreographic flow which are later eliminated as he achieves the mastery which one senses in him almost before it is displayed. During the creation of the work, Serge Diaghilev, for whose company it was being prepared, remarked to an acquaintance, 'What he is doing is magnificent. It is pure classicism such as we have not seen since Petipa.'

The Prodigal Son (Le Fils Prodigue)

Ballet in one act and three scenes. Choreography: Balanchine. Music: Sergei Prokofiev. Décor: Georges Rouault. First performed Diaghilev's Ballets Russes, Théâtre Sarah Bernhardt, Paris, 21st May, 1929. Serge Lifar (Prodigal), Felia Dubrovska (Siren), Michel Fedorov (Father), Léon Woizikowski and Anton Dolin (Servants).

As the ballet opens, two friends of the Prodigal are arranging provisions for a journey. The Prodigal comes out of the entrance to his home followed by two sisters who watch him anxiously. He leaps high in the air and looks off to a glittering future which he imagines for himself. He stops, suddenly confronted by his father who gathers the two sisters and the Prodigal to himself. The son obeys but reluctantly, and finally breaks loose of his family ties with a dramatic leap over the household enclosure to meet his future.

In the second scene, the Prodigal rushes into the strange and exotic city for which he has longed. Baldheaded revellers enter brutally and ominously. At one point they form duos with locked arms back to back and move across the stage like monstrous crabs scuttling in the semi-darkness. It shocks the Prodigal at first, but their self-seeking interest is lost on him and he joins in the revel. The Siren enters trailing a long red robe behind her and begins a seductive dance in which she luxuriates in her own voluptuousness. The robe is entwined around her body and then spread out behind her and finally she crouches down to the ground and covers herself completely with it. The Prodigal comes forward and whips the garment from her and offers himself as her partner. Before their duet, his friends do a spirited dance during which the Prodigal is transfixed at the sight of Siren. Their *pas de deux* is sensually expressive and her growing mastery over him is expressed at one point by an encircling movement which she makes around his body while slowly sliding downward to the floor. The seduction has been successful and the revellers now dominate the scene as they prepare to plunder their victim. The exhausted Prodigal is propped up against the banquet table and nothing is seen at first except the greedy hands of the revellers appearing out from behind the table to strip the Prodigal of his goods and even his clothes. The Siren snatches a medallion from his neck which she had previously admired. The Prodigal is left nearly naked without even his shoes.

In the last scene, returning home, he is clad in rags and supports himself with a staff. He is pressed down with weakness and shame and drags himself across the length of the stage unable to rise from his knees. The father is told of his coming and emerges to welcome back his son. The Prodigal crawls to embrace his father's feet and climbs up his body as one would ascend a tree. The father enfolds him in his arms and carries him back to his home.

The Prodigal Son was the last ballet Balanchine did for the Diaghilev's company. Its dramatic title role is demanding in terms of character portrayal, but one of the most rewarding for the male dancer. Serge Lifar, who first danced the role, achieved great success and currently Edward Villella of New York City Ballet has refined it into a masterful portrayal of youthful enthusiasm soured by unhappy experience. In portraying the episodic nature of the story, Balanchine devises some striking tableaux. One which combines a chilling impersonality and humour is formed by a compact group of revellers. They create a banked formation like the keyboard of a typewriter and face the Prodigal who extends his hand to greet them. Their hands dart out and back before he is able to grasp any of them. It is impersonally menacing.

One of the interesting sidelights in this work is the deft use which is made of a simple stage property. It is made to serve as the fence over which the Prodigal escapes, the hull of a ship, a banquet table, then the pillar upon which he is stripped and finally, the gate through which he crawls back to his father. In a symbolic way it forms a résumé of the entire tale.

Serenade

A ballet in one act. Choreography: Balanchine. Music: Tchaikovsky. Costumes: Jean Lurçat. First performed Students of School of American Ballet at estate of Felix Warburg, White Plains, N. Y., 9th June, 1934. Presented by producing company of the School of American Ballet at Avery Memorial Theater, Hartford, Connecticut on 6th December, 1934. 'Serenade' is now danced by many companies both in the United States and abroad.

Set to Tchaikovsky's *Serenade in C Major for String Orchestra*, the ballet was first created by Balanchine when he came to the United States in 1934. It utilizes the Tchaikovsky score but transposes the last movement into the third section of the ballet. It opens with diagonal lines of girls holding one hand aloft. In unison their hands drop downward as if in a gesture of farewell. Turning forward, the dancers sharply

assume the first and basic position of ballet with feet turned
out and arms softly rounded in front of them. They have left
one state and entered into the world of the dance. They form
small groups and move with spirited and flowing combinations
and at the end of the movement they return again to the
formation in which they started. A girl joins them and takes
her place in their ranks. A boy enters at the rear of the stage
and all of the others go off except for the late girl. The second
movement is their *pas de deux* during which the other girls
return. The principal girl is joyous and this mood is reflected
in the dance of the other girls. At the end of the movement
all go off.

At the start of the third section, five girls cluster in the
centre of the stage gracefully linking arms. A boy comes on
and dances with one of the girls, but then the group rushes
off and she is left lying face down on the stage. In the final
section, a girl, shielding the eyes of a boy from behind, guides
him to the fallen girl. She is drawn upward by him and they
dance together. The guiding girl returns and joins in a *pas de
trois*. They move together like reflections of one another.
Suddenly the mood is changed and the guiding girl once again
shields the eyes of the boy and he is led off, leaving the fallen
girl. She is gathered up by a cortège which bears her off.

Serenade was created at a time when Balanchine had few
good dancers and could only work with any of them erratically.
These circumstances account for the odd number of performers
in the various movements and even for the elements of the
choreography. Balanchine kept a fall, which happened to one
girl, in the ballet. He placed the lateness of another in the
fabric of the work. He added boys to the ballet as they appeared
at rehearsals. Throughout he tied the whole ballet together
with classic dancing.

There is no dramatic thread running through the work and
it is best considered as separate movements each having but
related short stories. The most dramatic section is the fourth in
which a man is torn between the girl who guides him (who
could be a surrogate figure for Fate) and the girl to whom he is

guided. In the other sections we find basically a celebration of the lyrical feeling of the Tchaikovsky score and the exuberance that the trained dancer can feel in the command of his craft. It is a ballet which has found favour with many companies and has been mounted by them successfully.

Ballet Imperial

Classical ballet. Choreography: Balanchine. Music: Tchaikov-sky, Piano Concerto No. 2 in G. First performed by American Ballet New York, 27th May, 1941. Revived by Royal Ballet, Covent Garden, 5th April, 1950 (with scenery and costumes by Eugeno Borman, replaced in 1963 with scenery and costumes by Carl Toms).

Ballet Imperial is Balanchine's tribute to Petipa, to the world of the Maryinski Ballet and to the attitudes and manners to be observed in the classic ballets and, arguably, in the Tsarist court.

FIRST MOVEMENT. *Allegro brillante.*

After the piano and orchestra have announced the opening theme the curtain rises to reveal eight couples facing each other in a diagonal; they exchange reverences, and then start to dance. Eight further girls enter and then a leading soloist comes on to prepare the way for the prima ballerina (a Grand Duchess announcing the arrival of an Empress). She dances to the piano cadenza in a series of flashing, brilliant incidents, and is later joined by her cavalier. They exit and there follows a *pas de trois* for the leading soloists with two male attendants; the movement ends with the return of ballerina and cavalier in a dazzling finale.

SECOND MOVEMENT. *Andante non troppo.*

The Empress's cavalier – like the Prince in *The Sleeping Beauty* awaiting the arrival of Aurora's vision – dances first with eight *corps de ballet* who form swinging arcs of movement. Then the ballerina appears to her prince, and they dance a loving duet, but finally the ballerina melts away with the attendants. The cavalier prince must exit alone.

THIRD MOVEMENT. *Allegro fuoco.*

The *corps de ballet* enter to the brilliant bouncing rhythms of a polonaise and soon the ballerina and her partner also appear. There follows a general section, and brief passage for the trio of soloists before the final dazzling conclusion for the ensemble.

Ballet Imperial is a ballet about ballet, about aristocracy, about the world of the Maryinski – as a theatre and as a social symbol. It is, like all Balanchine's works, compact of marvellous dancing, marvellously set on the score. Grand, lyrical, pyrotechnic, the second piano concerto of Tchaikovsky makes a perfect basis for this study in classicism as it was, and classicism as it is now.

La Sonnambula (Night Shadow)

A ballet in one act. Choreography: Balanchine. Music: Vittorio Rieti, after Bellini. Décor: Dorothea Tanning. First performed Ballet Russe de Monte Carlo at City Center, New York, 27th February, 1946, with Alexandra Danilova (Sleepwalker), Nicholas Magallanes (Poet), Maria Tallchief (Coquette), Michel Katcharoff (Host). The Royal Danish and Ballet Rambert also perform this piece as did the Le Grand Ballet du Marquis de Cuevas. New York City Ballet staged it on 6th January, 1960, with décor by Esteban Frances. Costumes: André Levasseur. Allegra Kent (Sleepwalker), Eric Bruhn (Poet), John Taras (Baron), Jillana (Coquette) and E. Villella in Harlequin dance. First performed London's Festival Ballet (décor: Peter Farmer), 20th March, 1967, Teatro La Fenice, Venice.

The ballet tells the story of a poet and a sleepwalker. The setting is the home of a rich Baron who is greeting his guests at a masked ball. A coquette, presumably his mistress, stands near him. Abruptly, an uninvited guest, a poet, arrives and the host greets him warily. The poet has eyes only for the coquette and scarcely responds to the host's welcome. The dance resumes and the couples pause for a series of entertainments. These are: a pastoral offered by two couples; a blackamoor pair who do a humorous variation ; followed by an eccentric and witty dance by Harlequin, who appears bothered by a stiff back.

After this diversion, the guests depart for the garden and the beginning of the meal, leaving the poet and the coquette alone. They dance a romantic duet which is interrupted by the return of the host and his guests. The host is obviously possessive of the coquette and takes her away.

Alone, the poet sees a girl in white coming towards him. She carries a candle, moving on point, sleepwalking. Thus she does not appear to see him. Their *pas de deux* is elaborately one-sided as the poet attempts to trap her time and again only to have her step out of his grasp or disappear effortlessly beneath his outstretched arms. He pushes her and she immediately takes the course he has put her on, gliding fluidly across the stage. The coquette returns to find the poet with another woman, the host's wife, and furiously tells the host, who thereupon murders the poet. He collapses in front of the guests and the sleepwalker gathers him in her arms and carries him off, the way she appeared, up the stairs of a tower to her room.

La Sonnambula or *Night Shadow* (as it was first titled), is a Gothic tale set in a large mansion. The relations of the principals have a murky obscurity that adds a dimension of mystery to the narrative. It is an unusual form of ballet in Balanchine's oeuvre which is ordinarily characterized by its clarity of relations. From these cloudy elements Balanchine has created a piece rich in portent. Some of the most strikingly effective movements have been created for the corps in a series of dances based on a roughly circular pattern. At one point of the evening, the masked couples demonstrate a subtly erotic interest in each other as they whip off their masks and flee, breaking out of the social circle. Everyone seems to have gathered at the ball only to flee away into private assignations.

Beneath the glittering show lurks unruly passion that finally erupts into violence.

The Four Temperaments

A ballet in one act, five parts. Choreography: Balanchine. Music: Paul Hindemith. Décor: Kurt Seligmann. Lighting: Jean Rosenthal. First performed Ballet Society, Central High School of Needle Trades, New York, 20th November, 1946. Revised version by Ballet Society at City Center on 9th February, 1948. First performance by newly styled New York City Ballet on 25th October, 1948. Décor and costumes (for American Ballet's South American tour) by P. Tchelitchev were not liked by Hindemith so ballet was not presented by them at that time. Also in repertoire of Netherlands National Ballet, Royal Swedish Ballet and Paris Opéra Ballet.

The ballet is divided into five parts as is its Hindemith score. The theme is stated in the opening movement and is then followed by the four developmental variations, 'Melancholic', 'Sanguinic', 'Phlegmatic' and 'Choleric'. The music was commissioned privately by Balanchine who had admired the composer's work.

Three couples, each representing different statements of the musical theme, dance the opening section. Their movements have a sharp angularity to them and each of the duets concludes with the atmosphere of an armed truce between the boy and girl. There is a general lack of finality to these three *pas de deux* which will only be resolved in the final section. This is followed by the first variation, the 'Melancholic'. A man dances dispiritedly until the tempo of the music changes and he is joined by two girls and then four other more menacing girls who stalk haughtily across the stage. However, at the end, his melancholy reasserts itself. The second movement, 'Sanguinic', is light and free and the man and woman move confidently to the music. The third variation, 'Phlegmatic', again finds a man on stage alone and in a listless mood. The tone of the music changes and he is joined by four girls, all of whom are roused to a joyous state. The severely contrasting 'Choleric' variation follows in which a single girl dances fiercely and untouchably. After this, the entire ensemble dances the finale which is climaxed with high lifts of the solo girls travelling from right to left across the stage between files of the corps.

The temperaments alluded to in the music and ballet itself are the humours of the body which the ancients imagined were the components of personality. It was presupposed that each and every person had a measured portion of each which would account for his particular disposition.

As envisioned by Balanchine, the melancholic and phlegmatic humours were particularly male and the enraged choleric, female. Only a man and a woman together could be representative of the well-adjusted sanguinic. At the conclusion, all of the temperaments were transformed into a forward looking amalgam as the leading girls rose and descended among the lines of the corps.

When it was first performed, the ballet had surrealistic costumes designed by Kurt Seligman that were later discarded for practice clothes in which the ballet has been performed ever since. The work is one which is thought of as being quintessentially representative of the New York City Ballet's style.

Bourrée Fantasque

Choreography: Balanchine. Music: Chabrier. First performed New York City Ballet in New York, 1st December, 1949. Costumes by Karinska. The music comprises: Bourrée Fantasque, the prelude to 'Gwendolyne' and the Fête Polonaise from 'Le Roi Malgré Lui'. (First performed by Festival Ballet, London, 18th August, 1960 – with new costumes by Peter Farmer in 1968.)

Like Gaul, *Bourrée Fantasque* is divided into three parts: the opening Bourrée is a danced burlesque that is witty, and entirely classical. Its humours depend on fans, upon bright, brilliant movements executed with entirely dead-pan expressions, and the mismatching of a very tall girl dancer with a diminutive partner. Everything is a joke: the ballerina's attempts to ignore her partner, his enthusiasm for his task, and the sheer strangeness of ballerinas' feet in block shoes (the boys get down on the ground and examine the girls' feet with the seriousness of stamp-collectors studying a penny black). The contrast with the second movement could not be more marked: it is lyrical, concerned with the eternal search for the ideal beloved, as a boy and a girl at first fail to meet and then are joined in a beautiful romantic duet.

Fête Polonaise is a bounding joyous finale, built on a crescendo that gathers tremendous momentum as the movement progresses. A ballerina flies across the stage supported by her partner who holds her arm as she curvettes and beats; the ballerina of the second movement enters with her troupe of dancers, and soon all three ballerinas, with their own groups are on stage. Balanchine here devises a breath-taking sequence of patterns: circles, stars and whirling formations, and the movement ends in a final spectacular mêlée as the curtain falls.

Agon

One-act ballet consisting of introduction and three parts. Choreography: Balanchine. Music: Stravinsky. Décor (lighting): Nananne Porcher. First performed New York City Ballet at City Center, New York, 27th November, 1957.

Agon is an original score composed by Stravinsky for Balanchine's ballet of the same name. It consists of twelve short pieces of a spare and sinewy quality which the ballet reflects. It is choreographed for twelve dancers, four boys and eight girls. As the ballet opens, the four boys stand at the back of the stage and whirl to face the audience. They perform a *pas de quatre* of athletic brilliance and leave the stage to eight girls. Their section is labelled a double *pas de quatre* in which they display their own athletic, but feminine exuberance. Finally they all dance together in a triple *pas de quatre*. A similar pattern on a smaller scale is then introduced in the form of a *pas de trois* for two girls and a boy. They dance together, the boy does a *sarabande*, followed by the two girls in a *galliard* in which he rejoins them. The second section contains three *branles*. The first with two boys is a brilliant mirror of the brass while the girl doing a *branle gai* introduces a Spanish flavour into the ballet and all conclude with a *branle double*.

This is succeeded by a linked *pas de deux* in which the couple are scarcely ever separated. It is a complex and involved *pas* that utilizes the space of two arm lengths extremely imaginatively. At the end, the four boys return to move upstage in sweeping movements and indicate the end of the ballet with a showman-like gesture of finality suggesting '. . . and there!'

Agon is the Greek word for contest and there is a strongly athletic atmosphere to the entire ballet. It is not the contention of the athletic field however, but stems more from a sexual competitiveness between boys and girls, each attempting to excel. The ballet is particularly interesting in its combination of classical dance gesture and contemporary aggressiveness. At one point the boys place one reposed arm across the chest in an aristocratic manner and at the same time prop a hand arrogantly on one hip.

The forms of the sections take their names from 17th century dances which Stravinsky imitated through his own 20th century sensibility. Balanchine alludes to them in the choreography but the work is strongly contemporary in feeling. It is one of the most successful of the Stravinsky/ Balanchine collaborations and occupies a high place in the canon of Balanchine's work.

Stars and Stripes (dedicated to the memory of Fiorello H. LaGuardia)

One-act ballet in five campaigns! Choreography: Balanchine. Music: John Philip Sousa (adapted and orchestrated by Hershey Kay). Scenery and lighting: David Hays. Costumes: Karinska.

First performed New York City Ballet at City Center, 17th January, 1958, with Allegra Kent, Robert Barnett, Diana Adams, Melissa Hayden, Jacques D'Amboise.

Stars and Stripes is a ballet done in *campaigns* rather than movements. It is a suitable designation of the martial spirit which pervades this bouncy ballet. The first *campaign* is performed to the march, 'Corcoran Cadets' and is danced by a majorette leading a corps of girls in a pert and somewhat immature evocation of the military panache. The dancers move throughout with a precise delicacy. The second *campaign* has a more aggressive attack and is lead with a bolder approach than was the first. It too features the dancing of a corps of girls. The third *campaign* is designed for the men of the ballet who move arrogantly and stylishly to one of Sousa's most vigorous marches, 'The Thunderer'. The group is led by a commander who darts rapidly in and among his performing 'soldiers' with confidence in their complete perfection of timing. Along with the vigour of their movements is added a joyous insouciance that creates a winning combination of fun and precision.

The fourth movement consists of a *pas de deux* between a splendidly costumed officer and his lady. It is performed to the music of 'El Capitan' and 'Liberty Bell'. The couple have the air of particularly successful patriotic acrobats. In their duet the man displays his athletic but somewhat gauche prowess by rising in leaps with deliberately unpointed feet. The juxtaposition of the softly executed leap and the right-angle profile of the feet is humorously effective. The lady affects an air of brassy grandeur. In the final *campaign*, all of the dancers join in a finale that concludes with the American flag being unfurled at the back of the stage.

Stars and Stripes when properly performed is one of Balanchine's most fluent ballets. It possesses a tongue-in-cheek jingoism that captures an era of simplistic patriotism. Balanchine has chosen few American composers whose work he has felt merited his attention. It is significant that John Philip Sousa was one of them. Sousa's music has a directness and

moral uprightness which Balanchine saw as typical of turn-of-
the-century America.

In *Stars and Stripes* he has done homage to that sensibility
which was best exemplified by Theodore Roosevelt's comment
that America 'should speak softly but carry a big stick'. The
choreography captures the vigour and also the sentimentality
of such a naïve moral stance. It is a ballet which Balanchine
is exceptionally careful in presenting. He deliberately refrained
from including it in New York City Ballet's tour of the Soviet
Union for fear that it would be misunderstood as a political
statement. Great Britain is one of the few nations outside the
United States in which its special qualities have been
understood.

Liebeslieder Walzer

*Ballet in one act, two scenes. Choreography: Balanchine.
Music: Brahms' 'Liebeslieder Walzer, Op. 52 & 55'. Décor:
David Hays. Costumes: Karinska. First performed New York
City Ballet at City Center, 22nd Novenber, 1960.*

Liebeslieder Walzer is a ballet in two sections comprised of
eighteen waltzes in the first naturalistic section and fourteen
in the second *timeless* portion. The music is scored for four-
hand piano. The musicians arrive first and sit at the piano at
the left of the stage; they are then joined by four singers. The
four couples who are to perform the ballet arrive in the formal
19th-century drawing room. The music and the dancers begin.
It quickly becomes apparent that they represent four distinct
and separate types of amorous engagements. There is a young,
eager, somewhat shy couple, another with a tinge of sadness,
a third with a more tranquil relationship, and a fourth with
elements of contention. The dances follow rapidly upon one
another and towards the end of the first section, the dancers
exit one by one until the drawing room is empty.

At the start of the second set of waltzes the decorative
candlelight is extinguished and the colour tone of the room is

changed from the warm intimacy of the first half into the cooler look of the infinite, removed from specific time or place. The dancers return and the women have changed into more theatrical ballerina costume. The waltzes of this section are more spectacular and have a considerably more airborne look to them. The tonality of the first scene has been expanded into a more flamboyant presentation. At the end of this section, the dancers return in the costumes they originally wore in the first part, listen quietly to the music of the last song, then politely applaud.

Liebeslieder Walzer is a curiosity inasmuch as it is that rare type of ballet, a ballet of manners. The atmosphere and relations of four couples during an epoch, suggestive of the Austro-Hungarian Empire, are explored and detailed with an almost novelistic intensity. The particular place is delineated with the polite breeding that one would expect to find in a modish treatise on conduct. The feeling persists that if the dance movements could be imitated properly one would not commit a social *faux pas* in a social gathering of that time.

The ballet lasts for just over an hour during which time there is a seemingly endless flow of dances in waltz time. Seen just as a technical exercise within the narrow confines of a single rhythmic pattern, *Liebeslieder* would astonish by its imaginative mastery; as a work of the creative imagination, it ranks with Balanchine's finest productions.

Don Quixote

Ballet in three acts and five scenes. Choreography: Balanchine. Music (commissioned): Nicolas Nabokov. Décor: Esteban Frances. First performed New York City Ballet, New York, at State Theater, 27th May, 1965, with George Balanchine (Don Quixote), Suzanne Farrell (Dulcinea), Deni Lamont (Sancho Panza).

The Cervantes novel provides the basic plot for this full evening work which opens in the Don's study. He dwells

among books of arcane lore through which he seeks to find the
significance of life. Having fallen asleep one evening, he
dreams of ideal beauty and the dark terrors of the night which
beset such beauty. In a dream he combats various monsters
and rescues beauty from them. In the morning, he is awakened
by a lovely peasant girl, Dulcinea, who comforts him and
washes his feet, drying them with her hair like the Magdalen.
He surges forth to right the wrongs of the world but is constantly disappointed by his labours. The boy he frees from a
cruel master turns on him, the prisoners he liberates attack
him and an innocent street carnival employing captive children,
which arouses his sympathetic wrath, collapses on him.
Restored to his senses, he is carried off to the local duke's castle.

In Act II, which is basically a series of *divertissements*, Don
Quixote finds himself among people with whom he has little
basic sympathy – nor they for him. He is taunted gently at
first, but then more viciously. His servant, Sancho Panza, feels
the malevolence of their hosts long before his master, but all
is brushed aside for the *divertissements*. These include a
savage couple, a highly refined and restrained couple and a
solo girl who does an erotic dance accompanied by a page who
tries energetically to keep a canopy over her during the dance.
The act concludes with a dance for the court, including Don
Quixote, who is insulted, assaulted and humiliated. He is
finally expelled from the great hall.

At the beginning of the third act, he and Sancho Panza find
themselves in a drugged sleep and bound in nets outside the
duke's castle. The Don has a dream of ideal beauty which
sustains him. It is a distillation of the beautiful beset
shepherd girl in the first act and the figure who comforted
him in the castle during the second act. Each of the
soloists in this dream ballet dance with a reserve that almost
makes the ballet within a ballet seem to have a restraining
curtain drawn across it. During the course of the ballet the
central girl is beset with various hindrances that bring her
tragically to her knees.

After this sequence, the Don and Sancho Panza move on to
adventures with the knight in glittering armour, tilting with

the windmills and assaulting a herd of swine. The wounded
Don is finally led into a litter upon which he is borne home
trapped like an animal. He dies in his own bed but is visited
with the spirits and visions of a variety of crusaders, starting
with the familiar military ones and concluding with the
spiritual knights of the soul. At the conclusion of the procession past his litter he dies. At the first light of day, his faithful
friends, including Sancho Panza and the peasant girl Dulcinea
come to mourn at his bedside.

Don Quixote is a flawed ballet saddled with an impossibly
eclectic score which is totally uncharacteristic of the type of
music which Balanchine is ordinarily attracted to. The music
has a sound track appropriateness but little purpose of its own,
other than to reflect the libretto. Despite the infelicitous
nature of the music, Balanchine has created a ballet of
immense power.

He continually draws the parallels between the totally dedicated artist and the martyred religious figure who is destroyed
for his own monomaniacal pursuits. The ballet is artistically
structured to reflect the progressive pilgrimage of the hero. In
the first act there is little but character dancing. In the second,
demi-character dancing, and in the third, there is mainly
classical dancing of a specially restrained order. The central
role is a mime non-dancing part which has most effectively
been portrayed by Balanchine himself who has danced it on
select occasions. *Don Quixote* reflects one of Balanchine's few
attempts to construct an evening-long dramatic ballet. It is not
entirely successful, but preserves a rough-edged power despite
its awkward transitions. It has something of the fascination of
a memoir although it is denied that the ballet has any auto-
biographical intent.

Jewels

*Ballet in three acts. Choreography: Balanchine. Music:
Fauré, Stravinsky and Tchaikovsky. Lighting: Ronald Bates.
Scenery: Peter Harvey. Costumes: Karinska. First performed
New York City Ballet, State Theater, 13th April, 1967.*

Jewels is a full evening-length work and has three distinct movements which are related conceptually, but not narratively. The ballet is plotless. Each of the sections is complete in itself, but together they create a trilogy of contrasting and complementary moods.

The first section, *Emeralds*, is dressed in green and performed to selections from Fauré's *Pelléas et Mélisande* and *Shylock*. This section features two couples, three soloists and a corps of ten girls. The ballet opens softly with a *pas de deux* during which the couple is backed by the corps moving sympathetically behind them. The girl does a solo variation of an aristocratic but understated nature. The second girl, who has a certain wistful loneliness, enters to do her solo. It creates a mood of sadness within the framework of a highly ordered society. Two girls and a boy enter to do a *pas de trois* that is vigorous and lean, moving with the assurance of young thoroughbreds. The second girl and her partner perform a *pas de trois* in which she accepts him with a somewhat resigned air. The movement ends with all of the soloists and the corps in a formal dance.

The second portion of the ballet is *Rubies*, and the entire mood of the piece is vigorous. There is a couple and a solo girl backed by the corps. The movement starts with the entire corps in a half-circle facing the audience. The girls rise on point and the boys also poise themselves for action. From this time on the movement will not have a moment of repose until the final chords of Stravinsky's *Concerto for piano and Orchestra* subside. It has a non-stop pacing reminiscent of the marathon dance contests of the 1930s. The corps is led at various times by the principal couple or the solo girl. Central to the movement is the *pas de deux* of the leading couple which has the playfulness and wayward sophistication of movie musicals in which formally dressed men and women occupied outlandishly scaled settings. Following their duet, the man leads the boys on a chase in which they pursue him in an imitation of the children's game of 'Follow The Leader'. The movement ends with an exuberant finale.

Diamonds is the concluding section of the ballet and is

arranged for a principal couple, soloist and large corps. The
music is the last four movements of Tchaikovsky's five-part
Symphony No. 3. It opens with the corps arrayed in curved
ranks, led by two soloists. The lines mesh into one another
and separate. The quality of the movement is classic and this
section sets the tone for the *pas de deux* of the principal couple
in it. The couple exchange a pledge of commitment to one
another that is done with a rarified nobility. The next section
finds them in a series of variations with the corps. The final
section is a polonaise for the entire ensemble which has the
sweep and dash of this character dance distilled into a crystalline
clarity.

Jewels – a three-act abstract ballet – is probably the least
likely type of work that anyone would pick for popular success,
and yet it has proven itself to be so with varieties of audiences.
It was introduced almost diffidently and after its première
became one of the most sought-after ballets in the repertory
of the New York City Ballet. Balanchine recalls that the idea
of the piece was suggested to him after he had seen the collection of precious stones owned by the jeweller, Claude Arpels.

Each section celebrates a differing mood. In the first, which
is highly structured and formally passionate, a French sensibility appears to be explored. The second section, although the
music was written by a Russian, has the driving, jazz-sympa-
thetic movement of the United States. In it, the sense of brute
energy is continually upheld. There is even a mechanistic
reflection of 'Sleeping Beauty' as the solo girl performs an
adagio surrounded by her four 'princes' who each hold one of
her arms or legs and move her through an intricate *pas de
cinq*. It has a sense of fun and the outrageous, ingeniously
combined, like a man adjusting his *boutonnière* in the centre
of a tornado.

Each of the three sections deals with the music of a country
in which Balanchine has spent considerable time. The final
section, *Diamonds*, has a refined purity of gesture that breathes
the spirit of classicism and seems to be a homage to the land
of his birth. The combination of the three movements which

culminates in *Diamonds* represents Balanchine at the height of his powers and inventiveness.

JEROME ROBBINS (b. 1918)

Native Americans, apart from Red Indians, are not the easiest people to find. Most Americans have come from somewhere else or their fathers or grandfathers did, so that most Americans receive a dual heritage, one old before they were born and the other in the process of formation. It is at this meeting point of the old and the new that Jerome Robbins has made his distinctive contribution to American Ballet. He has, in his work, concerned himself with bringing together expressive indigenous elements with the technique of classical ballet in a meaningful contemporary mixture.

Robbins, whose sensibility draws on an immigrant heritage as well as an American upbringing in the urban environment of New York, has become the foremost American-born ballet choreographer. Quotes from street games and sidewalk pastimes were spotted through early ballets such as *Fancy Free* and *Interplay*, and more recently, in *Dances at a Gathering*, the quotes have come from European folk dances. In each case expressive character movement has been woven together with the more restrained classical vocabulary to give Robbins' work its distinctive flavour. By turning rapidly from one form to another and juxtaposing them Robbins has inevitably created an element of humour in his works which adds a special charm to their presentation. No one can easily forget the sailors in *Fancy Free* doing brief excerpts from a classical *barre* exercise using a commercial bar to work from, or the 'choosing up sides' episode from *Interplay* as the boys and girls form teams.

For Robbins the most expressive and therefore the most natural movements are those of the character or *demi-caractère* sort; they reveal the person in the accents most congenial to him. Classical technique speaks in a more refined tone but is still vitally linked and draws sustenance from the less stylized movements. It is a relationship similar to the one between everyday speech patterns and the cadences of poetry. The poetical soars beyond the other but sinks its roots deeply into the rhythm of ordinary conversation. Robbins has endlessly combined aspects of the two into his ballets and into his other theatre work.

As a choreographer he has worked not only in the classical ballet but also on the dramatic stage that produced *West Side Story*, an updating of the Romeo and Juliet tale that once again tied a traditional form into a contemporary setting. The play was later made into a film which Robbins directed and for which he received several industry awards, including the first one ever given for choreography. *Fiddler on the Roof*, which was staged by Robbins with enormous success, once more dealt with the theme of a man at the crossroads of time. In this case, a father born into a traditional ghetto culture lives to see his daughters reject his values to create a new life of their own. Robbins' movements for the actors could not be exactly described as choreography or as plain stage direction but partook of both elements.

Pursuing further the direction which he had taken in *Fiddler*, Robbins proposed to establish 'The American Lyric Theatre Workshop' for which he received a government grant of $300,000. The projected workshop was to have created a combination of stage, musical and dance elements that would have been different from the current theatrical forms and one which was particularly reflective of the new American culture. After a few years of quiet work Robbins dropped the experiment and returned to the ballet stage. Little or nothing has been heard of the project and one must conclude that it failed to live up to Robbins' expectations.

His first work since turning his full-time attention to ballet again was *Dances at a Gathering* which was done for soloists and principals of the New York City Ballet in 1969. Robbins, who had been associate artistic director of the company from 1949 to 1963, and had produced ten ballets during that period, returned with a new-found depth to his work. *Dances*, which lasts for nearly an hour, is set to selected Chopin piano pieces and is accompanied by a solo player on stage. It places five couples on the stage, with only a cloud formation projected on the cyclorama for décor. The young men and women of the piece dance with one another in a joyous celebration of the fact that they are there and alive and interested in one another. It is the most impressive work that Robbins has done to date, effortlessly blending European folk dance steps in with the classical movements that provide the unifying framework for the piece.

The humour arising from this ballet has the quality of a deeply human statement about life and love and passing fancy. It is removed from the somewhat raw frenzy of *Interplay* and *Pied Piper* in which the classical form was bent and twisted almost for the impish sake of doing it. *Dances* indicates a mature talent at full and easy creative floodtide.

Fancy Free

Ballet in one act. Choreography: Robbins. Music: Leonard Bernstein. Décor: Oliver Smith. Costumes: Kermit Love. First performed Ballet Theater at Metropolitan Opera House, New York, on 18th April, 1944 with John Kriza, Harold Lang, Jerome Robbins (three sailors), Muriel Bentley, Janet Reed and Shirley Eckl (three passers-by).

The time is a summer evening in a large city. Three sailors on shore leave arrive with the intention of having an evening on the town. They enter into a bar with swaggering braggadocio and order three beers. One of the sailors is tricked into paying. They wander outside into the street and see a girl; they scuffle with one another and one of the boys is knocked down while the other two run off after the girl. Another girl walks by and the remaining sailor dances with her. It is an understated and softly endearing *pas de deux* which sees the reappearance of the other two sailors and the girl at its end. It is easy to see that there are only two girls and three boys so one of the boys will have to leave. They decide on a dancing contest in which the loser will leave the others alone.

One sailor does a vigorously energetic dance full of trick

turns, falls and stunts, designed to dazzle and intimidate the
other two. The second sailor does a completely contrasting
variation featuring the flow of long-spaced phrases touched
with gentle sadness. The third sailor performs a slinky variation with Latin rhythms. Its tempo picks up gradually until
it is in full swing, combining elements of both of the previous
variations. The girls are unable to decide which of the two
sailors are to remain and begin to argue with one another. The
sailors then start to brawl and the girls flee. The sailors pick
themselves up to see that the girls are gone. They are crest-
fallen and somewhat wary. They go outside the bar where
they see another girl as inviting as the first. They are guarded
in their response, pretending that they have learned their
lesson and will not be trapped as they were the first time. But
their false resolve holds for only a moment, then their enthusiasm bursts through and they exit chasing the girl. The
cycle is to begin again.

Fancy Free was Robbins' first ballet and was hailed as the
advent of a major new choreographic talent. It was also the
first collaboration between the choreographer and the composer Leonard Bernstein. The ballet is highly topical and
reflected a wartime situation familiar to audiences all over the
country. It has since become less immediate in its particulars,
but retains a thematic freshness. Robbins combined boisterous
city-bred gesture along with a balletic vocabulary to create a
vibrant character dance. It has a particularly American flavour
and was the start of a line of creative development in which
Robbins successfully united contemporary American movements with the more traditional ballet steps.

Interplay

*Ballet in one act. Choreography: Robbins. Music: Morton
Gould. First performed: 'Concert Varieties', Ziegfeld Theater,
New York, 1st June, 1945, with John Kriza, Janet Reed and
Jerome Robbins. First performed Ballet Theater at the Metro-
politan Opera, New York, 17th October, 1945. Décor: Oliver*

Smith. Costumes: Irene Sharaff. With Janet Reed, John Kriza and Harold Lang.

Interplay is a sportive ballet for four couples. It is set in no particular locale but pulses with the feeling of youthful enthusiasm. The enthusiasm is reflected in the bright pull-overs that the boys and girls wear, suggesting an American high school gathering place. All of the movements are some form of 'play', 'Free Play', 'Horse Play', 'Byplay' and 'Team Play' and all have a common denominator of interplay.

'Free Play' begins with the entrance of a boy followed shortly by his three friends. They frolic and imitate children's vaulting games and then lie on the ground with legs in the air as the first girl enters. Her friends follow and the boys follow them. They form couples and compete with one another.

'Horse Play' has one boy performing a solo while the other dancers relax around the edges of the stage. He combines a tongue in cheek insouciance with great technical prowess and ends with his arms thrown out to two of the girls.

The tone changes to the blues in the third movement, 'Byplay', as the lead couple dance their *pas de deux*. It, too, has elements of the unserious mixed with the highly important. They approach their affection for one another as a form of game akin to other less important games. In the fourth movement, 'Team Play', the couples divide up into teams and move to opposite ends of the stage. They issue challenges to one another, and each tries to out-leap, out-turn or out-spin the other. At the finale the girls join in line at the front of the stage with their feet planted firmly apart. The boys rush up from the back of the stage and slide through their legs to face the audience with their heads propped on their hands. The game is over.

In this ballet Robbins continued to explore the possibilities arising from the intersection of classical dancing and the vigorous pulse of the contemporary American scene. In 1945 when this ballet was premièred, jazz was the dominant feature of popular music and jazz movements are an integral part of this ballet. Robbins has repeatedly shown great skill in adapting contemporary dance movements and integrating them into his works. *Interplay* was one of the most successful of these and was the precursor to other ballets such as *New York Export: Opus Jazz* which he created for his own company, *Ballets USA*. Robbins alone among the serious ballet choreographers has been able to bring jazz movements into ballet without compromising the essential spirit of one or the other.

Afternoon of a Faun

Ballet in one act. Choreography: Robbins. Music: Debussy. First performance of revised version New York City Ballet, City Center, New York, 14th May, 1953. Set and lighting: Jean Rosenthal. Costumes: Irene Sharaff. Dancers: Tanaquil LeClercq and Francisco Moncion.

Afternoon of a Faun is an adaptation of Nijinski's scandalous ballet about a satyr's innocent lust for a young maiden. Robbins has taken the lovely Debussy music and recreated the ballet as the encounter between two dancers in a ballet rehearsal studio.

As the piece opens, a young man is seen curled upon the floor of the studio. The wall which would ordinarily hold the floor to ceiling mirror to be found in such a practice room is missing. It is the imaginary wall which faces the audience and the ballet will develop with the dancers seeming to regard themselves in it. He slowly unfolds his body, arches his back, puts one leg and then another in the air, flexes his foot and then with a sudden movement sits upright to look at himself. He has exercised his body to get the internal feel of it and now he wants to see what he looks like. He works further in front of the mirror and then curls up resting at the front of the stage at the left.

A soft wind makes the gauze walls of the studio flutter and a girl enters. She adjusts her simple practice costume and proceeds to luxuriate in the feel of her own body. The boy starts up and looks at her in the 'mirror'. She sees him and retreats to the supporting *barre* to begin a serious and non-frivolous warm up. He stands behind her and they begin their *pas de deux*. The girl maintains the innocence of the situation by never looking at the boy except for his reflection in the 'mirror'. Her attempts to do this lead to complicated and quietly desperate turns of the head that add tension to this softly-stated ballet. After they have been dancing for a while they kneel down and the boy kisses her cheek. She continues to look at him in the 'mirror' but touches her cheek reflectively and rises to leave on point. The spell has been destroyed. He lies down again and the ballet is over.

Faun is one of Robbins' most masterful creations. In it he has fused the restraint of the classic ballet vocabulary with other more obviously expressive movements. For the girl, the classical steps are a form of protection and a way for her to retreat from the advances of the boy who pursues her. Whenever she feels threatened in any way she assumes one of the classic positions and thereby erects a wall of reserve between herself and his presence. It is as if she were saying to him that she has really come to the studio for serious work and not for a romantic adventure.

There is a softness and hush in the air as the couple dance. It is a moment where the outside world is forgotten and two beautiful human bodies enter into a movement relationship. When the world (in the form of the boy's kiss) breaches the curtain, the dance is over and she must leave. Robbins has created more ambitious ballets, but none more perfect than this *pas de deux*.

The Concert

Ballet in one act. Choreography: Robbins. Music: Chopin, with orchestral arrangements by Hershy Kay. Costumes: Irene Sharaff. First performed New York City Ballet, City Center, New York, 6th March, 1956.

The Concert portrays a series of images suggested, to those attending a concert, by the pieces played. At the opening a pianist is seated on stage performing. A group enters individually each holding a collapsible chair. An enthusiastic woman sits as near as possible to the piano, a serious young man sits studiously down, a bored man with teeth firmly fixed on a cigar enters with his wife who is intent on improving his mind by exposure to good music. Others enter to complete the group.

As the music changes a woman rises in a dream ecstasy to do a solo, a man imitates a runner attempting to finish the course distance in the time it takes to play the Minute Waltz. There is some difficulty with seat numbers and an usher shifts many of the group around to accommodate a latecomer. The man with the cigar imagines how he will murder his wife and ends up injuring himself with a knife.

In addition to these pantomime sketches several dances of great humour were included as well as a serious solo for one girl. Of the humorous dances one which had a special delicacy was performed by six girls in flowing tunics. One girl was subtly out of phase with the others and managed to destroy the rhythm of their dance with cumulative missed cues. She would start early or perhaps later than the others and in trying to synchronize her movements obliterated any semblance of unity.

During the *Butterfly Study* all of the listeners to the concert emerged with filmy wings and scampered around the stage with clumsy and inept lightness. One by one they returned to their places and resumed the poses and expressions which they had at the beginning of the piece. As the music stops they applaud politely and return to the everyday.

The Concert underwent several revisions after Robbins originally created it. Basically, however, it has a loose enough structure to permit additions and deletions without harming the tone of the piece. An abbreviated version of it was even prepared for commercial television broadcasting which captured much of the original wit. Robbins took the commonplace situation of dreams arising from music and imaginatively showed the impact of Chopin on a series of ostentatiously ordinary concert-goers. The humour arose from the contrast between their civilian appearance and their dream idealizations. It is a piece permeated with gentle laughter and does not display the knife-edge of cutting satire.

Dances at a Gathering

Choreography: Robbins.   Music: Chopin.   Lighting: Thomas Skelton. First performed New York City Ballet, New York, 22nd May, 1969 (previewed at a Gala, 8th May, 1969).

Dances at a Gathering is a ballet for five boys and five girls. Each is identified only by the colour of the costume worn. The score is a selection of Chopin's piano music played by a pianist on stage.

At the beginning a single man enters an area that suggests an open field and walks slowly around looking up at the sky. There is only one piece of stage decoration and that is some vague cloud formations projected on the back cloth. The man lifts his hand and makes an arc in the air. His gesture combines greeting and curiosity. A couple enters and dances a playful duet, another couple performs a more serious dance. A spritely solo is danced by the first girl and then is followed by a strong-limbed aggressive dance by the man from the second couple.

As the ballet develops the combinations of dancers increase and a *pas de trois* follows the *pas de deux*. The dancers are introduced slowly, almost casually. They dance with a variety of partners rather than confining themselves to just one person. The momentum of the dance slowly accelerates until finally all of the dancers are on stage and their enthusiasm culminates in a spectacular *pas de six*, at the conclusion of which the three boys line up diagonally across the stage and the girls one by one are passed down the line. The first boy performs a simple lift on to the second who makes a more spectacular lift on to the third. The daring of the lifts increases until the last girl who comes through is thrown into the air executing a turn to be caught by the last boy.

Each of the dancers has a distinct personality which is

developed through the various combinations in which they are involved. At the end the man who came out first returns alone and kneels down to run his hand meditatively across the earth. All of the others join him and walk forward toward the front of the stage where they sweep their heads from right to left as if following the flight of something passing by. They form couples and walk slowly off.

The ballet is the production of a mature sensibility in sure possession of the craft of dancing and confident in its own inventive powers. *Dances at a Gathering* arises from that area in which classic dance intersects with character dancing. It is highly expressive and also highly conscious of the craft of disciplined movement which is classic dancing. One is made aware of the play which exists between the two as the dancers execute steps almost puckishly at times. At one point the lead man stands stage centre and performs a basic *barre* exercise a couple of times and then rockets off to continue his variation. The ballet lasts for about an hour and it is a tribute to Robbins' inventiveness that the time slips by imperceptibly.

There is no story to be found in *Dances* except perhaps the story of a group of people living a portion of their lives before us. The ballet opens with a glance at the sky that contains a welcoming wonderment. At the end a glance at the sky or something transitory in it lends a note of sadness to the ballet. Despite the fact that there is no narrative element to the work, the dancers come alive as persons in a way rarely seen in the ballet repertory. Most of the time they appear to be playing roles while in this ballet they appear to be playing themselves. The entire piece shows Robbins pushing further and further along the path of choreographic exploration that he trod in his first ballet *Fancy Free*. It is the problem of resolving how to pour the American experience into a European dancing vessel.

JOHN TARAS (b. 1919)

John Taras is almost impossible to talk to about choreography,

his own or anyone else's. He says with a disarming smile,
'Well, you know I'm a ballet master and not a choreographer.'
It is only partly true. Taras, who was assistant ballet master
with New York City Ballet, has unceasingly re-staged the work
of George Balanchine for ballet companies all over the world
and, with great skill, rehearsed the company in the Balanchine
repertory. Over the years, he has created a considerable
body of his own work, much of it for companies based in
Europe where he became ballet master at the Paris Opéra in
1969.

Under his favourite nom de plume of ballet master, he was
virtually the artistic director of the Grand Ballet du Marquis de
Cuevas for a decade during the 1950s and worked extensively
with French dancers and companies, producing a string of
opera *divertissements* and *pièces d'occasion*, in addition to other
somewhat more substantial ballets. One of his best known
works, *Piège de Lumière*, dates from this period and has
entered the repertory of many companies including London's
Festival Ballet and New York City Ballet. While it is Taras'
most publicized ballet it is by no means the strongest work he
has created. It is in a sense the distillation of a chic choreographic sleight-of-hand which achieves its effect by means of
production values rather than the inherent interest of the
choreography itself. The story is exotic, that of penal colony
prisoners and the egalitarian society they form in the forest
depths and their light trap invented to ensnare rare butterflies
for resale to eager lepidopterists. Costuming is brilliant and
the choreography features some incredibly difficult catches,
including one in which the kneeling male has his back to the
female and must catch her as she launches herself on to his
waiting back. But the impression that one has is of decorative
costuming and scenery rather than biting incisive invention.
The work by which he must be reckoned is that which was
produced before and after his association with the de Cuevas
Ballet.

It is unusual that Taras, who was born in New York, has
displayed a proclivity for thematic material that has best
found its expression in a style of dancing imbued with a

French sensibility and sensitivity for emotional nuance. His best work has been with rules and regulations that could be transgressed, but only at the expense of some emotional difficulty. He has often favoured such structured settings for his work. At one time or another he has chosen the cloister (*Arcade*), the prison (*Piège de Lumière*), the social sport, tennis, with its elaborate rules of conduct (*Jeux*), or even the burial field (*Shadow'd Ground*), to work out the destinies of his characters.

His most recent work for New York City Ballet, *Haydn Concerto*, featured two couples whose relations were worked out on what appeared to be an after-the-hunt gambol. The younger of the two couples effortlessly fell in rapturous infatuation with one another and the senior woman of the older couple found emotional interest in one of the retainers who attended the principals when they returned to the household. Their *pas* was replete with hints of social lines being crossed, but with the consequences put firmly in the background for the rapturous moment.

Taras has an uncanny sense for bringing out the latent conflicts in a situation and then exploring them at his leisure. One of his finest pieces to date was his re-telling of the original Nijinski ballet *Jeux*, with its evocative Debussy score. The time is late afternoon in the country. Two girls, who have more than a passing interest in one another, are surprised by the arrival of the young man with whom they have been playing tennis. His presence sets loose a host of competitive feelings which eventually destroy their own idyll. The air is heavy with portents of summer lightning and social uncertainty. Nothing is ever stated directly but is framed by being alluded to indirectly.

For his serious ballets, Taras is a painstaking workman who moves slowly and carefully and consequently his output of them has been relatively modest. At one time he worked for a year reading the ancillary correspondence between the original collaborators on *Parade* as preparation for his own proposed ballet utilizing the same Satie score. It was a bitter disappointment not to have been able to secure the rights to the music.

Almost alone among the choreographers who have worked with New York City Ballet, he has been concerned with the total production of his ballets from the choreography down to the costumes and set framing the action. It is once again attributable to a Gallic conception of presentation that demands choreography to be well dressed in order to be fully enjoyed. It is difficult to place John Taras' position in the spectrum of contemporary ballet, but it is clear that he possesses a finely honed sensibility that is unique among the current group of American choreographers.

Designs With Strings

Ballet in one act. Choreography: Taras. Music: Tchaikovsky, Theme and Variations from Trio in A Minor. Décor: George Kirsta. First performed Metropolitan Ballet, Edinburgh, Scotland, 6th February, 1948. Later staged for numerous companies, including American Ballet Theater, Royal Danish Ballet, London's Festival Ballet.

Designs With Strings is a plotless ballet for four girls and two boys that begins and ends in a silhouetted and motionless group pose. As the music begins, the dancers weave in and out among one another slowly, remaining anonymous as they are only seen in outline until the lights come up. On the fully lit stage, the group breaks in half with one boy and two girls on stage while the other trio leaves. They dance in a wistful mood and are then rejoined by the other three who add a more vivacious dash to the movement. Together the six dance at a fast accelerated pace.

A boy and girl dance a casual *pas de deux* after the others have made their exit. They find themselves alone with one another, not by design, but by accident, and dance with a playfulness and not with intense passion. This is followed by a *pas de trois* with another girl and two boys. It is in a more mature mood. There is a conflict seen in the boy who danced with both girls. The other dancers return and it becomes apparent that the situation has changed between all of them since the innocent start of the dance. The girl from the *pas de deux* tries to put her arms around the boy she had danced with, but he slips away and joins the other dancers. She follows him and the group reforms the same reposeful formation which they had at the beginning.

This was one of Taras' earliest ballets and the only work of his dating from the 1940s that is still in the active repertory. It announces some of the characteristics that are to be seen throughout his mature work. It has a modish and deft stylization and places its hero in a triangular relationship torn between two girls. Taras is fond of three-sided relations and used them again and again in such works as *Jeux*, and *Piège de Lumière* where the convict and the giant butterfly contend for the rarest female butterfly. The ballet makes imaginative use of the lovely Tchaikovsky score and shows Taras at his most skilful in handling the delicate and complex relations of this group of six people.

Ebony Concerto

Ballet in three movements. Choreography: Taras. Music: Stravinsky. Décor: David Hays. First performed New York City Ballet at New York City Center, 7th December, 1960, with Patrica McBride and Arthur Mitchell. The ballet was danced in practice costume.

Ebony Concerto is a realization of Stravinsky's score for clarinet and orchestra which was dedicated to band leader Woody Herman. The ballet was first produced as part of a 'Jazz Concert'. Four different choreographers each created a work, using totally independent scores. Of the four works prepared for the evening only Balanchine's *Ragtime* and Taras' *Ebony Concerto* have survived.

The piece opens with the principal couple and the small corps silhouetted against the cyclorama. It was an effect which Taras had already worked with in *Designs With Strings*. The opening movement is danced entirely in silhouette, making effective use of the depersonalization of the dancers to reflect the jazz rhythms of the score. The second movement for the lead male and female is an apache-like *pas de deux*. The final movement is again for the ensemble with a driving rhythmic intensity. There is no story, merely the reflection of the sound in spatial terms.

The work creates a hard-boiled ambiance. What warmth exists in the piece is understated compared to the sheer energy of the dancers reacting to the virtuoso score. Stravinsky, who was an admirer of clarinettist Woody Herman, and his band, wrote the music to combine a classic *concerto grosso* form with contemporary jazz accents. Taras reflected the accents of the pulsing score particularly effectively in the opening and closing movements. The dancers combined an all-out assault on space with a closely-reined emotional reserve. It is, like *Designs With Strings*, a plotless ballet, but it contains the hint of an underworld sub-culture with its own sense and set of values. The tension in the score, which links a clarinet soloist skittering around and through the formal structure of the form, found a sympathetic ear in John Taras.

Jeux

Ballet in one act. Choreography: Taras. Music: Debussy. Décor: Raoul Pène du Bois. Lighting: Jules Fisher. First performed New York State Theater, 28th April, 1966, with Edward Villella, Allegra Kent and Melissa Hayden.

Jeux begins in the late afternoon in which two women and a man have been playing tennis. The setting is a secluded area near a still pond. Two girls greet one another. The first is dressed in a short skirt and the other wears a cap and fashionably tailored trousers. They dance a duet that begins casually but develops into a closer relationship. Suddenly they are interrupted by a tennis ball which bounces across the stage. A young man runs in after it. There is some question as to whether the ball accidentally rolled in that direction or whether the young man deliberately threw it there.

He dances with one of the girls while the other watches with growing dismay. She comes out from behind the tree where she had concealed herself and implores the other girl not to become so involved with the man. The first girl does not choose to remain away from him. The second girl tears off her cap in anger allowing her long hair to flow down her back dramatically. She has destroyed her faintly boyish look. The man is attracted to her and they dance. The triangular relationship now deepens with each of the three reaching out to one or the other of the group at various times. The lighting now has dimmed to indicate that the afternoon has ripened into dusk and firefly lights are seen on the pond. The involvement of the parties has reached a peak. Another ball bounces across the stage breaking the mood. The young man runs off after it and after a moment's hesitation the first girl dashes after him. The second girl is left alone.

Jeux is the second ballet in the repertory of the New York City Ballet which is an updated version of a Nijinski original. The other is Robbins' *Afternoon of a Faun*. Both choreographers have kept the essential relations of the principals but have created totally new works. *Jeux* capitalizes on the social setting of an afternoon of play suddenly interrupted by the intrusion of a sensual element. The two girls are first seen in what appears to be a secluded spot where they can be together. But their budding idyll is destroyed by the implicit demands of another of the players. The young man brings with him the social situation from which they were attempting to withdraw. Taras creates a particularly effective trio for them in which they are closely linked but each appears to be responding to the person just beyond the one closest to him. It is one of Taras' most accomplished works and tells the story of this casual *ménage à trois* with great subtlety and precision.

GLEN TETLEY (b. 1926)

Like other American dancers, Glen Tetley studied both

classical ballet and modern dance technique, appearing with, among others, Martha Graham, American Ballet Theater and Jerome Robbins' Ballets USA. He made his first choreography, *Pierrot Lunaire*, for his own company in New York in 1962, and in 1963 went to work for two years as dancer and choreographer with the Nederlands Dans Teater, for whom he staged *The Anatomy Lesson* in 1964. Subsequently he created seven more ballets for this company, including *Field Mass*, *The Game of Noah*, *Sargasso*, *Arena* and *Circles*; in 1966 he staged *Ricercare* for American Ballet Theater and *Mythical Hunters* for the Batsheva Dance Company of Israel. The next year he began an association with the Ballet Rambert, mounting *Pierrot Lunaire*, *Ricercare*, and *Freefall* (originally produced in Salt Lake City in 1967) and creating *Ziggurat* and *Embrace Tiger and Return to Mountain* especially for that company.

Pierrot Lunaire

Ballet in one act: Choreography: Tetley. Music: Schoenberg. Décor: Reuben Ter-Arutunian. First performed Glen Tetley Company, New York, 5th May, 1962. First performed Ballet Rambert, Richmond Theatre, London, 26th January, 1967.

'In the antiquity of the Roman theatre began the battle of the white clown of innocence with the dark clown of experience. Pierrot and Brighella are their lineal descendants and Columbine their eternal pawn.' Tetley's programme note serves to introduce us to the theme of his ballet; at curtain rise we see Pierrot swinging high on the white tower of scaffolding that forms the set. He is wide-eyed, innocent, a dreamer, a moody introverted clown, and when Columbine appears he is seized with delight; her appearance is brief, but she returns with a clothes-line which she gives him to hold. He is in an ecstasy of delight but when he tries to kiss her, and then puts a hand on her breast, she slaps him, sends the laundry line whisking back into the wings, and leaves him. She returns again, cloaked, and Pierrot grovels, abjectly adoring. The third character appears, announced by the dark sonorities of the eighth poem, *Nacht*. It is Brighella, clothed in sombre colours; Pierrot plays with him, but Brighella soon achieves a dominance, and Pierrot's innocence is gradually destroyed by this confrontation with experience. Brighella now brings on Columbine, dressed in brilliant scarlet, and they tease and taunt Pierrot, and eventually attach cords to him so that he becomes their puppet. Next Brighella strips Pierrot of his white costume and puts it on over his own dark clothes; Pierrot lies defeated on the ground while Columbine and Brighella dance around the stage. He struggles to his feet and staggers across the stage to lean on the proscenium arch while the other two watch his suffering from the vantage point of Pierrot's tower. Pierrot mimes some fighting gestures, then lies exhausted on the ground. Slowly he gets to his feet, and climbs up his tower to join Brighella and Columbine at the top. They offer him back his hat, but he casts it aside and in a final gesture of strength he puts his arms round Columbine and Brighella, pressing their heads to his breast.

Pierrot Lunaire is an extraordinary and moving ballet – and an amazing first work. As with every Tetley ballet, it is full of allusions and analogies – not least with *Petrushka*, but whereas Fokine's creation triumphed only in death, Tetley's comes to terms with life and its torments. This Pierrot is the eternal victim, the dreamer forever wounded by experience, and the theme of Tetley's work is the education he undergoes at the hands of the bitch Columbine and the tough, worldly-wise Brighella. At the last, after being mocked and derided, after being stripped of everything including the identity of his traditional dress, with his domain (the Tower) invaded and taken over, he can still find strength to forgive and to accept the world.

The ballet gains enormously from the beauty of Ter-Arutunian's décor; Pierrot's white suit, white tower, white setting are wonderfully evocative of the moon-lit world of Schoenberg's *Pierrot*, and the costumes are admirable in shape.

Tetley uses the score with remarkable freedom, ignoring most of the Beardsleyesque imagery of Albert Giraud's poems, but he associates everything 'white' in the Commedia dell' Arte with Pierrot, and the dark elements and the feminine references serve respectively to identify Brighella and Columbine.

The Anatomy Lesson

Ballet in one act. Choreography: Tetley. Music: Marcel Landowsky. Décor: Nicolas Wijnberg. First performed Nederlands Dans Theater, The Hague, 28th January, 1964. Jaap Flier as the Man.

The ballet was inspired by Rembrandt's famous painting; at curtain rise we see seven men in dark clothes standing before a high, circular building with part of its upper stories cut away. The central building is turned round and the men take their places in the grouping round the body on the anatomy table that we know from the painting. The Man's body now moves down from the table and bends on to the ground; after a brief moment of activity, the Man returns to the table. The doctors cover the body with a cloth, then hold the cloth so that the body forms a pietà shape as if freshly deposed from the cross of his life. The Man, bare save for a loin cloth, now relives parts of his life; children pass, playing together, and he mingles with them – though never able to touch or communicate with them. His mother and wife appear and dance with him – he holds his mother in his arms so that she seems like a wooden Flemish Madonna – and throughout the ballet stalk two of the doctors who are now identified as the Prosecutor and his Assistant, inexorable judges of the Man's life.

In the final section, a procession of black-dressed men with women carrying gold laurel wreaths moves across the stage and takes up a position in the auditorium of the anatomy-theatre. They then leave the stage, and the body rests entirely alone on the dissecting table under its sheet.

In an illuminating BBC television version of *The Anatomy Lesson* Glen Tetley introduced the work with a brief commentary in which he talked of his desire to make this, his first ballet for the Nederlands Dans Teater, a specifically Dutch work. The movements of the children seen in the early moments of the Man's story were inspired by Dutch tiles; other groupings and poses found their inspiration in Dutch art. The ballet is a bold and extremely successful piece of theatre-craft; Tetley dissolves time, compressing incidents to extract maximum impact, exploring the tragedy of the Man on the table – to whom he gives a much more universal implication – with a wonderful compassion. The ballet is dominated by a superb performance of the central role by Jaap Flier.

Freefall

Ballet in one act. Choreography and décor: Tetley. Music: Max Schubel, 'Concerto for Five Instruments'. First performed Repertory Dance Theater, Salt Lake City, 1967. First performed London, Ballet Rambert, Jeannetta Cochrane Theatre, 13th November, 1967.

Freefall's title implies matters of weightlessness, of parachutists tumbling through the air, of bodies turning and falling; and Tetley's concern seems to be with setting his five dancers falling, and then observing what happens to them. They move and turn, buoyed up on strong currents, or straining against them, their movements by turns slow, languorous or fiercely energetic. They can seem like figures in a dream, having the curious lethargy of dream walkers; the designs that Tetley has devised, with their use of gleaming white and transparent polythenes, insist on the strangeness of the dancers and their surroundings. The action starts with a mutually complementary duet between a man and a woman (doubled by a reflection behind a sheet of perspex). They are somewhat encumbered as to boots and transparent jackets, but once these are removed, and the two men and three women of the cast are fully involved, there follows a sequence of solos and *pas de deux* that offer intensely stimulating choreographic ideas. There are a series of erotic partnerings that explore the dynamic and dramatic possibilities of male/female, male/male,

female/female duets, in which Tetley makes fascinating use of
the possibilities of movement slowed down by weightlessness,
and by the emotional as well as physical implications of the
title – never has the idea of 'falling for someone' been so
literally shown. But there is hatred, too, in these encounters,
and a tense dramatic quality; at times the ballet seems to
undergo a punning alteration from *Freefall* to *Free for All*.

Technically the ballet offered a remarkable view of Tetley's
ability to combine – to fuse is perhaps a better word – elements
from both parts of his own training – academic and Modern
Dance – to make a language that is entirely communicative
of his themes, and remarkably beautiful.

Ziggurat

Ballet in one act. Choreography: Tetley. Music: Stockhausen,
'Gesäng der Junglinge' and part of 'Kontakte'. Décor: Nadine
Baylis. First performed Ballet Rambert, Jeannetta Cochrane
Theatre, London, 20th November, 1967.

Ziggurats are those Assyrian brick structures which can still
be seen in Mesopotamia, rising like pyramids to the sky. In
essence they were temple-towers whose summit was the
meeting of earth and heaven, a place where man could most
nearly offer his sacrifice to God. For Glen Tetley, as his
programme note to this ballet suggests, they are also the
Hanging Gardens of Babylon, the stairway of Jacob's Dream,
and the Tower of Babel. All these ideas can be discerned in
Ziggurat, which like many of Tetley's ballets, offers cross-
references, allusions, dovetailed incidents that elide present
and past, *then* and *now*.

Ziggurat's theme is – arguably, since interpretation of this
kind of modern work is often a very personal thing – Man's
search for the Divine, his concept of a god, and his rare and
terrifying contacts with a deity, his terror if he finds that there
is no God, his attempts even to bolster up his faith by bolster-
ing up an image of a deity. At curtain rise we are presented

with seven men, naked save for a covering of fine looped thread, grouped in front of a structure of metal scaffolding, a temple in which sits the God-figure, the whole dominated by a large metal frame above. The men's pose recalls Assyrian frescoes, but their movements – agonized, terror-struck, a series of frantic dashes, mouthings of nausea with fingers to lips – denote a horror, a flight from dreadful pressures that implies, perhaps, the dilemma of modern man crushed beneath the ziggurats of his sky-scrapers. Their silent screams, frantic stamping and slappings, brief sequences of turns, – man seen in the terms of animals in flight from disaster – subside as the Godhead keels over sideways. The men place the fallen divinity on their reclining bodies, trying to revive him; as they carry him off stage a white screen descends and tilts over the stage, and the men remove the temple structure to the side of the stage and crouch within it.

A series of colour-film projections are now shown on the screen and on the white back-drop (the stage otherwise bare to the back walls of the theatre) and there follows a series of dances for one of the men and a group of white-clad girls. This gives way to a duet between the man and the Divinity, who returns to show the contrast between human and super-human. The stage is now bathed in red light and another of the men rolls a sheet of polythene across the stage to form a shining path on which he dances and where one of the women meets him in a voluptuous duet. After another group dance for men and women, the Divinity returns to join another man in the most beautiful section of the work, a struggle between Jacob and the Angel which is also a commentary on the basic father/son relationship. The women go off, the screens disappear, the scaffolding throne for the God is brought back, the men return, alone once more, and the God is propped back into his temple as the men assume the agonized poses of the work's beginning, and the curtain falls.

Ziggurat is by no means an 'easy' work; it is densely written, packed with imagery that speaks directly to us without any literary or dramatic undertones, though movement and gesture are immensely dramatic in themselves.

Tetley's view of man suffering and disoriented, still like an animal in his desperate frenzy, is moving, and most movingly expressed in dance.

Embrace Tiger and Return to Mountain

Ballet in one act. Choreography: Tetley. Music: Morton Subotnick. Décor: Nadine Baylis. First performed Ballet Rambert, Jeannetta Cochrane Theatre, London, 21st November, 1968.

T'ai-Chi is a system of Chinese callisthenics, 37 exercises in 'shadow-boxing' that were invented 1400 years ago, originally as a system of self-defence, in which an attacker's energy was used to confound him by a delicate appreciation of balance and falls. It later developed into a method of physical and emotional training, intended to create mental as well as physical well-being. Tetley saw a film showing Chinese performing these exercises, and was so intrigued that he studied the method and in *Embrace Tiger and Return to Mountain* (which is the name of the 17th of the exercises) he has taken *T'ai-Chi* as the starting point for a ballet. But this is no piece of mock-oriental knick-knackery; Tetley is inspired by the idea of a totally alien code of muscular and intellectual self-betterment brought into contact with western ideas of dance activity. In *Embrace Tiger*, coolness of manner, reserve – the cliché of the inscrutable oriental – are important, as is the electronic score by Subotnick – *The Silver Apples of the Moon* – music as cool and distant as its title.

The fusing of these elements, their translation into Tetley's own very personal movement idiom, makes for a ballet that seems both remote and immediate.

Tetley – and the ballet – starts with a basic *T'ai-Chi* exercise done by a cast of ten who pose, flex and stretch their bodies, and look very handsome in flame-shot leotards under a clear Chinese-white décor, with a silver floor that reflects light upwards and adds to the different 'feel' of the piece. The development of the ballet shows Tetley's extension of the basic attitudes of *T'ai-Chi*; as with others of his ballets, slowness and an unhurried exploration of muscular possibilities mark its style, the unfamiliar starting poses serving as a spring-board for Tetley's imagination. It is a ballet about dancers in reaction to one another both in duets and in group work; for much of the time the ballet's style has the kind of time-suspended quality seen in underwater swimming (also manifested in *Freefall*) with the same feeling of a strongly controlled muscular pulse behind it. Emotions are hinted at, balances and falls are as much a manifestation of personality as of physique, and in the closing section, where the score braces itself into a remarkable crescendo, so does Tetley's invention. Four men and a girl become involved in fierce eddyings of energy, like swimmers battling with submarine currents. But calm is at last restored; the exercises reassert their original purposeful control.

Embrace Tiger is a handsome and original work, suggesting more surely than one would have dared hope, that it is possible to make a fruitful cross-breeding between oriental and occidental attitudes to movement; best of all, it abounds in freshness of imagery.

ROBERT JOFFREY (b. 1930)

Robert Joffrey was born of an Italian mother and an Afghan father and grew up with the unlikely American name of Abdullah Jaffa Anver Bey Khan in Seattle, Washington, a region previously undistinguished for its contributions to the world of ballet. With the summer residence of the City Center Joffrey Company in recent years it has become a magnet attracting dancing talent from the entire northwestern United States. Before establishing his own company, Joffrey, who studied both modern dance and ballet, made his début in 1949 with Roland Petit's Ballet de Paris and later performed extensively with May O'Donnell's modern dance company. With such a diverse blending of background and dance

experience his choreographic approach has shown an un-
surprisingly eclectic cast to it.

The dominant character of Joffrey's wide-ranging ballets is
tasteful adaptation of *found* thematic materials. More often
than not he realizes the potential of a situation rather than
creating a ballet out of a rigorous personal frame of reference.
The ability to respond to so broad a range of experience has
enabled Joffrey to assimilate and recreate in ballets the most
contemporary phenomena – a 'rock and roll' mating ritual in
Astarte – or the delicacy of Near Eastern formality in *Gamelan*.
Often his inventive skill has been harnessed to produce ballets
which transform pictorial impressions into living works, such
as the Romantic era lithograph of Taglioni, Cerrito, Grahn
and St Léon which Joffrey enlivened into *Pas des Déesses*.

While his ballets do not appear driven by a dance (that is,
non-verbal) idea, his approach to the material he has selected
for treatment is consistently inventive and results in creative
ballets which are both highly original and faithful to the
initial suggestion. Joffrey's works are characterized by their
pleasing pictorial impressions and are appropriately framed in
terms of décor. Like the New York City Ballet, which preceded the Joffery Company as residents of the City Center
Theater, the younger company relies heavily on mood lighting
rather than expensive décors to set the emotional tone of its
works. Their designer, Thomas Skelton, has consistently lit
Joffrey's works with precise appreciation of their values.

The parallels between the two companies extend further
than just the light plots which both have used. Joffrey appears
to be following in Balanchine's footsteps as he creates his
company, but the timetable has been accelerated by about
fifty per cent. Joffrey established his own company in 1956
and achieved a permanent home at the City Center nine years
later in 1965 – it took Balanchine about a decade and a half to
reach the same status. New York City Ballet made a Russian
tour a dozen years after being established and Joffrey did it in
six. New York City Ballet created a summer residence for
itself four seasons after moving to its new home at State
Theater, and Joffrey did it after two seasons of residency at

its permanent home. Joffrey is a choreographer and artistic director in a hurry, and the youthful bounce of his company reflects it.

Because of the extreme diversity of Joffrey's work, it is not easy to anticipate the direction of his choreographic development. By way of contrast, before producing the mixed-media pop music extravaganza, *Astarte*, his most recent success, Joffrey's prior ballet *Gamelan* was a restrained formal piece of almost dreamlike understatement. Looking at his ballets, one is struck by the early appearance of his mature style and how little his handling of movement has changed since that time. One of his first and most successfully staged works, *Pas des Déesses* (1954) displayed a similar skill in devising movement as did *Astarte* (1968) which was conceived over a decade later. It is more enlightening to think of Joffrey's skill as having been formed early and his appreciation for the 'significant subject' as undergoing continual change. For example, *Gamelan* emerged after a tour of the Middle East and *Astarte* after Joffrey's residence in the Northwest and his subsequent exposure to the musical idiom of *raga rock* with its blend of Indian musical accents and *hard rock* rhythms.

Joffrey's output has not been particularly large compared with other choreographers, and has been restricted somewhat because of his other concerns as company administrator and teacher. In the latter role he has achieved particular acclaim both from professional dancers and pupils just beginning their training. Any dancer who has been coached by Joffrey has found the experience to be exceptionally helpful in interpreting roles. Similarly, he has a keen eye for promising young dancers and has ensured a continual flow of talented pupils into his school, and eventually, into his company.

Alone among American choreographers he has the personnel of two companies with which to work. In addition to the better known City Center Joffrey Company which bears his name, he is also the artistic director of the New York City Opera Ballet Company, for which he devises those short *divertissements* and dance movements necessary for opera production. None of the works that he has produced for the opera ballet has been of special distinction, but all have been suitable vehicles for the occasion. Membership in the 'opera' company is actually a form of apprenticeship which permits young dancers to obtain the feel of actual stage performance in small enough doses so that they are adequately equipped to appear with a full scale ballet company when their time arrives. His system is consistent with Joffrey's image of a Young Man In A Hurry, but it is a hurry that is careful, consistent and painstakingly precise.

Pas Des Déesses

Ballet in one act. Choreography: Joffrey. Music: John Field. First performed Kaufmann Auditorium, Y.M.H.A., New York, 29th May, 1954, by the Robert Joffrey Ballet.

Pas Des Déesses opens with the appearance of four dancers as they pose for a 19th-century lithograph, and closes in the same fashion, with the three ballerinas grouped around the male dancer, Arthur St Léon.

The ballet begins as the ballerinas break away from the static lithograph pose and begin to dance a short variation. St Léon comes to each in turn and invites her to dance with him. There is some suspense as he selects his first partner, the Danish ballerina Lucile Grahn. Each of the others was hoping to be chosen first. They exit hesitatingly as the first *pas de deux* begins. They cast overpolite glances at Grahn as they move out of the performing area. When they have finished the others return and do a brief reprise of their group dance. St Léon returns from escorting Grahn off, and selects Cerrito for his partner. She is a vivacious and pert dancer who lacks decorous restraint. One of the most memorable portions of their *pas de deux* comes as St Léon pulls her by the hand and she leaps into the air tucking her feet underneath her in mock surprise. After their spirited duet St Léon dances with Taglioni. He enters with her on his shoulder, and the *pas* develops with an ethereal buoyancy, reminding one of the perfection of Taglioni in *La Sylphide*. When their duet is over St Léon enters to do his solo variation which is full of the turns and jumps that were absent from the dancing of the ballerinas. At the end of this variation he leads them all to the back of the stage, gently drawing them like a team of horses. They cluster around him and the ballet ends.

Joffrey created this ballet near the start of his career as a choreographer, and immediately displayed a sense of period style that was perfectly suitable to this evocation of the Romantic ballet. The ballerinas had been rivals in their time and Joffrey chose to emphasize the humorous aspects of their competition rather than address himself to the fiercer side of their rivalry. Each of the ballerinas is exceptionally polite to the others and each subtly vies for the attention of St Léon, hoping to steal a march on her colleagues. They constantly attempt to upstage one another by prolonging their exit from the stage when the other is preparing to dance. The ballet has travelled widely in the repertory of several companies, including the Ballet Rambert, for whom Joffrey staged it the year after its première.

Gamelan

Ballet in one act. Choreography: Joffrey. Music: Lou Harrison. Décor: Willa Kim. First performed Robert Joffrey Ballet, Kirov Theatre, Leningrad, 15th October, 1963.

Gamelan, subtitled *Eight Choreographic Essays*, is the sketch of a pastel world of people whose clothes give them a faintly alien appearance. Each of the eight parts is connected by a man with a staff who performs a brief introductory variation between the dances. At the beginning he presents the entire company who then politely go off.

The first section, *Pas de Deux with Entrances and Exits*, is for the lead couple who are framed by the comings and goings of nine boys and girls. It is a device which is repeatedly used in this work. The following section, *Pas de Deux for Three*, has the male framed and gently opposed by another male who does not come too close to the couple, but remains at the edge of their area of movement. Again, in *Solo Accompanied by One*, the lead girl has a complementary figure on stage with her. Later, in *Double Solo*, the lead man will find himself similarly followed by another man. Pervading the entire ballet is a sense of gauze-covered mistiness. The dancers seem to inhabit a world which is buffered by velvet, where excess is discouraged. At the end, the entire company assembles on stage and the man with the staff draws a long flowing cloth across the front of the performing area to indicate that the ballet is over.

The designation of the ballet as *Eight Choreographic Essays* clearly indicates the choreographer's intention to discourage viewers from seeking a continuous narrative throughout the piece. Each of the movements is tied with the others by means of a common approach rather than by a logical linkage. The clothing suggests a Near Eastern but non-specific locale. The basic costume is leotard and tights in varying muted colours covered with a short garment of diaphanous material.

In *Gamelan*, Joffrey successfully creates the atmosphere of an exotic but basically sympathetic society. The work is obviously designed as a performance situation and does not make any attempt to imitate life by portraying actual situations. This ballet is art interpreting life, but opening with a parade as one might expect from performers, and then closing with the assembled company being concealed by a curtain. It has the feeling of a court entertainment. The music is imitative of the sound produced by an Indonesian percussion ensemble and contributes strongly to the mood of mysterious formality that pervades the work.

Astarte

Ballet in one act. Choreography: Joffrey. Music: Crome Syrcus. Film: Gardner Compton. Set and lights: Thomas Skelton. Costumes: Hugh Sherrer. First performed New York

City Center, 20th September, 1967, City Center Joffrey Company with Trinette Singleton and Maximiliano Zomosa.

As the ballet opens the sound of a rock and roll group is heard. Red and green coloured lights sweep over the audience and a stroboscopic light flickers on and off intermittently. A large, irregularly shaped white screen on the stage has the puffed and punched look of bread dough. Suddenly the lights stop their questing across the audience and focus on a young man seated in the stalls. He rises as if mesmerized and proceeds to walk slowly down the centre aisle towards the stage. As he ascends the stage a bank of lights flash on and off registering his passage from the normal existence into a new and special condition.

A girl in vibrantly patterned leotard and tights appears at the opposite end of the stage from him. She glows with the purple phosphorescence produced by an ultra-violet beam. He stares at her and begins to remove his outer clothing never once letting his eyes wander from her. When he has stripped down to a brief dance belt, he advances to meet her. She is aloof and they begin their *pas de deux*. At first he is awed by her and then with growing violence forces her into submission. She moves away from him and then begins her own mental assault upon his senses until she has broken him into submission. He turns from her and the screen lifts to allow him passage. He walks out of the stage area as unseen hands open doors in his path and exits on to the street behind the theatre.

During the time that he is on stage colour films from a series of projectors show images of him and the girl in street clothes and in performance costume. Groups of dancers in *discothèques* are also shown in similar gaudy clothes. When he leaves, a film of him leaving is shown. When he has completely disappeared from the theatre the performance is over.

Astarte was the Phoenician goddess of fertility and sexual love, and Joffrey updated the image to that of a contemporary sex queen with a psychedelic aura. The combination of live performers, film image, rock and roll music along with the superlative lighting design of Thomas Skelton combined to form a living mixed-means theatricality. The piece has a particularly contemporary look, assaulting the eyes and ears with the immediacy of environmental sight and sound.

At the core of the work, however, beneath all the theatrical cosmetic, is a viable and interesting *pas de deux*. It is not done in the traditional form of opening, variations and coda. For the end result of the encounter is to send the young man stunned into the street and not into a unifying coda. After the initial introductory and exploratory grappling, the young man asserts his muscular mastery and then the goddess dominates him. The effect upon him is to create dumb wonder over what has transpired. The dance is so soundly conceived, though, that other interpretations are possible and viable. The originator of the role, the late Maximiliano Zomosa, danced as if he were participating in a pagan ritual in an atavistic throwback. *Astarte* is significant in that it was the first ballet to adapt avant-garde experimentation for inclusion in the repertory of a major company.

Chapter Eight

French, Dutch and Soviet

SERGE LIFAR (b. 1905)

Born in Kiev, Lifar first saw dancing when he had occasion to watch a class at the school Bronislava Nijinska had opened in that city. He was so overwhelmed by the sight that he knew that he had to become a dancer, and joined Nijinska's classes. Barely a month later Nijinska left for Europe to assist in the Diaghilev staging of *The Sleeping Beauty*, and Lifar was left to work as best he could. Three years later Nijinska sent word to her school that the five best boys should be sent to Paris to join the Diaghilev Company. Since one of those selected had disappeared, Lifar pleaded to be the substitute, and in 1923 he arrived in Europe. His rudimentary technique doomed him at first to ferocious hard work to make up for his inadequacy, and after unflagging study with Cecchetti he started to show the beautiful style and prowess that made him one of the greatest dancers of his time. He soon attracted the attention of Diaghilev, and was featured in increasingly important roles – notably in the two Balanchine ballets, *Apollo* (1928) and *Le Fils Prodigue* (1929) – roles which indicate something of his range and qualities even then. In 1929 he made his début as a choreographer with a revival of Stravinsky's *Le Renard*, which earned considerable praise, but with the death of Diaghilev in that same year, the whole company disbanded. Lifar was then asked to stage a version of Beethoven's *The Creatures of Prometheus* at the Paris Opéra, and the success of this production led to his engagement as premier danseur and *maître de ballet* there, a post which he retained until 1959. His reign at the Opéra, and no other phrase will really convey the importance of his reputation and achievement, saw him raise the ballet company to a position of excellence that it had not known since the great days of the Romantic era. He has produced over a hundred ballets, and his work at the Opéra revitalized both the teaching and the reputation of ballet in France. In his most celebrated roles – in ballets he created for himself, like *Icare*, *Joan de Zoarissa* and *David Triomphant*, and in the classics (he was a fine Albrecht in *Giselle*) – he showed himself a performer of magnetic presence, and he worked with two of the greatest ballerine of our time at the Opéra: Yvette Chauviré and Nina Vyrubova, besides creating a fine company of dancers. Political agitation about his war-time activities to keep his company functioning led to his departure from the Opéra for two years after the Liberation in 1944, but he returned in triumph and continued there, with a brief break, until 1959. It is significant that thereafter, the Opéra ballet company has steadily declined in importance and productivity.

Noir et Blanc (Suite en Blanc)

Ballet in one act. Choreography: Lifar. Music: Lalo (from his ballet 'Namouna'). First performed Paris Opéra, 23rd July, 1943.

Suite en Blanc is a display piece, designed to show off the stars and the prowess of a fine company. Its music is taken from Lalo's beautiful score to *Namouna*, a ballet by Lucien Petipa, first staged at the Opéra in 1882, and the titles of each of the numbers are those of the original score. At the Opéra it was given against plain curtains, but with rostra on which the dancers are first seen posed at the beginning; they exit leaving three girls in long tarlatan skirts, who dance the *Siesta*. Their exit is succeeded by two men who leap on and announce the arrival of a ballerina who joins them in the *Pas de Trois*, and there then follows a *Serenade* for another ballerina plus eight *corps de ballet* girls. Next comes a *pas de cinq* for a third soloist with a quartet of men, which in turn gives way to *La Cigarette*, a ravishing solo for the chief ballerina with the rest of the women in the company grouped behind. Next comes the big male solo, a *mazurka*; then a *pas de deux* for the principal ballerina and her partner, to be succeeded by another ballerina solo for yet another star dancer, *La Flûte*; a final general dance brings the ballet to a close.

Lalo wrote the ballet score for *Namouna* within a period of four months in 1881; alas, despite the enchantment of the score, the ballet was not a success and it was taken off after fifteen performances (Debussy, then aged nineteen, was so vociferous in his enthusiasm for the work that he was forcibly ejected from the theatre). The story had to do with slave girls, pirates and true love in 17th-century Corfu. Lifar turned to the score in 1943 to make this grand show-piece of a ballet, retaining many of the titles to the numbers from Lalo's original score (hence the valse lente is still called *La Cigarette* because in the original ballet the heroine, Namouna, snatched a cigarette from the mouth of her lover: the *Siesta* is a prelude to Act II and showed freed slaves taking what must have been a well-earned rest). The *pas de deux* did not exist in the original, and was put together by Lifar from pages from the score. Lifar's most exciting quality as a choreographer has always been an heroic boldness; as a theorist and apologist for dancing he has written at great length, and in works like *Icare* (which has no score, and is danced to rhythm accompaniment from drums and other percussion) he has made fascinating experiments. *Suite en Blanc* preserves some of the finest of his inventions; it bears all the hall-marks of the Lifarian style: dancers working in parallel formation; feet placed in Lifar's own invented sixth and seventh positions; sharply held bodies; brilliant use of beaten steps. All this gives a very fair view of a notable and influential figure in the ballet of our time.

DAVID LICHINE (b. 1910)

Russian born, David Lichine made his debut with the Ida Rubinstein company and also worked with Pavlova. When the de Basil troupe was founded in 1932, he joined as soloist and created many important roles in the repertory, and also choreographed ballets, notably *Francesca da Rimini*, *Protée* and

Graduation Ball. After the war he created two fine works for Les Ballets des Champs-Elysées: *La Création* (which was performed in silence) and *La Rencontre*, which had a superb décor by Bérard, and featured Jean Babilée as Oedipus and Leslie Caron as the Sphynx. He also composed two ballets for Festival Ballet. He is married to Tatiana Riabouchinska and is now working in the USA.

His only ballet still in repertory in Britain is:

Graduation Ball

Ballet in one act. Choreography: Lichine. Music: J. Strauss (orch. Dorati). Décor: Benois. First performed de Basil Ballet Russe de Monte Carlo, Sydney, 28th February, 1940; revived for London's Festival Ballet, 9th July, 1957.

The curtain rises to reveal the gilded and chandeliered splendour of a drawing room at a girls' school in Vienna in the 1850s. The junior students are in a fine frenzy of excitement preparing for a ball at which they expect the cadets of a nearby military academy. One girl has discovered a swansdown powder-puff and as the senior girls watch amusedly, the juniors share the delights of random powdering. Suddenly they remember their manners as the Headmistress – a forbidding looking lady (though the role is often danced by a man) enters; the young cadets now make their entrance, escorted by their Headmaster, a whiskery, stiff-jointed though still gallant, General. At first both groups are on their best behaviour but soon the ice is broken – one girl with pigtails shows a lot of merriment – and before many moments the cadets and girls are waltzing joyously. Now the Headmistress and the General return for the formal entertainment: a series of *divertissement* dances. These include a Romantic *pas de deux* for La Sylphide and James; a Drummer; and a dance-step competition in which two girls try to outdo each other in brilliant turning steps. There follows a general *perpetuum mobile*, and all this time a flirtation of slightly creaking roguishness has been blossoming between the General and the Headmistress. After a final general dance the cadets take their leave and the girls go up to bed and dream of their conquests. One of the cadets and the junior girl creep back, determined to bid a last farewell – but the Headmistress is there to forestall them and they scuttle off as the curtain falls.

This is an enchanting, high-spirited ballet, with choreography bouncing sweetly along on the delights of the Strauss score. Over-enthusiastic playing can spoil it, for Lichine has created a remarkable evocation of innocent and endearing fun; but with sensitive playing it can be an unalloyed delight. It was first seen in London given by de Basil's Original Ballet Russe, to fine effect – and with one unforgettably elegant performance by Nicholas Orlov in his created role as the Drummer in the *divertissement*. Festival Ballet staged the piece with considerable care in 1957, and the Benois set, reproduced under that master's own supervision, looked particularly pleasing. The ballet also features in the repertory of the Royal Danish Ballet where it is given a loving and careful production.

ROLAND PETIT (b. 1924)

Born in France, Petit was trained at the Paris Opéra, but left in 1944 to join with Kochno and others in the foundation of Les Ballets des Champs-Elysées. For them he choreographed those early ballets – *Les Forains, Le Rendezvous, Les Amours de Jupiter, Le Jeune Homme et la Mort* – which so excited European audiences in the immediate post-war years. In 1948 he formed his own company, Les Ballets de Paris, for whom he created *Les Demoiselles de la Nuit, Carmen,* and many other works; he staged *Ballabile* for the Royal Ballet, worked in Hollywood, and formed yet another company in 1953: Les Ballets de Roland Petit for whom he created *Le Loup, Deuil en 24 heures,* etc. During the next eight years he revived this company intermittently, staging ballets like *Les Belles Damnées* (1955), *La Chambre* (1955), *La Rose des Vents* (1958), *La Dame dans la Lune* (1958), the three-act *Cyrano* (1959), *Maldoror*

(1962), among others, as well as producing shows for his wife Renée Jeanmaire, and working at La Scala, Milan. He returned to the Opéra in 1965 to stage another long work, *Notre Dame de Paris*, and in 1966 he devised *L'Eloge de la Folie* for Les Ballets de Paris; he mounted *Paradise Lost* for Fonteyn and Nureyev at Covent Garden in 1967, and *Turangalilâ* (to Messaien's symphony of that name) at the Opéra in 1968, in which year he also made a version of Scriabin's *Poème de l'Extase* for Nureyev at La Scala, Milan. In 1969 he staged another work for Fonteyn and Nureyev at Covent Garden, the appalling *Pelléas et Mélisande* – to the Schoenberg symphonic poem of the same name.

Roland Petit's theatrical gifts, which have served him equally well in the cinema and the music hall as well as on the ballet stage, have made him one of the best known choreographers of the post-war years. That his choreography rarely matches his theatricality is his tragedy; ideas abound, but their expression seems markedly inferior to the initial inspiration.

Le Jeune Homme et la Mort

Ballet in two scenes by Jean Cocteau. Choreography: Petit. Music: J. S. Bach (an orchestration of the Organ Passacaglia and Fugue in C minor). Décor: Wakhevich. First performed Les Ballets des Champs-Elysées, Théâtre des Champs-Elysées, Paris, 25th June, 1945. Jean Babilée as The Man, and Nathalie Philippart as Death.

The scene is a Paris attic, coarsely furnished, with a rope hanging from a rafter. A young painter in stained overalls reclines, smoking, on a bed awaiting the arrival of his girl friend. When she arrives, clad in a yellow dress, he leaps to greet her, but she is chilly and unresponsive to his ardour. He dances frantically, leaping over chairs and tables, but she remains coldly indifferent. Their emotional battle continues until the girl changes her tactics; she becomes gentle and affectionate, and gradually leads the man to the hanging noose of rope. She forces him to look at it, then pushes him away and rushes out of the room. Left alone the man bursts into a frenzy of anger and frustration that sends the furniture flying across the room. But the attraction of the rope is now present in his mind; he climbs on a stool, fixes the rope round his neck, kicks the stool away and with a tremor of the legs is dead.

The walls of the room fall away, showing the white-masked figure of Death walking along the rooftop. The man releases himself and joins her; she takes off her mask, places it on his face, and reveals herself as the girl he has loved. They move off together over the Paris roof-tops.

The ballet was designed as a vehicle for the prodigious gifts of Jean Babilée, a dancer whose extraordinary elevation matched his dramatic power. He made an unforgettable figure of the young man, turning and soaring with a savage neurotic energy, his body always moving with the superb grace more usually seen in the larger members of the cat family. Babilée was an unforgettably brilliant artist, whose presence in the early Champs-Elysées seasons was a guarantee of success for any work in which he appeared. The ballet was an extremely clever confection devised by Cocteau: during rehearsals the dancers worked to a jazz score, and only on the first night was the Bach *Passacaglia and Fugue* substituted: the contrast between the fierce stage action and the marvellous order of Bach's inspiration gave an extra force to the ballet.

Les Forains

Ballet in one scene. Choreography: Petit. Book: Boris Kochno. Music: Henri Sauguet. Décor: Christian Bérard. First performed Les Ballets des Champs-Elysées, Théâtre des Champs-Elysées, Paris, 2nd March, 1945. Roland Petit, Janine Charrat, Ethery Pagava.

A troupe of strolling players enter a street, pulling with them a cart loaded with all the paraphernalia of their show; behind them walks their leader carrying one of the girls. Gently he puts her down, claps his hands and the troupe burst into activity. They erect an improvised stage, take off their tattered overcoats to reveal their stage costumes. Clowns and dancers warm up, and several passers-by stand and watch. Now the stage is ready and the artists give their show: it includes a clown, an acrobat, a skirt dancer, a juggler, a girl in a hypnotic trance and a pair of Siamese twins. The magician, who is the leader of the troupe does his last trick by producing two doves which fly round the stage, and the whole company joins in a finale. There is a smattering of applause from the onlookers for the exhausted artists, and the conjurer comes round with the hat to make a collection; as he approaches the crowd they turn away and leave. The strolling players are left alone; mournfully they pack up their traps, fold up their stage and leave as sadly as they arrived.

This earliest and best of the many enchanting works that figured in the first seasons of the Ballets des Champs-Elysées is a tiny masterpiece of atmosphere. Beautifully decorated – as were all the works of those seasons – wonderfully under-stated in its effects, *Les Forains* seemed to bring alive the circus folk of Picasso's Blue period; essentially pathetic beneath the tawdry brilliance of their acts, these strolling players were presented with wit, humour and a great deal of sympathy.

Carmen

Ballet in five scenes. Choreography: Petit. Music: Bizet. Décor: Antoni Clavé. First performed Les Ballets de Paris, Prince's Theatre, London, 21st February, 1949. Renée Jeanmaire as Carmen, Roland Petit as Don José.

Scene I: A Street in Seville.

The crowd wander past, talking and occasionally dancing; interest is suddenly aroused when a girl scuttles down a staircase hotly pursued by Carmen. They bite and scratch, urged on by the crowd, and they are only interrupted by the arrival of Don José who comes to the rescue of Carmen's by-now-defeated opponent. But as he makes to arrest Carmen he is thunderstruck by her passionate beauty; instead of leading her away, he makes an assignation with her for that evening.

Scene II: The Tavern.

Don José enters the tavern which is the rendezvous for customers who seem either very bored or very lively; to the music of the *Habanera* he dances a *zapateado* of sorts, and then Carmen appears on the bar. She is lifted down and, carrying a fan, her hair and shoulders powdered with gold, she dances a fiercely erotic variation. At its finale she kneels at José's feet; he gathers her up and takes her to her bedroom. In their absence the customers dance and when Carmen and José return, they join in the dance. At its close, José envelopes Carmen in his cloak and takes her away.

Scene III: Carmen's Bedroom.

José pulls back the curtains that have shut out the morning light. He washes (drying his hands on the curtains) and Carmen lies revealed on the bed, luxuriating in her own physical beauty. José, at first seemingly indifferent to her charms, is soon excited by her body, and there follows a duet of the most explicit sexuality. As they lie exhausted, three of Carmen's friends enter and invite them into the street.

Scene IV: A Street, by night.

Carmen and José enter with their companions, preparing to rob a passer-by. Carmen gives José a dagger and then he is left alone; a drum beats ominously; José stamps to its rhythm; a cloaked man enters, José leaps on him and stabs him. Carmen and her accomplices enter, snatch the dead man's purse, and exit, with José in pursuit.

Scene V: Outside the Bull-ring.

A group of girls stand outside the Bull-ring awaiting the arrival of their hero, the Matador (called a Toreador in the ballet). When he arrives he greets the girls, but is more intrigued by the indifference of Carmen who is standing to one side. She gazes fully at him, and José, entering, sees this glance and the effect it is having on the Toreador. The Toreador leaves to enter the Bull-ring, and José rushes up accusingly to Carmen and tries to strangle her. She defies him

and they now become adversaries, each seeking to dominate
the other. Their *pas de deux* is a duel to the death, and it is
José who contrives to stab Carmen. She dies in his arms, as
hats tossed from the arena fall at his feet.

Carmen created a frenzy of excitement when it was first
staged that has never really died down. Petit's most famous
ballet, it is far from being his best, but its bravura, the passion
and almost clinical detail of its love duets, Clavé's superb sets
as well as the magnificent performances of Jeanmaire and Petit
as the lovers, have earned it a place in ballet history. The
choreography is rarely memorable but it is more than com-
pensated by the superb stagecraft that informs the piece.

Le Loup

*Ballet in one act. Choreography: Petit. Book: Jean Anouilh
and Georges Neveux. Music: Henri Dutilleux. Décor: Carzou.
First performed Ballets de Paris, Théâtre de l'Empire, Paris, 17th
March, 1953. Roland Petit as the Wolf, Violette Verdy a. the
Bride.*

Scene I: A forest glade near a church.

At curtain rise we see a forest setting with a caravan at one
side where a wolf-trainer and a gypsy girl are demonstrating
to a crowd of peasants how a man can be turned into a wolf.
They perform the trick on a peasant boy, having already shown
the trick with a Wolf-man. A bridal procession enters on the
way to a church; the Groom is attracted to the Gipsy Girl,
and the Wolf-trainer changes him into a Wolf and then
restores him to his orginal shape. So strong are the Gipsy
Girl's charms that the Groom creeps from the church to be
with her, and the Trainer contrives to substitute his Wolf-man
for the Groom. The young Bride is thus married to him
without realizing the deception, and she leads him back to
her house.

Scene II: Outside the house.

Amid general rejoicings, the Bride dances with the Wolf-man whom she thinks is her husband; suddenly she is made aware of the Wolf-man's true nature. At first horrified, she gradually feels compassion and love for him, and when the Trainer and the Gipsy Girl bring back her real Bridegroom, she rejects him. The assembled guests are shocked at this, and separate the pair, but they flee into the woods, pursued by the crowd.

Scene III: A forest.

The Wolf and Girl rush through the forest with the hunt in full pursuit. The villagers finally corner the pair; armed with rakes and spears they attack the Wolf-man, and stab him savagely. The girl rushes forward to protect him and is killed too. The villagers bear away the dead girl, and the Wolf-trainer drags off the corpse of the Wolf.

The ballet starts with the advantage of a wonderfully imaginative libretto and some of the most beautiful designs of the post-war years – Carzou's spiky forest scene and handsome costuming as well as the horrifying shapes of the rakes and farm implements that are used to kill the lovers. The score is cinematic stuff, and Petit's choreography rarely explores the emotional and pathetic possibilities of the tale to the full. Like so many of his ballets, though, the intensity of his theatrical vision is very effective.

MAURICE BEJART (b. 1928)

Born in Marseilles, Béjart was trained in his native city and in Paris, and danced with several companies – notably Mona Inglesby's International Ballet and the Royal Swedish Ballet. He formed his first company, Les Ballets de l'Etoile, in Paris, but in 1957 it was re-named Le Ballet Théâtre de Paris, and for these two companies he made some thirty ballets – notably *Symphonie Pour un Homme Seul*, to a *musique concrète* score by Pierre Henry. In 1960 he was invited to direct the ballet at the Théâtre Royale de la Monnaie in Brussels, and this formed the company which he still directs: Les Ballets du XX siècle. For them he has mounted nearly forty works, as well as staging a version of *Le Renard* and producing *The Damnation of Faust* for the Paris Opéra. Béjart is concerned with a total theatre concept of the dance: his lengthy stagings – of such works as Beethoven's 9th Symphony, his *Messe Pour le Temps Présent* and the *Four Sons of Aymon* – have earned him rapturous acclaim in certain circles on the continent, and vast audiences. His few ballets seen in London some years ago – in particular a stunningly obvious realization of *Le Sacre du Printemps* – are probably no longer any proper guide to his creativity, which has made him the most discussed figure of ballet's avant-garde on the continent. His 1964 staging of *The Damnation of Faust* at the Paris Opéra and of Flaubert's *Temptation of St Anthony* for Barrault's company in 1967 have also added to his reputation as a stage producer.

He is represented in the British repertory only by Western Theatre Ballet's production of *Sonate à Trois*.

Sonate à Trois

Ballet in one act. Choreography: Maurice Béjart, based on 'Huis Clos' by Jean-Paul Sartre. Music: Bartok (Sonata for Two Pianos and Percussion). First performed Ballets de l'Etoile, Essen, April, 1957.

A man and two women find themselves trapped in an hotel room which they cannot leave; love is impossible between them since their desires are a horrifying circle in which each is in pursuit of another who loves the third member of their trio. The room and their relationships are their Hell.

Béjart's realization of Sartre's *ronde infernale* is done with commendable simplicity; the room is bare save for three chairs, the dancers wear simple day clothes; it is their passions and anguish which must occupy our attentions. With three strong interpreters – and with Western Theatre Ballet it has always been well cast – *Sonate à Trois* has a vulgar efficiency, though its choreographic manner seems over-stressed and obvious.

A NOTE ON DUTCH BALLET

Each of the two leading ballet companies in Holland boasts a gifted young Dutch choreographer, and although the expansion of ballet in Holland is very much a post-war manifestation, the liveliness of the contemporary dance scene there is witness to the seriousness of much of the creativity.

The more experimental of the two companies – Nederlands Dans Theater – has made a great name for itself during the ten years of its existence, thanks to the complete modernity of its creative policies, the excellence of its dancers and the richness of its choreographic output. The company aims at producing ten new ballets each year – a phenomenal achievement which it maintains with seeming ease – thanks to the very considerable gifts of its two artistic directors and choreographers: Hans van Manen (b. 1932) and Benjamin Harkavy (b. 1930), with additional works created by Glen Tetley (*q.v.*) during his years with the company, and by several other distinguished modern choreographers. In 1969 Harkavy left the company to become joint director of the Harkness Ballet in New York, his place in Holland being taken by Glen Tetley.

The Dutch National Ballet is altogether different in character and aspirations; it is a large company with a large repertory that ranges from the classics and Fokine repertory, to revivals of famous modern works as well as creations by its own principal choreographer, Rudi van Dantzig, among others.

HANS VAN MANEN (b. 1932)

Solo for Voice I

Ballet in one act. Choreography: Hans van Manen. Music: John Cage. Décor: Jan van der Wal. First performed Nederlands Dans Theater, Circus Theatre, Scheveningen, Holland, 13th December, 1968.

The cast of this ballet numbers three: a female singer and two dancers. The motive force of this ten-minute work is the soprano who, holding a microphone, moves about the stage 'singing' (if that is the word) a gibberish score by John Cage, which seems more like a cadenza for voice in its free-form structure than anything else. The dancers are seen in a *pas de deux*, and it is the particular distinction of the ballet that their actions seem inspired – even created – by the vocalizing of the soprano. The voice is an integral part of the choreography; it seems to wind itself round the dancers, urging and goading and cajoling them in their amorous duet, as if charting out the course they must follow. At the end the dancers leave the stage and the singer retires; the effect of the ballet is exciting and original.

Van Manen's necessarily very considerable output of ballets (necessary because the economics of Nederlands Dans Theater demands a prodigious schedule of new ballets each year) includes a remarkable series of plotless pieces that offer a novel view of dance as emotion, as mirror of man's passions and fears. The shape of their dramatic structure, their interior logic is dictated by his feeling for emotional truth revealed in movement. In *Three Pieces* (1968) he treats of adolescent desires and imaginings with a delicate wit and a total absence of solemnity. The ballet has a white, radiant air and a choreographic vitality that make it irresistible viewing.

Five Sketches (1966) is a duet that starts with a long section of smooth elegant dancing; just before the end of the ballet the two dancers abandon their 'official' stage presences and for a moment become their ordinary selves. The ballet then continues in more serious and disturbed mood – the dancers seem like Adam and Eve after the Fall. In *Dualis* (1967) he contrasts two couples with attendant *corps de ballet:* one pair are 'sophisticated' with the girl in point shoes; the other couple are barefoot and their dances suggest a stripping away of conventional attitudes to reveal the darker passions that underlie even the behaviour of the first couple.

In writing about *Metaphors* (1966), van Manen noted that he was inspired by the vivid contrasts to be found in the score (Lesur's *Variations for Piano and String Orchestra*), and these generated for him a feeling of great tension which he sought to express in the conflicts (dynamic as well as emotional) between the dancers; *Metaphors* hints at relationships beneath its fluent, easy dance manner, and at its most intense – in a sequence of double work for two men, each alternatively acting as partner to the other – it suggests a superficial elegance masking a profound disquiet. 'Watching the complete ballet at one of the final rehearsals,' wrote van Manen, 'I discovered that the choreography filled me with a dual sense of joy and melancholy – perhaps a little like observing the end of one's youth.'

RUDI VAN DANTZIG (b. 1933)

Moments

Ballet in one act. Choreography: Rudi van Dantzig. Music: Webern. (Six Bagatelles and Five Pieces for String Quartet). Décor: Toer van Schayk. First performed Holland, 1968.

A plotless ballet, *Moments* offers a danced visualization of the succinct power, the terse allusive sonorities of the Webern score. With a cast of seven dancers, van Dantzig achieves a series of fluid encounters that seem like the changing patterns in a kaleidoscope. The choreography is clear, simple in its dynamics, beautifully imaginative in mirroring the fascinating intervals of the music. Dancers meet and part, embrace and separate with emotion that seems reduced to its essence, depersonalized but still potent. One male dancer is recurrently seen apart from the group, and the ballet is filled with a sense of dramatic intensity that has been as purged and refined of all non-essentials as the music itself.

Van Dantzig was at one time represented in the British repertory by *Jungle*, a fine work that was staged by the short-lived London Dance Theatre in 1965. *Jungle* drew parallels between life in a tropical forest and human behaviour. Its four sections: dawn, noon, twilight, night, showed the dramas that are played out among the forest creatures, the bursts of emotion, the fights, the ceaseless warfare and the struggle for existence itself. The movement was excellently characterized in human terms and the later development of the ballet showed more and more clearly its application to our own society. Van Dantzig avoided any of the romantic parallelism of a Walt Disney Wild-life Adventure; his view was more ferocious and more honest. His scavengers and predators obeyed laws that obtain also in our world – as the programme note stated: 'When night comes we don't know whether it is the return of darkness or a darkness created by people around us . . . ourselves.' The total effect was brilliantly theatrical, and the dance language, which showed a classicism flavoured with Modern Dance borrowings, could depict not only the savagery of the animals, but also a touching lyricism.

A NOTE ON SOVIET BALLET

With the revolution of 1917, Russian ballet – always a mysterious and glamorous thing to Western eyes – became even more mysterious because of the isolation in which it has worked until the last decade. Two invaluable studies recently published, *Era of the Russian Ballet* by Natalia Roslavleva (Gollancz, 1966) and *The Art of the Dance in the USSR* by Mary Grace Swift (University of Notre Dame Press, 1968) offer a fascinating guide to the post-revolutionary period, and are mutually complementary. The father-figure of Soviet ballet must be accounted Alexander Gorsky (1871–1924). Appointed regisseur in Moscow in 1900, he restaged many of Petipa's works (not to the old gentleman's satisfaction it would seem) and succeeded in making them more dramatic by melting what may have been the frozen classical perfection of the St Petersburg style into a warmer and more humanist manner. He started with *Don Quixote*, then made the first of five versions of *Swan Lake* in 1901, and proceeded to create a repertory in Moscow that offered a marked contrast to the academic perfection of St Petersburg. In 1910 came *Salammbô* (it did away with tutus – unthinkable crime) which was an effective summing up of Gorsky's desire to liberate and heighten dramatically the *ballet à grand spectacle* of Petipa. Gorsky's dramatic ideals for the ballet had been in part inspired by his association with Stanislavsky and Nemirovich-Danchenko, as well as by the excellence of the stagings at the private opera performances in Moscow put on by the millionaire Mamontov. Under his guidance the Bolshoi Company emerged from the inanition that seemed to threaten its very existence, while in St Petersburg the departure of Petipa after the failure of *The Magic Mirror* (1903) had left that great company without any sustained choreographic guidance. The maintenance of the repertory there was left in the hands of Sergueyev, and various choreographers – notably Fokine – made short ballets for the company, but it was not until the immediately post-revolutionary years that the St Petersburg ballet recovered the sense of purpose that it had known under Petipa. With the Revolution the whole attitude to ballet in Russia underwent a total reorientation. One of the greatest figures of this time – and one of the most influential men in the history of ballet in the twentieth century – was Anatol Lunasharsky, the first Soviet Commissar of Enlightenment. Soviet ballet's debt to Lunasharsky is incalculable: a great lover of all the arts, a notable critic, Lunasharsky made it his task to preserve the arts and make them worthy of the proletariat: 'While I am People's Commissar this work of introducing the proletariat to the possession of all human culture shall remain my first task.' The battle was not easily won; many activists sought the destruction of the classic ballet, and it was only after prolonged discussion that the forces of conservation (with the outstanding teacher Vaganova well in the vanguard) triumphed – a triumph notably helped by the debut of the first great Soviet ballerina, Marina Semyonova. During the 1920s a vast amount of experimentation took place in ballet: Feodor Lopukhov, Kasyan Goleizovsky, Nikolai Foregger all seemed inspired by the new creative excitement of the time in their choreography. It was during this period that the first successful Soviet ballet – *The Red Poppy* – was staged (Bolshoi Theatre, 1927). In 1930 Vassili Vainonen created *The Age of Gold* in collaboration with two other choreographers in Leningrad and two years later staged his greatest success *The Flames of Paris*. (In 1949, he also produced a charming comedy *Mirandolina*, based on Goldoni's *La Locandiera*.) In 1934, Rostislav Zakharov made his choreographic debut with *The Fountains of Bakhchisarai* which was based (like three other of his ballets: *The Prisoner of the Caucasus* (1938), *Mistress into Maid* (1946) and *The Bronze Horseman* (1949)) on themes from Pushkin, and in 1945 he made a version of *Cinderella*. One of the greatest dancers in Soviet ballet, Vakhtang Chabukiani, also started choreography in the 1930s – producing *The Heart of the Hills* in 1938 and following it the next year with *Laurencia*. Another fine dancer, Leonid Lavrovsky, graduate of the Leningrad school, also took up choreography in the thirties, creating *Fadette* (1934), *Katerina* (1935), and *The Prisoner of the Caucasus* (1938), producing his major ballet, *Romeo and Juliet*, in 1940. Thereafter he composed several short ballets – notably *Paganini* (1960) and a version of Bartok's *The Miraculous Mandarin* – as well as a staging of Prokofiev's *The Stone Flower* (1954). Another dancer at the Kirov, Konstantin Sergueyev, now Director of the company, has also produced ballets, including a version of Prokofiev's *Cinderella*, and *The Path of Thunder* (a ballet about apartheid) as well as revising and editing the Kirov's classic productions. Asaf Messerer, the celebrated Moscow dancer, has created several works, including the notably successful *School of Ballet*, and Leonid Yacobsen, a Leningrad-based choreographer, first worked on the 1930 staging of *The Age of Gold*, but his major ballet did not come until 1941 with *Shuraleh*. Later he was the first to make an attempt at the score of *Spartacus* (a ballet that has subsequently had many choreographic lives, including alternative versions by Moyseyev and Grigorovich).

Of the younger generation of Soviet choreographers, two in particular deserve attention in this necessarily brief (and rather breathless) introduction. Igor Belsky, born in 1925, made his first large ballet, *Shore of Hope*,' for the Kirov Ballet in 1959, and with *Leningrad Symphony* (1961) – to the first movement of Shostakovich's Seventh Symphony – he produced a searingly moving portrayal of the agony and ultimate triumph of the heroic people of Leningrad during the war years when the Nazis were besieging the city. A contemporary of Belsky's, Yuri Grigorovich (born in 1927) made his first big ballet with a version of Prokofiev's *The Stone Flower* (1957) for the Kirov and followed this with *Legend of Love* (1962). Appointed Director of the Bolshoi Ballet in 1966, he has provided a complete restaging of *The Nutcracker* as well as a new version of *Spartacus*.

We have made no attempt in this brief outline to do more than mention some of the most significant figures in Soviet ballet; there are many more working both in Leningrad and Moscow and in the numerous ballet companies to be found in all parts of the Soviet Union: the works of Natalia Roslavleva and Mary Grace Swift, as we have noted above, are an invaluable guide to further study.

Further Reading

However much ballet one sees on stage or television, books are a way of deepening and continuing the enjoyment at home. Through books one can explore new aspects of dance, or prepare with better knowledge to re-see a well-known classic. One might start, for example, with a basic library to add to *Ballet, for All*:

BASIC LIBRARY

The Choreographic Art: Van Praagh and Brinson, A. and C. Black, £3.

The Dancer's Heritage: Guest, The Dancing Times, 15s.
A History of Ballet and its Makers: Lawson, Pitman, £2 5s.
A Dictionary of Ballet: Wilson, Cassell, 18s.

The Dancer's Heritage and *A History of Ballet and its Makers* are essential for anyone planning to take the GCE 'O' level Ballet examination, while *The Choreographic Art* is equally important for anyone teaching the examination. *The Choreographic Art* is really two books in one since its first half deals with ballet history and the second half describes how ballets are created on stage – so each half covers exactly one of the two GCE ballet papers. It is also a book which includes much of the material on which Ballet for All's theatre and television programmes are based. For quick, easy reference to facts and details, though, nothing can beat G. B. L. Wilson's *Dictionary*.

SPECIAL INTEREST

After covering the subject in general you may find particular periods or kinds of ballet attract your interest. Here are some suggestions:

Early History
Background to European Ballet : Brinson A. W., Sijthoff (Leyden, Holland) £1 10s.
Noverre: Letters on Dancing and Ballets: trans. Beaumont, Dance Horizons, £1 12s.

Romantic Ballet
The Romantic Ballet in Paris : Guest, Pitman, 5 gns.
Bournonville and Ballet Technique : Bruhn and Moore, A. and C. Black, £1 5s.

Classical and Russian Ballet
Era of the Russian Ballet : Roslavleva, Gollancz, £2 5s.
The Art of the Dance : Swift, University of Notre Dame Press, 15 dollars.

Diaghilev
Ballet Russe. The Age of Diaghilev : Haskell, Weidenfeld and Nicolson, £1 1s.

Modern Dance
Isadora Duncan. The Russian Years : Schneider, MacDonald £2 2s.
Introduction to the Dance : Martin, Dance Horizons, £2.

For Younger Readers
Every Child's Book of Dance and Ballet : Ed. Franks, Burke, 16s.

Periodicals
The Dancing Times : monthly, 3s. 6d.
Dance and Dancers : monthly, 5s.
Ballet Today : bi-monthly, 2s. 6d.

All the above books and periodicals are in print at the time of writing, so can be obtained through most local bookshops or newsagents. In case of difficulty, however, there are two book services specializing in ballet. They are: Ballet Bookshop, 9 Cecil Court, St Martin's Lane, London, WC2; or Dancing Times Book Service, 18 Hand Court, London, WC1.

Finally, the Royal Ballet's Ballet for All organization directed by Peter Brinson at the Royal Opera House, Covent Garden, London, WC2, provides:

(1) A small travelling theatre company of actors and Royal Ballet dancers able to bring well-presented theatrical performances to small theatres and school stages. These performances aim to introduce ballet, inform and entertain through special ballet-plays which combine music, dancing and speech.

(2) Individual lecturers and small demonstrations.

For details of both these services and their availability to local authorities, art societies, schools and other organizations write to: The Director, Ballet for All, at the Royal Opera House, Covent Garden, London W.C.2.

The authors and publishers regret that due to the difficulty of fitting in the production schedule of this book with the television programmes to which it is related, it was not possible in this edition to include the index which was prepared for the book. The index will be included in all future editions.

A SELECTION OF
POPULAR READING IN PAN

FICTION

☐ FREDERICA	Georgette Heyer	(25p)	5/–
☐ BATH TANGLE	" "	(25p)	5/–
☐ BLACK SHEEP	" "	(25p)	5/–
☐ KINGS OF INFINITE SPACE			
	Nigel Balchin	(30p)	6/–
☐ NOT AS A STRANGER	Morton Thompson	(40p)	8/–
☐ HORNBLOWER AND THE 'ATROPOS'			
	C. S. Forester	(30p)	6/–

NON-FICTION

☐ THE DOCTOR'S QUICK WEIGHT LOSS DIET Irwin Maxwell Stillman M.D.			
	and Samm Sinclair Baker	(25p)	5/–
☐ GIPSY MOTH CIRCLES THE WORLD (illus.)			
	Sir Francis Chichester	(30p)	6/–
☐ MY LIVELY LADY (illus.)	Sir Alec Rose	(30p)	6/–
☐ BALLET FOR ALL (illus. As Shown on TV)			
	Peter Brinson and Clement Crisp	(40p)	8/–
☐ RING OF BRIGHT WATER (illus.)			
	Gavin Maxwell	(25p)	5/–
☐ LORDS OF THE ATLAS (illus.)	"	(40p)	8/–
☐ THE DAM BUSTERS (illus.) Paul Brickhill		(25p)	5/–
☐ ENGLISH PROVERBS EXPLAINED			
	Ronald Ridout and Clifford Witting	(25p)	5/–
☐ NICHOLAS AND ALEXANDRA (illus.)			
	Robert K. Massie	(50p)	10/–
☐ THE LEFT-HANDED BOOK (illus.)			
	Michael Barsley	(30p)	6/–

Obtainable from all booksellers and newsagents. If you have any difficulty, please send purchase price plus 9d. postage to P.O. Box 11, Falmouth, Cornwall.

I enclose a cheque/postal order for selected titles ticked above plus 9d. per book to cover packing and postage.

NAME...

ADDRESS...

....